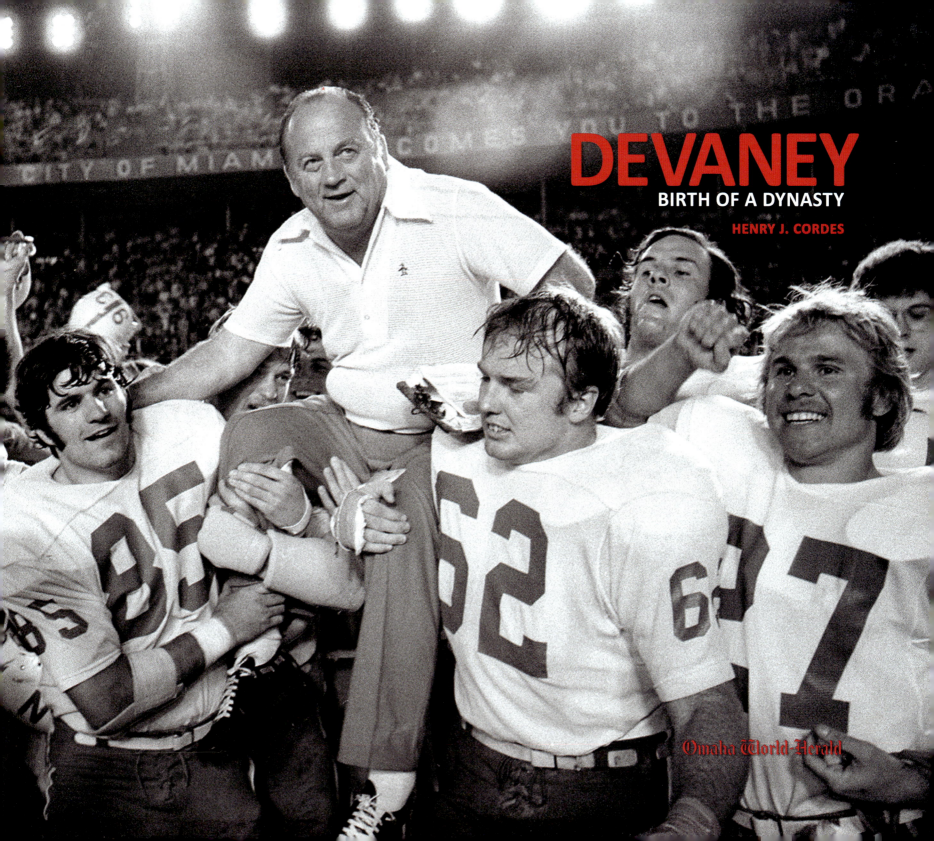

DEVANEY
BIRTH OF A DYNASTY
HENRY J. CORDES

Omaha World-Herald

Nebraska's Johnny Rodgers and Larry Jacobson celebrate Rodgers' punt return for a touchdown against Oklahoma in the Game of the Century.

2	**Death of a Salesman?**
28	**The Coordinators**
40	**Shaping Up**
48	**In Search of Help**
56	**Super Sophs**
66	**Teetering on the Brink**
76	**The Quarterback Shuffle**
86	**Norman Conquest**
94	**Black and White**
104	**Dawn of a New Age**
118	**Devaney's Problem Child**
132	**The Jerry and Van Show**
142	**They Might Be No. 1**
154	**Opportunity Knocks**
160	**A Night to Remember**
176	**Standing by His Man**
186	**Great Expectations**
198	**Storm Brewing on the Plains**
208	**Don't Look Back**
220	**One for the Ages**
236	**Going on a Bear Hunt**
248	**A Bittersweet Ending**
262	**Epilogue**
272	**Acknowledgments, index & credits**

Omaha World-Herald

EDITOR
Dan Sullivan

DESIGNER
Christine Zueck-Watkins

PHOTO IMAGING
Jolene McHugh

EXECUTIVE EDITOR
Mike Reilly

PRESIDENT AND PUBLISHER
Terry Kroeger

All rights reserved. No part of this book may be reproduced, stored in a retrieval system, or transmitted in any form or by any means, electronic, mechanical, photocopying, recording or otherwise, without prior consent of the publisher, Omaha World-Herald Co.
Copyright 2014

Omaha World-Herald Co.
1314 Douglas St. Omaha, NE 68102-1811
First Edition
ISBN: 978-0-692-31859-1
Printed by Walsworth Publishing Co.
Marceline, MO

On the title page: Jerry List (85), Mike Beran (62) and Joe Blahak (27) help Bob Devaney celebrate his final victory, a 40-6 win over Notre Dame in the 1973 Orange Bowl.

Death of a Salesman?

DECKED OUT IN A BRIMMED FELT HAT, Cornhusker letterman's jacket and a scowl as wide as the state of Nebraska, Bob Devaney looked on as the University of Oklahoma's Steve Owens turned the football field in Norman into his personal playground. It was November. 23, 1968. And the star Sooner back romped to a Big Eight Conference-record five rushing touchdowns that day. He left his cleat marks all over the chests and backs of Devaney's humbled defense — and also stomped the life out of any lingering interest the Liberty Bowl had in this wobbly University of Nebraska team.

The Husker defense wasn't even the most inept unit on the field that day. By some margin, that was the Nebraska offense, which picked up only seven first downs and saw the Sooner defense take an interception back for a score. The Ruf Neks, the all-male Sooner pep squad that fired off shotguns after each score, were making Owen Field sound like a war zone. At the end, as the student section behind the Nebraska bench mockingly serenaded Devaney and the Huskers with "Happy Trails to You," the scoreboard read Oklahoma 47, Nebraska 0. In Bob Devaney's storied coaching career, this was the lowest moment.

> **"We got a couple bad calls against us."**
> — Devaney, years later explaining why his 1968 team lost to Oklahoma 47-0

Of course, Devaney would later joke about it. Give the gregarious storyteller an audience, and perhaps a drink, and he'd spin a tale of bumping into a woman that afternoon on his way to the Nebraska locker room after the game. "Pardon me, ma'am, I meant no offense," he told her. "Coach, your defense stinks, too," came the punch-line reply. Never one to take himself too seriously, Devaney was often at his funniest after a loss.

But as Devaney had been finding out during this long 1968 season, the boosters who attend the Monday Extra Point Club luncheons in Lincoln don't laugh at your jokes quite as much when the losses start to pile up. This one was particularly hard to laugh off — a complete humiliation, televised to the entire nation at a time when few games made it to the airwaves. By the end, the ABC network had switched to a roundup of national scores in a desperate effort to cling to its audience. The shellacking also capped Devaney's second consecutive mediocre 6-4 season at Nebraska and his second straight 3-4 record in the Big Eight.

Soon there were rumors of boosters in Omaha starting up a petition to force Devaney's ouster. To the coach's critics, it didn't matter that during his seven seasons at Nebraska, he'd won four titles in the rugged Big Eight — precisely four more than the school had won over the previous two decades. Or that despite the recent stumbles, his career winning percentage still ranked above anyone else's in the college game — higher than such coaching luminaries as Woody Hayes, Ara Parseghian, John McKay and Paul "Bear" Bryant. Indeed, where would Nebraska football have been at that moment had it not been for Bob Devaney? At the time he arrived in Lincoln in 1962, there had been little reason for fans to have any expectations at all for the Nebraska football team.

A glum Devaney watches the final moments of a humiliating loss to Oklahoma in 1968, with assistants George Kelly, left, and Mike Corgan.

The Cornhuskers, in striped shirts, battle the University of Chicago in 1906. Coach Amos Foster led NU to a 6-4 record in his only season as coach.

Coach Fred Dawson's teams beat Notre Dame in 1922 and 1923.

TO BE SURE, THE PRAIRIE SCHOOL founded near the banks of the Salt Creek in 1869 had seen some proud moments in its gridiron history. Students had first picked up the brutal game in 1890, opening with a 10-0 victory over the Omaha YMCA. The Omaha World-Herald that day took particular note of the fan interest in the new sport, reporting that several hundred "came out to see the boys enjoy themselves and break each other's shins." Over time, the sport would appeal to the nature of the rugged, hardworking people who scratched their livelihood from the earth. Big Red fever was born.

For the next half-century, the University of Nebraska would suffer only three losing seasons and six times would go unbeaten, becoming known far and wide as a Great Plains cyclone you'd be wise to steer clear of. Bummy Booth's Cornhuskers won 25 in a row between 1901 and 1904, including a 1902 team that didn't surrender a single point. Jumbo Stiehm (pronounced *Steam*) and his "Stiehm Rollers" ran off an unbeaten string of 34 games between 1912 and 1916. Notre Dame's Knute Rockne and his fabled "Four Horsemen" backfield lost only two games between 1922 and 1924, both of them in Lincoln to coach Fred Dawson's scrappy team. Illinois' Red Grange, the famed "Galloping Ghost," was but a wisp of a spirit against the stout Huskers in 1925. Grange reportedly retreated to the sidelines in tears.

As a monument to their gridiron success, Nebraskans in 1923 built Memorial Stadium, a stately gray campus football cathedral that they proudly packed every fall. The success continued under Coach Dana X. Bible, whose scarlet-clad crusaders won six Big Six Conference titles between 1929 and 1936. Biff Jones followed with two more league crowns, and after the 1940 season he took the Cornhuskers to their first-ever bowl game. That Rose Bowl invitation was huge for Nebraskans, proving that the school was finally recognized as more than just a regional power. Classes were canceled, and students rallied on the steps of the State Capitol. They egged on the governor until he joined them in singing the school song and its prideful opening line, "There is no place like Nebraska."

Biff Jones' 1940 team went to the Rose Bowl.

Nebraska's Lloyd Cardwell hauls in a pass from Henry Bauer before racing in to score during a 19-13 victory over Kansas in Lincoln in 1935. Cardwell, dubbed "the Wild Hoss of the Plains" by then-World-Herald sports editor Frederick Ware, helped lead NU to Big Six football titles in 1935 and 1936.

Even decades later, the Jan. 1, 1941, Rose Bowl was still proudly celebrated. In fact, Devaney had been in Lincoln for five years before he learned that Nebraska had lost the game.

But with the onset of World War II, Nebraska's football fortunes took a bitter turn. You can partly blame the War Department. The University of Nebraska was one of a few big colleges in the country without a naval officer training program, which provided schools a steady flow of able student-athletes at a time most other young men were going off to war. Even coach Jones answered his nation's call, never to return to Lincoln. The war's happy conclusion in 1945 did not end Nebraska's football misery. From 1941 to 1961, the Huskers endured 17 losing seasons, dropping 125 games — second only to Kansas State among major colleges. It hurt Nebraskans deeply to see the team that gave them so much pride fall into oblivion.

Memorial Stadium in 1940. Nebraska's first game there, in 1923, was a 24-0 victory over Oklahoma. The official dedication a week later was spoiled by a 0-0 tie with Kansas.

Bill Jennings' 1961 Nebraska team went 3-6-1, a record noteworthy only in its consistency with his five-year record of 15-34-1. A year earlier, Jennings had famously chided Nebraskans for their inflated expectations for both football and life in general. He told an Omaha business crowd that a state with a population of just 1.5 million could never be great at anything. "We can't feed the ego of the state of Nebraska with the football team," Jennings proclaimed. But the Board of Regents did have higher aspirations. At the conclusion of the 1961 season, the regents sacked Jennings.

A month later, on a cold December day, longtime NU administrative aide Carl Donaldson was dispatched to the Lincoln airport with orders to pick up a salesman who'd be arriving on the 3:30 plane from Denver. Donaldson didn't know who "Mr. R. Roberts" was. Or that the man he was picking up was actually Bob Devaney, a candidate for the school's football coaching vacancy. Donaldson's bosses didn't lie about one thing, though. The mystery man was indeed a salesman. There were few better salesmen anywhere than Bob Devaney. And in a remarkably short time, he would become the savior of Nebraska football.

"Men, you don't have to win... Sometimes the price may be too high."

— Bill Jennings, speaking at the Omaha Benson High football banquet three days after he was fired

ROBERT S. DEVANEY WAS BORN April 13, 1915, in Saginaw, Michigan, the son of a Great Lakes mariner. His father wasn't around much, taking off in March each year and not returning again until the lakes froze over. Saginaw was a dirty industrial town then, and Devaney lived a hardscrabble childhood. The oldest of three boys, he was a scrappy kid who ran with a rough crowd. As he'd later say, a few of his friends "ended up working for the state, and not voluntarily." He was twice himself arrested in his young adult years, once for hopping trains and another time for a brawl he incited when he felt he'd been cheated out of some booze.

Devaney was no standout athlete growing up. He started on a ninth-grade basketball team but went the entire season without scoring a point. In high school, he wouldn't letter in any sport until his senior year, though he did ultimately start on the football, baseball and basketball teams at Arthur Hill High School. He also did some boxing on the side, showing off some quick hands that made him see himself as a potential lightweight champion. That is, until he got the heck beat out of him by a fighter with a traveling carnival who was taking on all comers. It seemed to Devaney that the carny pugilist packed something besides just stuffing in his gloves.

Devaney never cared much for school. So after graduating from Hill High in 1933, he took a job casting auto parts in a Chevrolet foundry. But after three years of making $17 a week performing hot and grimy manual labor, he found that he liked factory work even less than school. A chemist at the foundry fortuitously took Devaney under his wing, introducing him to the football coach at nearby Alma College.

Devaney, who starred at Alma College, said, "There wasn't any such thing (as a scholarship) in those days at small schools. I nearly quit school two or three times because of financial trouble."

DEATH OF A SALESMAN? 7

Devaney married Phyllis Wiley in 1936.

At the time, Alma was one of the smallest schools in the country playing college football. Devaney donned a leather helmet, losing a few teeth in his first game. But he proved a tenacious end who during his senior year was named team captain and MVP. In those college years, Devaney waited tables and pumped gas to help pay his way. At Alma, he also met Phyllis Wiley, and the two were soon married. Under Phyllis' guidance, if not direct intervention, Devaney's grades improved considerably. He left Alma in 1939 with his degree.

That fall, Devaney took a job teaching history, math and geography and coaching football at Big Beaver High, near Keego Harbor, Michigan. The school had gone winless the previous four years, and there were so few players out for the team that Devaney had to don pads himself to have enough guys to scrimmage. The new coach proved no immediate success. "We'd lose once in a while — once a week," he'd later quip.

But Devaney in the end scratched out two winning seasons at Big Beaver before moving on to bigger jobs in Saginaw and then Alpena. It was at Alpena, on the cool, misty shores of Lake Huron, that Devaney created a Michigan high school power, going 52-9 over seven seasons.

By 1953, Devaney had been coaching high school ball for 14 years and at age 37 was thinking of getting a master's degree and moving into school administration. That's when he got a life-changing phone call from Michigan State's Duffy Daugherty. Would he accept a position on the Spartan staff? Devaney had just gotten back from a lake fishing trip and wondered years later how differently his life could have turned out had he not been home to take that call. Devaney jumped at the offer. Daugherty would become Devaney's closest friend and mentor, teaching him the college game.

Devaney's 1961 Wyoming team tied Kansas, which later beat Nebraska.

Then after four years with the powerhouse Spartan program, Devaney in 1957 landed his first college head coaching job. He headed west to the Rockies, taking over the program at the University of Wyoming.

As at Big Beaver, he wasn't coming into an ideal situation. Wyoming was the least populated state in the Lower 48 states. The Cowboys had been winning, but it had been with the help of some big-city bad apples the previous coach had brought in. Some of these guys didn't even have high school degrees, just certificates indicating that they'd attended classes some, and they were now running roughshod over the campus. One of the hooligans in an early practice took a swing at Devaney. The new coach reared back and, with a single punch, knocked him out cold. Devaney had few problems after that, on or off the field. Often sporting a cowboy hat on the sidelines, he again won big, going 35-10-5 in five seasons in Laramie, with four Skyline Conference championships. The last of those titles came just as the Jennings era was ending in Lincoln.

Nebraska's search for Jennings' replacement was in the hands of Athletic Director Tippy Dye, newly arrived at the school from Wichita State University. Dye had originally hoped to bring the Wheatshockers' successful football coach with him. But after a couple weeks of deliberation, Hank Foldberg disappointed his former boss and instead went to Texas A&M.

Back to the drawing board, NU Chancellor Clifford Hardin worked an old connection from his days as agriculture dean at Michigan State. He called Daugherty. Would the coach be interested in a change of scenery? Daugherty declined, but he did give Hardin the number of a guy in Wyoming.

After Devaney's covert arrival in Lincoln in late December 1961, he was taken on a tour of the NU campus, which sprawled with no architectural theme or clear plan north of downtown Lincoln. On its western edge loomed Memorial Stadium. Devaney took it in while wearing a borrowed overcoat to ward off the cold. He headed over to Selleck Quadrangle, the men's dorm where most of the players lived. Then he retreated to a dark room to view recent Husker game film. He wanted to see what kind of personnel would be awaiting him if he decided to accept the challenge.

Athletic Director Tippy Dye, left, with Nebraska booster Bob Elliott. Dye was hired as A.D. after the NU Board of Regents fired football coach Bill Jennings.

DEATH OF A SALESMAN?

Later, he attended a dinner at the chancellor's home, where school officials promised to provide whatever Devaney needed to build a winner in Lincoln. "Bob, if you come here and win, you'll never be sorry," said Regent Clarence Swanson, a former Husker All-American. "These people want to win that much." Devaney had gotten similar encouragement earlier from his old mentor, Daugherty. If you can win in Nebraska the same way you did in Wyoming, Daugherty told him, "things could go big."

That prospect ultimately sold Devaney, who saw a higher ceiling in Lincoln than in Wyoming. By January 1, he had accepted the job and a salary of $17,000 a year, although it would take more than a month before the hiring became official. The regents in Wyoming were livid that Devaney was walking out on them after they'd privately guaranteed him his job for life. They initially refused to release him from his contract, with one regent later admitting that they just wanted to make Devaney sweat for a while. Finally, in early February 1962, Dye and Hardin could officially announce Nebraska's new football coach.

Nebraska Chancellor Clifford Hardin was secretary of agriculture under President Richard Nixon from 1969 to 1971.

> "Usually when you come into a place where there has been some dissatisfaction, you don't inherit a team as good as we did."
>
> — **Devaney at his first Big Eight press gathering**

Nebraska Regent Clarence Swanson was an All-American end for Fred Dawson's 1921 team.

The 46-year-old coach who first faced the Nebraska media was a rather unimpressive, dumpy-looking man, baldish and with little sense of style. His rumpled, ill-fitting clothes, with no discernible color pattern, later caused one Sports Illustrated writer to liken him to Willy Loman, the aging, fading protagonist in Arthur Miller's "Death of a Salesman." Devaney would defend himself, suggesting that the scribe's powers of observation had been somewhat diluted during his visit to Lincoln. "I won't say the writer drank a lot while he was out here," he said, "although it was mostly my liquor."

Wisecracks like that one helped Nebraska fans take an immediate liking to the new coach. If nothing else, this new guy was entertaining. "My hope is to win enough games to please the alumni, but not so many as to draw an NCAA investigation," he said at one of his first meetings with reporters.

NU fans didn't even know how to pronounce the new coach's name, many reading it in the papers and assuming it was De-VANE-ey. It took World-Herald columnist Gregg McBride to clarify the matter, coming up with a rhyme to help people get it straight. "Get up off your fanny," he wrote, "and help Bob Devaney."

But that writer also could have pointed out that Devaney also rhymed with uncanny. There would be no better word to describe the miracle Devaney would work during his first year on the Nebraska sideline.

Devaney said privately that he couldn't believe the talent he found on the Nebraska roster, with a fast and powerful running back in Bill "Thunder" Thornton, a strong-armed quarterback in Dennis Claridge and a future NFL All-Pro lineman in Bob Brown. Bill Jennings could recruit, Devaney told his fellow coaches, but the players needed some direction, more focus and a morale boost.

He immediately overhauled the team's psyche. Practice under Jennings had been a menial grind, often lasting three or four hours. Devaney's teams practiced two hours or less, and there was never any "We're staying out here until we get this right." His philosophy was that if they didn't pick it up today, they would tomorrow. At a Devaney practice, the work was crisp, well-organized and spirited. "We work, and we work hard," lineman Bob Taucher said. "But Coach Devaney always has something funny to say at just the right time." During the season, he never scrimmaged, figuring the boys got hit enough on Saturdays.

Bill "Thunder" Thornton was a co-captain for Devaney's first team, in 1962.

Devaney also brought in the Duffy Daugherty offense, a power running game with some play-action passes thrown in — considered a multiple attack for the time. That was music to the ears of Husker fans, who long had grumbled about Jennings' conservative and predictable ground attack.

In the 1962 opener against the University of South Dakota, Devaney had Claridge come out throwing on the first play. "That'll show them we mean business," Devaney growled to an assistant, pointing his thumb toward the west stands. And indeed, the fans roared, not seeming to mind that the pass fell incomplete.

A World-Herald reporter that day noted how orderly and businesslike the Nebraska sideline was compared to the confusion and turmoil of recent years. The coach even used instant Polaroids shot from the press box to study opponent formations. The Huskers went on to demolish the Coyotes 53-0. In his very first game, Devaney registered the largest point total and biggest victory margin by a Husker team in 17 years.

The 1962 staff, from left: George Kelly, Mike Corgan, Jim Ross, Devaney, Carl Selmer, Cletus Fischer, graduate assistant Harry Tolly and John Melton.

Just a week later, the Huskers returned to Devaney's home state for a date in the Big House against the University of Michigan. Devaney respected the Wolverines, but as a Michigan State man, he sure didn't like them much. In front of more than 70,000 hostile fans, Thunder Thornton scored twice despite a bum shoulder, helping NU ground out a workmanlike 25-13 win.

When the conquering heroes returned to Lincoln, 2,500 excited fans came out to greet them at the airport. Thousands of others jammed up traffic halfway to downtown Lincoln. It had taken Devaney all of two games to put Nebraska back on the national map. People were stunned.

The Huskers didn't drop a game that first year until early November, falling at home to Missouri 16-7.

By then, Devaney had created such fervor among the Nebraska faithful that a sell-out crowd of 36,501 showed up. It marked the start of a home sellout streak in Lincoln that would stretch into the 21st century.

Before Devaney arrived, banks in Lincoln sometimes would buy up Husker tickets cheap and leave them on the counters for customers, free for the taking. But in the decade after Devaney's arrival, the athletic department would move to expand the stadium five times, doubling the capacity to 76,400 in an effort

NU's Dave Theisen (23) looks for running room against Michigan, with help from John Kirby (68) and Rudy Johnson (31).

to accommodate all the Big Red euphoria. The old edifice came to be called "The House That Bob Built."

Devaney's first team would go 9-2, including a respectable third-place finish in the Big Eight. And it would become just the third team in school history to play in a bowl.

The Gotham Bowl in New York City against the University of Miami, Florida, wasn't exactly a top-tier affair. The Huskers were invited at the last minute, just 11 days before the game, and a New York newspaper strike assured that the game would get little publicity in the city. The bowl's financial troubles prompted university officials to keep the Huskers' plane on the tarmac in Lincoln the day before the game until the check for the team's expenses cleared the bank.

Game day — Saturday, December 15 — dawned cold and snowy, the field frozen solid. It was believed that fewer than 1,000 fans came out to historic Yankee Stadium to brave the conditions, though organizers generously listed the crowd at more than 6,000. Not surprisingly, there would never be another Gotham Bowl.

In the locker room before the game, Devaney apologized to his players for getting them into "this crummy deal." It didn't seem like it would be much fun. But then he told them the situation reminded him of his days as a back-alley fighter growing up in Saginaw. "There's nobody there to watch," he told them, "but the toughest son of a bitch is going to win." The players roared with laughter. And then they went out and had a blast.

In a back-and-forth thriller against the Hurricanes and golden-armed quarterback George Mira, the Huskers pulled out a 36-34 victory. The NU celebration on the field afterward matched any the Yankees could muster after a pennant. The happy Huskers carried Devaney off the frozen turf, the first of many such trips he would take as Nebraska's coach.

Devaney rides off the field at Yankee Stadium in triumph after Nebraska beat the Miami Hurricanes in the 1962 Gotham Bowl.

Indeed, 1962 was just a start. Devaney's Huskers would go on to win or share the next four Big Eight titles, breaking Oklahoma's longtime domination of the league. His teams dropped just two conference games during that time, compiling overall records of 10-1, 9-2, 10-1 and 9-2. The Huskers played in two Orange Bowls, a Cotton Bowl and a Sugar Bowl and in each season finished in the Top 10 in the national polls. The Big Eight would never again be called "Oklahoma and the Seven Dwarfs."

Despite that success and a career winning percentage second to none among active coaches, Devaney still wasn't afforded the national respect of a Bryant or McKay. One scribe would term him "the most anonymous winning football coach in America." There's no doubt that three straight bowl losses from 1964 to 1966 hurt his standing. His undefeated 1965 team actually had a chance for a national title in the Orange Bowl after the top two teams lost their bowls. But the Huskers fell flat against Bryant and Alabama, which claimed the prize.

Such results left many national pundits with the impression that Devaney and the Huskers weren't quite ready for prime time. At best, they were an unknown quantity. At worst, they were a paper tiger that beat up lesser, overmatched opponents. Still, given the decades of suffering in Lincoln, around Nebraska the Devaney name was golden. Husker fans were likewise ready to give the man a lifetime contract.

As amazing as Devaney's success in Lincoln was by that time, those who played for and coached with the man say there was nothing mysterious about it. In the end, it came down to the considerable force of his personality.

Players simply loved to play for Devaney and relished his physical, hard-nosed style of football. While his own brawling days were behind him, he still would regularly go to the campus athletic center, Schulte Field House, to work over the heavy punching bag. That was typical of Devaney's mindset. He liked his guys to hit hard. As Daugherty had taught him, "Football is not a contact sport — it's a collision sport. Dancing is a contact sport."

Ed Pavoris (61), Walt Barnes (50) and Kelly Peterson (30) push Devaney into the shower after the Huskers earned an Orange Bowl invitation with a 29-20 win over Oklahoma in 1963.

But amid the hard knocks, Devaney kept things fun, light and loose. With a twinkle in his eye, he'd threaten a player that if he kept missing tackles he would make him a javelin catcher on the track team. He'd tease the linemen that he was going to have to start recruiting 110-pound running backs because they'd be the only ones who could get through the holes the line was creating. Or he'd tell one of his jokes, many of which weren't repeatable in polite company. When he really got the guys roaring, you could hear the laughter across campus.

Some head coaches at the time kept a distance from their players, not wanting personal feelings to get in the way when it came time to decide who was playing. That wasn't Devaney's way. He made a point of establishing personal connections with all his players. He'd encourage them to stay on top of schoolwork. He'd remember mom's name and ask how she was. Off the field, there was a loose accountability. The coach was willing to overlook a minor transgression but generally expected guys to go to class and stay out of trouble. Players respected that Devaney was straightforward and honest.

Devaney was a master motivator, seeming to have the perfect sense for which buttons to push. When the coach arrived in 1962, he quickly saw great potential in Brown, his massive 6-5, 259-pound guard. But he also thought the lineman was too soft. One day during spring practice, Brown arrived at his locker to find his equipment missing. He sought out Devaney for an explanation. "I've been talking it over with the other coaches, and we think it's best you give up contact sports," Devaney told him. "We recommend golf, or maybe tennis." Brown got the message. He went on to become one of the most fearsome linemen in the game, a consensus All-American who ultimately had his No. 64 jersey retired by the Huskers.

Years later, Devaney's son told of the time the Huskers had an awful first half and then were puzzled when their coach didn't appear in the locker room for his halftime instruction. Devaney finally popped his head in the door five minutes later. "Excuse me, I'm looking for a football team," he told them. "Is there one around here? I haven't seen one today." The team Devaney was looking for showed up in the second half.

Adrian Fiala would never forget a Sunday in 1967 when Devaney had the players back on the practice field after an embarrassing loss to Kansas. "Fiala," Devaney said as the linebacker walked by, "you should have bought a ticket to get into that game yesterday." The words left such an impression that Fiala wrote them out and taped them to his locker for future motivation.

Sometimes a player needed a more gentle lift. Tight end Jim McFarland later recalled his lowest moment as a Husker. He was laboring in anonymity on the scout team in 1967, wearing a green jersey and taking his lumps from the likes of all-conference middle guard Wayne Meylan. One day after practice he lingered in the freshman locker room of Schulte Field House, feeling beaten and wondering whether he was good enough to play at Nebraska.

Bob Brown played at both offensive guard and linebacker in 1963. The Huskers switched to two platoons in 1964.

Devaney walked by and seemed to sense McFarland's flagging spirit. "Jim, I've been watching you in practice, and you're doing some good things out there," Devaney said. "You keep it up, and you'll play a lot of good football for us." The words came just at the right moment for McFarland and would become one of his fondest memories in an all-Big Eight career at NU.

Devaney also knew there were times a coach needed to really let players have it, especially if they weren't giving the effort he expected or repeatedly made mental mistakes. Some of his meltdowns were epic and unprintable, at least in full. Almost every player had at least one story of a time he faced Devaney's red-hot Irish fury.

One classic example came when Devaney stormed over to defensive tackle Carel Stith during a 1966 scrimmage. "Caroline! Are you going to hit that guy with your purse, or are you going to knock him on his ass?"

Receiver Guy Ingles recalled how in 1968 he talked Devaney into letting him return punts. The general rule was that if the punt was coming down inside the 10, you were to let it go and hope it bounded into the end zone for a touchback. The first time Ingles fielded a punt in a game, he looked down and was aghast to see that he was straddling the goal line. The panicked Ingles managed to get the ball out to the 12. Back on the sideline, Ingles was standing among teammates when it seemed the Red Sea parted, revealing an angry Bob Devaney. "Ingles!" he roared, "I thought you said you knew what the hell you were doing back there!"

Devaney understood, though, that there was a line between merely dressing down a player and shattering his confidence. He knew how to tread it. Almost inevitably, soon after such blowups, Devaney would have his arm around the player, offering words of encouragement. "You're my man," he'd say. "Get in there." Devaney never stayed mad.

His manner engendered respect and genuine affection in his players. There was nothing players feared more than letting Devaney down. As Johnny Rodgers would later put it, "You would rather slide bare-ass down a razor blade than disappoint Coach Devaney."

Devaney talks to struggling quarterback Fred Duda on the sidelines against Oklahoma State in 1965. Duda led the Huskers to a score with 38 seconds left for a 21-17 win.

Devaney's personality also made him formidable on the recruiting trail. He had no trouble selling his program, assuring parents that if their kids worked hard, above all, they'd get a great education at Nebraska. Three-quarters of his players got their degrees.

He could relate to families from all walks of life, discussing grain prices with a farmer or the stock market's vagaries with a broker. Devaney well understood, though, that the key to hauling in recruits was winning over their mothers. When offered a cookie while working a recruit's living room, he would ask the kid's mom for the recipe, declaring it without doubt the best cookie he'd ever tasted. When he went to West Virginia to recruit receiver Tony Jeter, Devaney ended up seated next to his mom at an organ, singing hymns. Once Mrs. Jeter heard the charming coach belting out "Bringing in the Sheaves" in his Irish tenor, she wouldn't listen to talk of her son going anywhere else. Devaney liked to joke that such efforts usually resulted in the mom enrolling at Nebraska and the player going to Missouri. But there's no question he got more than his share of blue-chippers.

Devaney once told a magazine writer he had a simple formula for winning: "Recruit like hell, then organize." Though Devaney had no formal business training, he possessed impressive skills for building and running an organization. He was the true CEO of Cornhusker Football Inc., an inspiring leader who hired great people, set the vision, delegated responsibilities and steered the enterprise forward.

In the Bob Devaney School of Management, you trust your people. Devaney had learned back in his high school coaching days that if you wanted to win in football, you can't do it all yourself, and you'd be stupid to try. So he hired coaches who knew football and were great teachers, and he let them coach. He found that the more credit and responsibility he gave his assistants, the more pride and dedication they put into their work, and the better they performed. He placed faith in his staff to get players ready. "You know what to do," he'd tell his coaches after they'd worked up their game plan for the week.

Devaney kept abreast of what his assistants were doing, asking the right questions. And if there were disagreements, he'd have the final say. Everyone knew who was in charge. During practice he'd roam from station to station carrying a clipboard, with the players trying to keep an eye on where he was. In the rare cases he'd step in to offer his advice or criticism, players knew they'd better listen. "Devaney was the man," Rodgers recalled. "He was running the show, Jack."

Devaney's coaches were fiercely loyal, thanks in large part to the respect he showed them. NU didn't see the constant churn of assistants typical at most schools. All six of the full-time assistants Devaney hired at NU in 1962 were still with him in 1968. Four of them — Jim Ross, John Melton, Carl Selmer and Mike Corgan — dated back to Devaney's Wyoming days. Ross had coached with him at Alpena.

Tony Jeter, both a football and academic All-American in 1965, said his parents were impressed that Devaney "showed enough interest in our family to sing church hymns along with us. I wouldn't have believed it if I hadn't seen it."

Each coach on the staff was unique and in many ways a character. But there was little friction among them, because Devaney kept them pulling in the same direction. And no one in his organization was more important than anyone else. Whether a coach, a trainer or the maintenance guy in the red polka-dot hat who tended to the grass practice fields, Devaney treated them all the same. And together, they won.

Devaney kept a book on his desk titled "What I Know About Football" and would encourage guests to thumb through its pages — all of which were blank. But he did know the finer points of the game and was both competitive and confident. Sometimes during film study, his coaches would express concern about the threat the Huskers faced that week. Devaney was more likely to turn off the projector at the end of the session and pronounce, "God, if we can't beat these guys, we ought to quit coaching."

Devaney and assistants John Melton, left, and Jim Ross review game film. Dr. Bert Hooper of the NU College of Dentistry was credited with originating the filming of football games in the 1920s for coaches' later review.

If Devaney did lose, it tore him up inside. But at least outwardly, the losses didn't seem to linger long. It was always on to the next game, his confidence unshaken. Recalled Tom Osborne, the longtime assistant who would later succeed Devaney as Nebraska's head coach: "I don't think Bob ever went into a game he didn't think he would win."

That kind of confidence also rubbed off on his players. Devaney was rarely one to make big speeches at halftime or before kickoff, believing team confidence founded on some trumped-up pep talk crumbles as soon as adversity strikes. Devaney firmly believed preparation and execution were what won football games.

Devaney each fall would ask the incoming freshmen whether they'd ever had a coach say after a loss that the team had still played a good game. Every hand would go up. "That's bull!" Devaney would blurt in response. "If you had played a good game, you would have won. You lost because you made more mistakes than they did." Devaney and his coaches focused during the week on teaching players to eliminate mistakes so he wouldn't need to make grand speeches on game day.

While everyone in the Nebraska program shared in the great success of the Devaney years, no one enjoyed it more than the head coach himself. Game days were particularly special, with Devaney, the other coaches and staffers and their wives all reconvening afterward at Lincoln's American Legion club for a night of dinner and dancing.

In that bygone era, the club was the entertainment hub of Lincoln, filled to capacity each night by members of the Greatest Generation. Though Devaney was not a veteran, club manager Bob Logsdon had given the coach an honorary club membership early in his tenure at NU, and the two became close, lifelong friends. The Husker staff and spouses would frequently sit together at a long table in the middle of the huge dining room. "It was one big family," Joan Bryant, the wife of NU sports information director Don Bryant, would recall of those halcyon days. "And Bob was the foundation of it."

Over drinks at such gatherings, the natural raconteur would hold court, telling story after story. Devaney, as most everyone knew, was no saint. Whether at the club in Lincoln or out on the road, he'd enjoy a highball or three, usually starting with a screwdriver and then moving to other favorites like Kahlua Supreme or Brandy Alexander.

Devaney gathers his team as it prepares to take the field in 1965.

The drinking sessions often would extend long past the legal closing time — not a problem when some of the city's top law enforcement officials also are part of the festivities. And with the close relationship in those days between coaches and the old-school reporters who frequently joined in the merry-making, Devaney could afford to be a bit of a rascal without fear that it would blow up in the papers. "Put it this way," recalled his son, Mike Devaney. "My dad worked hard, but he also played hard, and he enjoyed life."

Stories of Devaney's late-night exploits on the town would over time become the stuff of legend. But those who knew him best say he was largely a social drinker. Who, after all, was more social than Bob Devaney? Not surprisingly, some of the most colorful stories Devaney told revolved around the times he and his buddies were at a bar and "stayed longer than we intended."

Nebraskans related well to Devaney, who never held himself above anyone and was easy to like. He, Phyllis and their two kids lived in an unpretentious brick house in southeast Lincoln, a city of 150,000 that still considered itself a small town. He was listed in the phone book and would greet strangers he met on the street. Devaney always tried to keep his personal success in perspective. He'd frequently borrow a line first made famous by his friend McKay: "There are 800 million Chinamen who don't give a damn what happens to the Nebraska football team on Saturday afternoon."

Fans in Lincoln send off Devaney and his team for the 1965 Orange Bowl.

Nebraskans would frequently hear such witticisms from Devaney as he made the rounds in the state during public appearances. From Omaha to Scottsbluff and from Beatrice to Butte, Devaney logged thousands of miles each year selling the program and entertaining fans. He collected a tidy sum in speaker's fees for his trouble, supplementing a modest salary that was nothing like the millions he would have raked in had he coached in more modern times.

But he also knew the fans' Big Red passion contributed directly to the success of his program. It was a force of nature that assured a steady flow of home-grown talent, an athletic budget that lacked for nothing and a home-field advantage that was second to none.

In a state without any pro teams to dilute the interest, these people were as football crazy as fans you'd find anywhere. Men came to games in red cowboy hats or fedoras, red ties and red blazers, while the ladies were decked out in red scarves, red shoes and Go Big Red buttons. It all combined to turn the game-day crowd into landlocked Lincoln's celebrated Sea of Red. As Sports Illustrated would put it in 1970, Devaney "harnessed the region's old-fashioned Americanism, dressed it up in red and put it in the stadium to cheer his team."

Even with all the stadium expansions after his arrival, there never were enough tickets to go around. People had been known to stop at the NU ticket office on the way to or from funerals to inquire about the availability of the dearly departed's season tickets. Beyond buying tickets, fans joined the Extra Point Club, for annual donations of as little as $1, and the Touchdown Club, for the heavier hitters giving over $100. Local auto dealers in the Wheel Club made sure Devaney and his coaches cruised the state in comfortable rides. And Nebraska farmers and ranchers who were members of the Beef Club annually donated some 200 head of prime cattle to the athletic department.

Donald Schultze, left, and Larry Schultze cheer on the Huskers at a 1965 game.

Those corn-fed steers would be turned into prime rib, steaks and other beef cuts devoured at the Cornhusker training table.

More broadly, Devaney's football program became part of the very culture of the state, almost akin to a state religion. Across Nebraska, nearly all activity stopped on Saturday afternoons as fans headed to Memorial Stadium or turned their ears to the game call on the radio. As native Nebraskan and Kennedy White House aide Ted Sorensen once put it, "Nebraska is a good place to be from, or to die, or to be a football fan."

It seemed Devaney had found a comfortable home in Nebraska. He'd been offered other jobs but always figured he had a good thing going in Lincoln. The regents in 1967 handed him added responsibilities as the school's athletic director, seemingly cementing his place in the university and state.

But the relationship between Devaney and NU's passionate fans was tested some that very fall when the 1967 Cornhuskers finished an uncharacteristic 6-4, tied for fifth in the Big Eight. The team struggled all year to score, a glaring weakness that became apparent in the first scrimmage of fall camp. The first-team offense picked up only one first down against the No. 2 defense — and that was on a roughing-the-punter penalty.

Still, it was easy to consider the season a bit of a blip. It was a young team — NU had only seven returning starters, by far the fewest in the league. And they were playing in a much improved Big Eight, with Kansas, Missouri and Colorado all rising. Three of the four losses had been by seven points or fewer, including one in which the Huskers had a touchdown called back. A break here or there, and they easily could have won eight or nine.

Nebraskans weren't necessarily happy about 6-4. However, given the Devaney record, they were willing to be forgiving. Before a big crowd at the last of the weekly Omaha booster breakfasts that season, Devaney got them laughing when he expressed surprise that no one had presented him with a suitcase that morning. He then thanked the fans for "sticking with us."

But then came 1968. Though the record once again would be 6-4, the season revealed that there were cracks in the program's foundation far deeper than even Devaney had realized. The Huskers lost at home to both Kansas and Missouri to fall to 3-2. Even the wins to that point had come in Herculean struggles. It took late field goals to beat both Wyoming and Minnesota. It later took a last-minute touchdown to dispatch a so-so Oklahoma State team. Scoring for this team, Devaney's seventh, was again at a premium. The offense often appeared clueless and lost.

Colorado crushed Joe Orduna (31) and the Huskers 21-16 in Lincoln in 1967.

DEATH OF A SALESMAN?

Then on a cold, gray November afternoon in Lincoln against Kansas State, the Huskers seemed to hit rock bottom. Facing the perennial Big Eight doormats — a team that had not won a conference game in four years — the Huskers were shut out 12-0. The game wasn't even as close as the final score indicated. The Huskers were dominated on both sides of the ball. What's more, the homecoming loss was Nebraska's third straight in Memorial Stadium, something that had not happened since Jennings' last year in 1961 (and which, incidentally, has not happened since). Indeed, the loss to KSU had the feel of a Jennings flashback.

The crowd of 67,000 started leaving in stunned silence with five minutes on the clock. The only sound at the end was the pop-pop-pop of dismayed fans dispatching their red balloons, which were traditionally released in a popular spectacle after the Huskers' first score. Rather than face flak from angry fans, Osborne and fellow assistant Melton lingered in the press box afterward, faces buried in their hands. "I am at a loss to know what happened," a shell-shocked Devaney said. Indeed, as the 47-0 thrashing at Oklahoma two weeks later would prove, he really had no answers.

Devaney always knew there was pressure to win in college football, keeping his sense of humor about it. One of his favorite stories on the banquet circuit was of a coach who got tired of telling his players to go out and win for their moms or in the memory of some unfortunate soul who'd recently suffered an untimely death. Just go win for yourselves, the coach told the players. The team proceeded to get killed in the first half. That caused the coach to offer a new message at halftime. "OK, since you don't want to win it for yourselves, how about winning it for me, the eight assistant coaches and our 27 children."

Kansas State's Mack Herron escapes from Nebraska's Bob Liggett in the Wildcats' 12-0 victory in Lincoln in 1968. The crowd left early. "The walkout was a rare and almost frightening sight," The World-Herald reported.

In another frequently used line, Devaney would tell booster groups he knew they were with him, "win or tie." They were laughing so hard, he'd say after the room erupted, because they knew it was true.

Now the situation in Lincoln was no laughing matter. Both the fans and the university's regents were growing restless. Despite Devaney's past successes, there was talk on the street that the game had simply passed him by. One Lincoln letter writer noted that with Devaney wearing the hats of both athletic director and coach, the regents needed to "inject themselves into this dilemma before all that has been gained is lost."

Oklahoma corrals Nebraska's Mick Ziegler in the Sooners' 47-0 win in Norman in 1968.

The Lincoln Journal in an editorial after the K-State game had cautioned fans against overreacting, reminding them of Devaney's seven-year record. The paper also noted it was "only a game," pointing out that the Huskers "are not determining the fate of mankind." The World-Herald's editorial writers days later expressed admiration for the Journal's sentiment but noted that those finely chosen words "won't convince that rabid breed of extremists" who believe the fate of mankind truly does revolve around the happenings at Memorial Stadium. Devaney had himself to blame for the madness. He had created the monstrous expectations.

As Devaney spoke at the Extra Point Luncheon after the Oklahoma loss, his tone was more wistful than confident, and it was devoid of humor. "We'd like it to be better," he said of the 6-4 record. "We don't expect compliments."

To Devaney's assistants, it was clear these last two seasons had been hard on their boss. The happy-go-lucky coach seemed to age before their eyes. What if he was Willy Loman, his career now in hopeless decline? Death of a salesman, indeed.

It's unclear at what point the rumors of a petition to oust Devaney surfaced, or how serious the drive really was. If it indeed existed, the petition never got up enough steam to ever make its way into the newspapers. No coaches spoke publicly of any petition until more than a decade later. Melton joked about it, saying the Huskers had been so bad he had been tempted to sign the thing. Dean Kratz, an Omaha attorney who in 1969 was among the city's most prominent university boosters, said in a 2014 interview he never laid eyes on such a document.

"It certainly was a weak effort, if it was tried," Kratz said. "But people were upset, no question about it."

In a 2014 interview, Osborne said coaches at the time were "very much aware" of the petition and the fan discontent driving it. And even if there was not much real momentum to fire Devaney at that point, there was much pressure on the head coach to fire some assistants. "People took that real seriously," Osborne recalled. "I took it seriously because I was one of those guys." That memory would stay with Osborne throughout his long coaching career, a lesson in how little job security there is in football. The long winter of 1968-69 would be a time of great anxiety for everyone in the program.

In the face of such pressures, though, Devaney held firm. He was staying. Any creeping self-doubts were overwhelmed by his resolve to make things right. And true to his trademark loyalty, all his assistants were staying, too. "If one guy goes, we all go," Osborne recalled Devaney telling his staff as they huddled in the wake of the Norman debacle. "I'm not having any sacrificial lambs."

But as Devaney met with his coaches in the Husker football offices, on the second floor of the NU Coliseum, there was a sense of urgency. Warren Powers, at the time a graduate assistant, decades later recalled how plain-spoken and serious Devaney was as he laid out what was ahead for coaches during this critical off-season. "We're not going to continue like this," Devaney said. "We need to get our asses in gear."

Devaney well knew his program stood at a crossroads. If they were ever going to get things turned around, major changes were in order.

> "I would suggest that Devaney go back to being head coach and relinquish the job of athletic director. I don't believe one man can do justice to both positions."
>
> **— An Omahan writing to The World-Herald's "Voice from the Grandstand" column**

Assistant coach Mike Corgan talks with Dick Davis (45) and Joe Orduna (31) on the sidelines in 1968. Devaney refused to fire staff members in reaction to dissatisfaction with the Huskers' second straight 6-4 season.

The Coordinators

TOM OSBORNE SAT ALONE IN THE DARKNESS of a tiny film room in the Nebraska football offices, the shaft of light from the projector barely illuminating his youthful face. Osborne clutched a controller in his hand as he intently watched black and white images of Steve Owens galloping through the Nebraska defense.

Devaney puts his squad through calisthenics during spring practice.

Several times during each play, the Husker coach hit a button on the controls and reversed the film's direction. That caused Owens and the other players to miraculously spring back to their feet and run backward to their original positions. Then Osborne would play it again, going back and forth and back and forth in a monotonous whir.

With each replay, Osborne's eyes would focus on a different part of the screen, a different Oklahoma player. He'd intently watch what each player's assignment had been and translate it into X's and O's on the notebook in front of him.

Such film study, of course, is a staple of football. Coaches spend countless hours every year breaking down the tendencies of their opponents. Few loved that aspect of the game more than Osborne, who often took a portable projector and reels of film home with him at night. Unlike that projector, Osborne had no off switch. His tireless viewing of film years later as head coach at Nebraska would reach epic proportions.

But this time Osborne wasn't scouting a future foe. He was studying the inner workings of Oklahoma's I-formation offense, planning to incorporate some of its concepts into an offensive attack of Osborne's own creation.

During the 1968-69 offseason, Bob Devaney and his coaches re-examined the Husker program from top to bottom. They looked at everything from how they practiced to their game-day morning rituals. He dispatched several assistants to other programs to study best practices his team might adopt. He was open to anything. And while Devaney refused to listen to those calling for him to fire coaches, he did decide to shake up some responsibilities on the staff. In the end, it's arguable that no one's duties changed more than his own.

Devaney at practice in 1969 with quarterback Van Brownson and assistant Tom Osborne, who was retooling Nebraska's offense.

Up to that time, Devaney had never employed offensive or defensive coordinators — assistant coaches specifically designated to oversee operations on one side of the ball. Though still a recent concept in football, such coordinators had been coming into increasing use in college and the pros around that time. In the past, Devaney's style had been to work with all his coaches to draw up weekly offensive and defensive plans and then to make most of the game-day strategic decisions himself.

But during this 1968-69 offseason, Devaney decided it was time to, in effect, fire himself from that duty and name de facto coordinators on both sides of the ball. These coaches' primary jobs would be coming up with and implementing the weekly game plan on offense or defense. And despite Devaney's longtime associations with several assistant coaches who had decades of coaching experience, he boldly handed those coordinator jobs to the two most junior coaches on his staff: Tom Osborne and Monte Kiffin.

Looking back now, it seems almost fated — or perhaps just plain luck — that Devaney had those two young men already working in the NU football offices. Devaney arguably could have scoured the nation and not found better candidates for the jobs than the two native-born Nebraskans who were mostly anonymous outside of Lincoln. Osborne ultimately would become universally regarded as one of the most innovative offensive minds in football, his schemes copied in college and the pros alike. And Kiffin would prove to be a defensive whiz who designed much-emulated defenses during a decades-long NFL career, winning a Super Bowl in 2003 with the Tampa Bay Buccaneers. At this point, though, they were just two enthusiastic young coaches who regularly played handball together in Schulte Field House.

Osborne starred in track, football and basketball at Hastings College. He won both high school and state college athlete of the year awards from The World-Herald.

Osborne had grown up a standout athlete in Hastings, less than two hours west of Lincoln. Schoolmates called him "Yak" because he talked so much, an ironic nickname to those who would know the quiet and introspective man as an adult. He grew up across the street from Hastings College, where both his grandfather and father had played football. The younger Osborne also took to the game, playing so much football with his friends on the campus lawn that the school president at times would chase them off.

The tall and gangly redhead became a three-sport star in high school and was named The World-Herald's prep athlete of the year. He then became the third-generation Osborne to play for hometown Hastings College.

Despite the little school's low profile, the brother of a scout from the NFL's San Francisco 49ers spotted him during the small-college Mineral Water Bowl in Excelsior Springs, Missouri. The wide receiver went on to play two seasons with the Washington Redskins, starting some games and ranking third on the team in receptions in 1961.

In January of 1962, Osborne found himself at a turning point in life. He was slowed by a chronic hamstring injury and was in a minor dispute with the Redskins over the $500 he was supposed to have been paid for exhibition games the previous season. Though the team offered him another contract for 1962, Osborne decided it was time to move on. The cerebral Osborne enrolled as a student at the University of Nebraska with plans to pursue a doctorate and become a college professor.

But the 24-year-old budding academic wasn't quite ready to leave football behind. He wrote to Devaney, who just days earlier had been hired as the Husker head coach, and asked to serve as a graduate assistant.

While the coach responded that he already had all the assistants that he needed for the coming season, he was aware of a problem at Selleck Quadrangle. Some of Bill Jennings' players had taken over a portion of the dorm, essentially tossing the resident counselors out. If Osborne would move into the dorm and ride herd on the Selleck ruffians, he'd be able to eat his meals for free at the team training table.

Osborne accepted. That winter and spring, he broke up a few fights and restored order in Selleck while also volunteering as a coach during spring ball. And by the fall of 1962, Devaney named Osborne a full-fledged graduate assistant.

Osborne straddled the fence between football and academia for the next several years. He taught graduate and undergraduate courses during the morning and then coached in the afternoon. He was extremely dedicated to both pursuits, impressing his bosses with his work ethic, and he was popular with his students and his players.

After completing his doctorate in educational psychology in 1965, the man Nebraskans later came to call "Dr. Tom" was torn. He very much enjoyed teaching, and the psychology department offered him a job as a professor. But the pull of football was strong.

Osborne again talked to Devaney and threw out a proposal. If you can match the $10,000 salary I would receive as a professor, I'd like to instead become a full-time coach. At the time, there were no NCAA restrictions on how many assistant coaches a college team could have, the number limited only by a school's willingness to pay for them (Oklahoma years later would have an assistant whose sole job, from the best Osborne could tell, was to recruit all-world high school running back Billy Sims). Devaney made the best hire he'd ever make, naming Osborne the coach of the Huskers' offensive ends.

Devaney called Osborne "a real brilliant young man" in hiring him full time.

THE COORDINATORS 31

By that time, Devaney had recognized that there was something special about the earnest young Osborne. Personalitywise, they didn't share a lot in common. Osborne was a teetotaler who couldn't muster up a curse word stronger than "dadgummit." He wasn't one to spend much time around the Legion club. "Tom and I never went out together and did foolish things," Devaney would later say.

But Devaney also was quick to recognize the genius of Osborne when it came to football's Saturday chess matches. There was an air of quiet detachment about him, as if great thoughts were swirling around in his head. And he was meticulous in his preparations.

Nebraska's power-running game at times featured two lead blockers for the running back.

Devaney years later would tell an acquaintance that he knew as early as 1964 that Osborne was the coach he wanted to succeed him as head coach one day. In the spring of 1969, Devaney had not yet told Osborne that, but he did see that the 32-year-old was at the moment the perfect man to serve as his first offensive coordinator. He wanted Osborne to not only take over the Husker offense but give it a major retooling.

In his early years in Lincoln, Devaney had been served well by the Daugherty offense he'd first learned at Michigan State: a power running game utilizing a full-house backfield and an unbalanced line. A left halfback, a fullback and a right halfback were lined up side by side behind the quarterback. And on the line, a guard and both tackles were together on one side of center, providing more bodies and girth to that side of the field. Many of the running plays predictably would go in that direction.

Devaney's philosophy was, "We're gonna run it on you or be damned." The coach had a well-earned reputation for teams that played stout defense, avoided mistakes and then pounded you into submission with the running game. One writer appropriately had dubbed Devaney's Huskers "the ponderous pachyderms of the plains." If the Huskers threw the ball a dozen times a game, that was a lot. The offense had evolved a little by 1968, with NU running plays from several different formations. Power running, however, remained Nebraska's bread and butter.

It was clear now, though, that Devaney's bread and butter had gone stale. A second straight year in which the offense averaged fewer than 16 points a game — capped by the big goose eggs in losses to K-State and Oklahoma — made that painfully obvious. Defenses began recognizing that Nebraska rarely passed out of the unbalanced line and were using blitzes and other pressure defenses to stop the Huskers' run game.

Devaney now wanted a more diverse and wide-open attack, featuring a quarterback who could both run and throw. And he trusted Osborne to come up with it. "Bob came to me and said, 'I want you to redesign the offense,'" Osborne recalled in 2014. "I don't want to make myself to be any more than I was, but that's what I did."

Quarterback Frank Patrick looks for end Tom Penney (85) after faking a handoff to Ben Gregory (22) in 1967 against Kansas. Much of Devaney's early passing attack was based on the defense's expectation of a run.

The focus of Osborne's new offense became the I formation. The origin of the I, in which the quarterback, fullback and halfback are lined up vertically behind center, one behind the other, is unclear. But it had been popularized in the early 1960s by John McKay's University of Southern California Trojans.

Behind a powerful I-formation offense, USC won national championships in both 1962 and 1967. The same day the Huskers were getting pasted by Oklahoma's I-offense in Norman, USC's O.J. Simpson was wrapping up the 1968 Heisman Trophy with a huge 200-yard game. His national record 1,800 yards and 23 touchdowns made him the runaway winner of the honor for college football's best player.

Devaney first had added the I to his arsenal of formations before the 1967 season, but the Huskers rarely used it. Osborne during this 1968-69 offseason fully embraced the I, studying its use at Oklahoma and USC and adding his own variations.

Osborne's I featured an elaborate option run game with either the quarterback, fullback or I-back carrying the ball. There also would be power sweeps to the I-back and roll-out passes by the quarterback. Instead of a third running back in the backfield, a wingback, or flanker, would be deployed in the slot between the end and tackle, able to go out for passes or carry the ball on inside reverses. It created lots of possibilities for deception.

Frank Patrick hands off to Ben Gregory from the I-formation in 1967 against Kansas. "We don't want to get caught behind the times," Devaney said of the new offense in the spring of 1969.

In one creative Osborne twist, the Huskers would break out of the I during obvious passing situations, the I-back moving into the slot as a second flanker. In this "spread" offense, the quarterback could get the ball to any of the backs and ends to use their speed. While some versions of the spread had been around since leather helmet days, it appears that few, if any, major programs were running it at the time. The combination of the spread with the new Nebraska I made for a versatile run-pass offense to attack a defense.

But the most innovative part of the new Osborne offense was the elaborate system of audibles he developed. It was in many ways ahead of its time.

For every play in the new Nebraska playbook, there was an alternate set of plays the quarterback could check into at the line of scrimmage. It all would depend on how the defense was aligned. A play called in the huddle could be doomed to failure before it even started if it was run into the wrong defense. The Osborne audible system counted on the Husker quarterbacks being able to recognize the defense and getting the Huskers out of the "dead" play and into one that instead created a mismatch in the Huskers' favor. An audible literally could spell the difference between a major offensive breakdown and a length-of-the-field touchdown.

In some cases the audible simply might reverse the direction of the play, going to the side of the field where five defenders were lined up rather than six. Other times it was a whole new play. For example, to exploit how the defense was lined up in the secondary, a "46 iso" — a simple handoff to the I-back through the left-guard hole — could be turned into a "51 pass," a rollout pass to the wingback.

To make the change, the quarterback at the line of scrimmage would call out "46" — the number of the play called in the huddle. That was the signal to everyone that the play was now changing. Then he'd call out "51," the number for the new play. Whenever an audible was called, the Huskers knew, the snap count always would be on the second hut, regardless of the count called in the huddle.

The players who first would learn the system in 1969 had no idea just how groundbreaking it was. And while Osborne as a head coach would become known for his devastating, ground-pounding running game, this offense under Devaney would make Osborne a guru of football's passing game.

Notable as it would seem today, Osborne's role in transforming the Husker offense at the time fell largely outside of public view. He continued to be listed in media guides as merely Nebraska's offensive ends coach, his profile among the lowest of all the Husker coaches.

While it might seem odd now, it wasn't for the time. The media back then often portrayed head coaches as mythic, larger-than-life figures who hands-on managed all aspects of their programs. And Devaney did little to disabuse Husker fans of such notions. It would be years before Devaney publicly gave Osborne credit for running the offense during his final years on the sidelines. "We didn't call him the offensive coordinator," Devaney said in a 1992 interview, "but that's what he was."

Not all the coaches on Devaney's staff approved of the new offense, preferring to stay with the old unbalanced line. And throwing the ball around surely went against Devaney's conservative grain. He generally held to the old football maxim that when you throw a football, three things can happen, and two of them are bad. "There are some good things that happen when you pass," he had said in 1967, "and some things that aren't so good."

But sometimes the mark of a good leader is his willingness to change. Devaney liked what he saw in the plan, and he trusted Osborne. He told the young coach to implement the changes. Over the fruitful years to come, Devaney would come to rely heavily on the young assistant to have the offensive unit ready to play each week. Then on Saturdays, Osborne would sit high in the press box watching the game plan play out like moving pieces on a chessboard. He'd tweak things as they went along and sometimes send down play calls by headphone to a coach standing with Devaney on the sidelines. The Husker offense was Osborne's baby.

George Kelly left Nebraska for Notre Dame before the 1969 season, the first of the original staff to leave.

THE COORDINATORS 35

Similarly, Devaney decided it also was time to hand over defensive-coordinating duties and overhaul what Nebraska was doing on that side of the ball. He turned to a 28-year-old who had just spent the previous two seasons helping coach Nebraska's freshman team.

"Monte, do you think you're ready to take over this defense?" Devaney asked young Monte Kiffin.

"Yeah, hell yeah, I can do it," replied Kiffin. It was a response that would come to typify the enthusiasm and confidence Kiffin brought to the football field each day.

Under Devaney, the Huskers already had established a storied defensive tradition with its "Blackshirts" — the nickname given the starters on the defensive side of the ball. Today, the most ardent of Nebraska fans are familiar with the history of how the Blackshirts name came to be during Devaney's reign. But the story was less widely known during Devaney's time. Fans of that day might have surmised the unit's moniker came from World War II-era fascist thugs. But it actually was the product of a thrifty shopping choice at a Lincoln sporting goods store.

In 1964, Devaney decided to finally switch Nebraska from single platoon football to separate offensive and defensive units. To sort things out in practice, he initially had defensive players wear gray vests. But he soon wanted more contrast with the offense's white jerseys. So running backs coach Mike Corgan was sent to a local sporting goods store to get jerseys in some other shade. Corgan found a set of pullovers that just happened to be black, and they were on sale. Corgan knew a bargain when he saw one.

Coaches in practice soon after started to refer to the first-team defense as "the black shirts." About a month later, a World-Herald story picked up on that, referring to Husker defenders by the "Black Shirts" name. The Blackshirts tradition was born. And over time, it would develop its own mystique within the world of college football. Helping build the legend was the stoutness of that 1964 defense. Ranking second in the country, it was the first great Nebraska defense in the modern era.

The 1967 Blackshirts had been another great unit, setting a school record by limiting teams to a nation-low 158 yards a game and posting four shutouts in 10 games. The 1968 unit had been solid, too, surrendering just 16 points a game. Still, after watching the way the Sooners' Owens plowed through the Blackshirts in that last game in 1968, Devaney decided it was time for some major changes. And in Kiffin, he had the right man for the job.

Kiffin had grown up in a football family, the son of the high school coach in Lexington, Nebraska. And from an early age, he loved Cornhusker football. He would head out east on U.S. Highway 30 with his dad in the fall and pay a quarter to sit in the bleachers of the then-open south end zone at Memorial Stadium, known as the knothole section.

Kiffin turned out to be a pretty good player himself. Bud Wilkinson, coach of the Oklahoma teams that dominated the national football landscape during the 1950s, flew into Lexington one day to recruit the powerful lineman. But Kiffin instead accepted Jennings' offer to play for his beloved Huskers.

Monte Kiffin was a three-time all-stater in basketball at Lexington High.

Kiffin was a junior on Devaney's first Husker team and didn't play a lot that year. In fact, what he would be most remembered for was what came to be known as "the milk truck incident" — a transgression that kept him home from the Gotham Bowl.

There was an official party for the seniors on the Monday night after the regular season ended, and Kiffin was part of a big group that ended up at an all-night cafe. At 3 a.m., they started back for campus on foot, cutting through the parking lot of Roberts Dairy in Lincoln. Kiffin noticed a milk truck, its cab empty and the engine running.

"Hey guys, let's take this truck home," Kiffin imprudently suggested. Several guys piled in, Kiffin got behind the wheel, sounded the horn and drove off to Selleck Quadrangle. The police rousted the groggy Kiffin out of bed hours later.

Devaney suspended him for the bowl but didn't kick him off the team, allowing him back for his senior year. Kiffin went on to start at both offensive and defensive tackle on the Big Eight champion team in 1963. He always would be grateful to Devaney for the second chance.

Devaney thought a lot of Kiffin, too, enough to name him a graduate assistant when he was done playing and give him a full-time job with the freshman team in 1967. During those years, Devaney became like a second father to Kiffin. "I owe everything that's happened to me in my career to Coach Devaney," the veteran coach would say decades later.

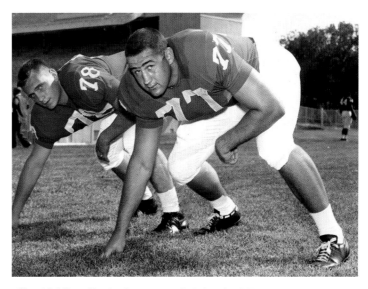

Kiffin with fellow offensive lineman Dennis Carlson in 1963.

Shades of that crazy, unpredictable, milk truck-jacking side of Kiffin were what made him such a great coach. While he was clearly a skilled tactician, what set him apart was the passion he brought to the field.

Kiffin believed in only one speed — all out. And he didn't just preach it. He'd actually run the stadium steps with his players. When they did the grueling "up-down" drill — running in place, diving to the turf, and then springing back to their feet as fast as they could — he would lead them, popping back up 50, 80, even 100 times. Sometimes while demonstrating techniques during practice, he would tackle the running back without the benefit of helmet or pads. Legend has it that during one scrimmage, Coach Kiffin dove headlong to recover a fumble just before an offensive player could get his hands on it. This guy absolutely lived for football.

The Blackshirts related well to their young coach and came to mirror his intensity. One player from the era later recalled a running back protesting after a Blackshirt unloaded on him during what was supposed to be a half-speed drill. Kiffin jumped to his player's defense. "What the hell is wrong with you? You've got pads on," Kiffin barked at the back. "Don't bitch about it. Play the game." It was no wonder the Blackshirts wanted to play so hard for "Coach Kif."

Kiffin years later said he wasn't sure why Devaney turned to such an inexperienced coach to coordinate the Husker defense. Jim Ross — the respected gentleman who was Devaney's right-hand man, longest-serving aide and best friend — voluntarily left his spot on the defensive staff at that time. He instead took over the freshman team and assumed some of Devaney's athletic director duties, allowing the head coach to devote more time to football. John Melton, the veteran linebacker coach who had been with Devaney since Wyoming, may not have wanted the coordinator job, Kiffin surmised.

Not only did Devaney pick Kiffin, he hired Kiffin's buddy, roommate and former teammate — ex-Husker defensive back Warren Powers — as a full-time assistant for the defensive backs. Devaney told Kiffin to work with Melton and Powers to put the new defense together. "You would have thought Bob would go out and hire someone from a Top 10 defense," Kiffin recalled years later. "But he believed in his people."

As with Osborne, Kiffin was not publicly named defensive coordinator. He wouldn't actually get the title officially until Osborne became the Huskers' head coach more than four years later.

Soon after receiving his new assignment, Kiffin boarded a plane and flew to the University of Georgia. The school at the time was utilizing the "Monster" defense that Frank Broyles had developed years earlier at Arkansas and that Devaney decided to emulate. The Monster essentially was a 5-2 defense that deployed a defensive back — the monster back — in a sort of hybrid, roving role. The monster would line up on the tight end side of the field and could play back to defend against the pass or move up into the box to help against the run.

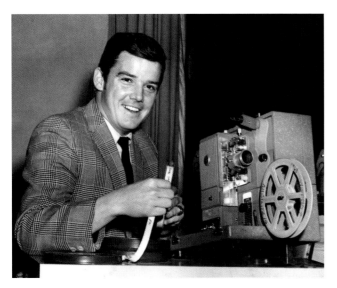

Warren Powers joined the staff as a full-time assistant in 1969.

Devaney and Kiffin liked the concept's versatility and adopted it as the signature for the new Nebraska defense. For the rest of the Devaney era — and for two decades to come after — the term "monster back" became part of Husker football vernacular.

The twin hires of Osborne and Kiffin weren't the only big moves Devaney would make during this critical offseason. But none would have a bigger impact on the future fortunes of Nebraska football. Still, the only hint that there had been any coaching shake-up during the 1968-69 offseason came in February, when the NU Board of Regents approved the contracts of Powers and Thunder Thornton — a new offensive aide for the freshman team. A World-Herald account of the hires noted that Kiffin likely would be moving up from freshman duties to work with the varsity, but only as a defensive line coach.

Keen readers a few weeks earlier might have noticed another signal that Devaney had bigger things in store for both Kiffin and Osborne: Of all the returning NU coaches — including the head coach himself — the only ones who would be getting raises after that dreadful 1968 season were those two junior staff members.

Nebraska monster back Al Larson (20) stuffs a Georgia back in the 1969 Sun Bowl with help from Mike Wynn (90). Blackshirts Ken Geddes (37) and Jerry Murtaugh (42) also are on the spot. The Huskers had devised their new defense in 1969 after studying it at Georgia the previous winter.

Shaping Up

THE HUSKER PLAYERS SHARED PERPLEXED, what-the-hell-is-this glances the first time assistant coach Cletus Fischer led them down to the handball court in Schulte Field House, just north of Memorial Stadium. An old wrestling mat had been spread out on the floor. And in the middle of the mat sat a wooden ax handle.

Following Fischer's instructions, the Huskers paired off, and the first two knelt down on the mat, each grasping one end of the ax handle. Then Fischer, a Husker offensive line coach, blew a whistle. That started a violent flurry as the players battled to wrest away the ax handle — by whatever means necessary. There weren't a lot of rules. In the free-for-all, the Huskers would twirl, yank, push, shove, grapple, lash out and brawl. One Husker years later would describe it as MMA — mixed martial arts fighting — before there was MMA. Indeed, what players came to simply call "the ax-handle drill" very quickly proved a blood sport. There would be numerous broken noses, wrenched limbs and other physical carnage during the fierce gladiatorial combat. "It probably wasn't the best idea in the world," Tom Osborne would concede years later.

But for players, the ax-handle drill was the first and surest sign that after that 1968 season, nothing was going to be the same in the Nebraska football program. In another key offseason change, Devaney for the first time implemented a required program of winter conditioning. And thanks to that new resolve from Devaney — with a major, unexpected contribution months later from a bodybuilding pole vaulter on the Husker track team — the conditioning program over time would revolutionize the way college football players everywhere prepared their bodies for future seasons.

Devaney with 1969 assistants Monte Kiffin, Bill Thornton and Cletus Fischer, creator of "the ax-handle drill."

After that miserable 1968 game in Oklahoma, Devaney warned returning players that they'd better have their jockstraps on tight. "I can tell you there had better be some changes around here," tight end Jim McFarland recalled him saying, "because there were a lot of candy-ass football players on the field." Jerry Murtaugh, a linebacker, said the message was something like, "God help all of you that are coming back next year. Your soul belongs to the Lord, but your ass is all mine." Regardless of Devaney's exact words, it seems clear he intended to put them through their paces. They soon learned just what he had in mind.

Prior to 1969, spring practices had been the only off-season conditioning for some players.

As coaches took stock of the program in the wake of the OU loss, Devaney sent trainer George Sullivan and Fischer to visit a high school in Lawrence, Kansas, and to Louisiana State University. Both schools were running offseason football conditioning programs, a rarity at the time. It's almost unthinkable now, but at Nebraska and most places, players would just show up for practice in the spring and in the fall, and the coaches would hope they would have done something to stay active. Devaney wanted Fischer and Sullivan to check out the schools' programs and launch something similar in Lincoln.

Nebraska's new offseason conditioning was an official class required of all football players, with an hour's university credit as part of the deal. In reality, it was a football version of boot camp. Sullivan was listed as the instructor, and he and Fischer took the lead in designing and running it. Players would learn that Devaney and the coaches were taking this new endeavor very seriously. It would turn out to be among the hardest hours of credit any of them would earn in college.

George Sullivan

Three afternoons a week at 3:30, players reported to the lower level of Schulte, a big open room with three-story, cathedral-style windows that spectacularly bathed the space in fading winter light. The players were dressed in what they called Gib's Grays — university-issued gray sports gear named for Gib Babcock, the equipment manager who handed them out each day. While the program was run by the assistant coaches, the general attitude driving it came straight from the top. "As long as we live, a total whipping like Oklahoma will never happen to us again," recalled defensive back Dave Morock. "It was a whole new attitude, and it was from Bob Devaney."

Dave Morock

First, players lined up and went through a battery of stretches. They then divided up into groups and rotated through eight stations, pushed and prodded at each to move faster, work harder or squeeze out one more rep. The stations were spread between Schulte and the dirt running area beneath East Stadium, a damp old-school space that years earlier had been dubbed "Mushroom Gardens." There, players ran through several drills intended to lengthen their running stride and improve their speed and agility. At another station, run by Warren Powers, players donned a harness like a horse and ran, a partner behind them providing resistance to help build leg strength and drive. The pace was intense, and it wouldn't take long before those gray uniforms were darkened by sweat.

Then there was Coach Fischer's ax-handle station. Osborne believes Fischer borrowed it from Alabama. Sullivan recalled that Fischer or someone on staff had picked it up in the service. Regardless, it soon became clear to players what the drill's purpose was: to instill some fight and aggressiveness into the Huskers. "It was a nasty drill," recalled walk-on quarterback Steve Runty. "But football is a nasty game."

Beyond the brute strength and savagery involved, Runty and other players would recall there was strategy, too. Sometimes instead of pulling on the handle, players would surprise the opposition and instead charge forward. Their opponents' own momentum would land them flat on their back, desperately trying to hold on. Morock recalled doing that to one underclassman and running right over him. Morock got the ax handle, while the other guy got a major split in his upper lip. "There was nothing really wrong with it," he said of the drill. "You figure the coaches would have stopped it before somebody died."

Defensive lineman Ken Geddes did everything he could to avoid such maiming. "If you got to fighting around with that stick, it was dangerous," he said. "I just tried to get the guy down and then just sit on him until they blew the whistle."

Bob Newton remembered a more aggressive tactic he used against fellow offensive lineman Donnie McGhee. "When they blew the whistle, I tried to shove the ax handle right into Donnie's neck," he said. "It was gruesome."

Guys would hold onto that ax handle for dear life. There was no shame if the 30-second match ended in a draw, but there was in getting beat. Especially when you had coaches and teammates gathered around the mat, hooting and hollering as if watching the proceedings in the Roman Coliseum. Some players dreaded the drill, while others relished it with animalistic fury. But no one was fonder of it than Coach Fischer. "He loved that drill," Sullivan later recalled. "It was the only way to have contact during the winter."

Weightlifting was only a small part of the new conditioning program that first winter after the 1968 Oklahoma debacle. Players spent about five minutes at a station where they lifted crude, makeshift barbells fashioned from concrete-filled coffee cans. Nebraska obviously wasn't set up for much weightlifting. But just a few months later, in August 1969, that would change.

Boyd Epley arrived in Lincoln in the summer of 1967 with dreams of becoming a national champion pole vaulter. The Beatrice, Nebraska, native had been a standout at a junior college in Arizona, setting a national junior college record and attracting the notice of Husker track coach Frank Sevigne. By 1968, the Husker aerial daredevil had cleared 15-feet, 1-inch to break the school's indoor record and seemed ready to scale even greater heights. But that spring, he missed the pad during a practice jump and broke his foot, an injury that knocked him out for the rest of the season. Then in November 1968 while preparing for his senior year, he injured a disc in his back during a practice takeoff. That mishap again left Epley on the sidelines — but would also come to alter his life in ways he never imagined.

Injuries had sidelined Boyd Epley in both high school and college.

SHAPING UP 43

Boyd Epley set state records in a 1972 weightlifting meet.

Epley decided to take a redshirt year during the 1968-69 school year and use the time to rehab his back. Weightlifting became a significant part of his program. At the time, the NU athletic department had a dingy weight room, not much bigger than a bedroom, adjacent to the training room in Schulte. Used mostly by athletes rehabbing from injuries, it was modestly equipped with a universal lifting machine featuring about four stations, a barbell with about 400 pounds of loose weight and four dumbbells. Epley hit the weights hard with the hope of getting back on track. To that end, the effort proved a failure. Doctors would never clear him to vault again.

But along the way, he became enthralled with weightlifting, particularly with the way it was transforming his body. In a relatively short time, he'd become a virtual Charles Atlas, whose familiar bodybuilding ads appeared on the back covers of comic books.

Before he started his lifting regimen, Epley never would have been confused with the 97-pound weakling who got sand kicked in his face in the Atlas ads. He weighed a solid 170 pounds. But afterward Epley packed so much muscle on his 205-pound frame that he could bench press more than 350 pounds. Soon he would be entering bodybuilding contests, a year later finishing second in a 13-state "Mr. Iron Man" competition.

"Sevigne wanted to kick Boyd off the track team," Sullivan recalled. "He was always lifting weights and oiling himself up." But others were more enamored with Epley's chiseled physique — including some members of Bob Devaney's football team.

At the time, most football coaches — including Devaney — frowned upon any kind of weightlifting for their players. The old myth was that lifting would make players muscle-bound and take away their speed and athleticism. Nonetheless, a handful of Husker players did lift, either because they were rehabbing injuries or were weights zealots like Epley.

Epley would sometimes bump into them during his daily visits to Schulte. Some of them at first thought he was odd. Who was this guy who shaves his legs? — a bodybuilder's trick to show off muscle definition. But they also could see that he was a lot stronger than they were. "Oh, my Lord," Murtaugh thought when he saw how much Epley could bench press. "I want to be like this guy."

Then one day during the spring of 1969, Epley walked into the weight room a half hour later than normal and found a half dozen football players just sitting there. "What are you guys doing?" Epley asked. "Waiting for you," they replied. Turns out, without Epley's notice, they had taken to following him around and mimicking his routine. From that point on, Epley started to informally work with them, passing on the finer points of lifting he had picked up. One thing Epley emphasized was combining their lifting with intensive stretching exercises. That would keep their new muscles from binding them up and slowing them down.

Epley came in to lift one day during the spring or early summer of 1969, when he was summoned to the adjacent training room to take a phone call. On the line was assistant football Tom Osborne. "Are you the guy who has been showing the players how to lift weights?" he asked.

Osborne requested that Epley come to his office, where he also found offensive line coach Fischer.

Epley thought he might be in some trouble, knowing how most coaches felt about lifting. Instead, Osborne and Fischer offered him a job. Would Epley be willing to teach the football team to lift? They'd pay him for it — $2 an hour to work with players for a total of six hours a week.

Epley told them he was just a student, but they didn't care. He told them there wasn't enough equipment, but Osborne said that wasn't a barrier either. Bring me a list of the things we'd need, Osborne told him. Epley went home and prepared that list, taking care not to ask for too much. It was mostly some barbells, squat racks and benches. The next day he presented the list to Osborne, who immediately handed it to the football secretary and asked her to order everything. Epley couldn't believe how easy it had been, proving that the coaches really were serious about this. Realizing that money was no object, Epley immediately told Osborne he'd forgotten to bring the second page of his list. With a knowing grin, Osborne told Epley to let him know what else they needed. Epley asked for more equipment, including some dumbbells. Sometime later, a wall was knocked down in Schulte to double the size of the still-modest weight room.

Epley's strength program included in-season weightlifting.

Everything was now set. And on Aug. 15, 1969, less than a month after Neil Armstrong first walked on the moon, Boyd Epley became a different kind of pioneer. With his $12-a-week job, he officially became the first paid weightlifting coach in the history of college football. It was the modest beginnings of "Husker Power."

It would be four more years, under head coach Osborne, before Epley himself got the actual title of football strength coach at Nebraska. It also would be a while before coaches would require all Husker players to lift. For now, it would be encouraged, especially among the linemen, who would quickly become Epley's most devoted disciples. But Epley would go on to become an innovator in developing new training techniques, physical tests and equipment. He'd rebrand weight training as "strength training" and turn strength coaching into a recognized profession of its own.

Within a decade, the university would build the world's largest weight room, a 13,000-square-foot iron palace beneath West Stadium that became the envy of every football program in the land. On the wall of that "Strength Complex," Epley would prominently display words that defined the philosophy that guided him from the start: "Combine Running, Stretching and Lifting — If You Dare to Be Great."

The day Boyd Epley was hired, all of college football changed — as did the fate of Bob Devaney's football program at Nebraska.

But as Epley assumed his new duties in 1969, he still faced some doubters — most critically Devaney himself. While Osborne had become convinced that a weight program was the way to go, they still needed to persuade the head coach to go ahead with what they all would have admitted was a human-subject experiment. Before the hiring was finalized, Osborne asked Epley to sit down with Devaney.

Epley still vividly recalled the meeting years later. Devaney was seated behind his desk in a big leather chair. Epley was so nervous his legs were shaking. Osborne had Epley explain his philosophy about lifting, how he felt he could help make the football team both stronger and faster. Devaney expressed some skepticism, noting that since his days at Michigan State with his friend Duffy Daugherty, he had never believed in lifting weights. In the end, the dubious Devaney said he'd be willing to give it a try. Then he pointed a wary finger at Epley.

"But if anybody gets slower," he said, "you're fired."

> "They are in better shape as a group than they were last year. For the most part, the linemen came back pretty trim."
>
> —Bob Devaney after the first day of fall practice in 1969

Nebraska players push heavy bags as part of conditioning before practice.

In Search of Help

BOB NEWTON ROLLED HIS 240-POUND BODY out of bed in Nebraska's Harper Hall dorm. It was January 1969, the first day of the university's "spring" term. Spring, however, was kind of a far-off notion on this cold and blustery day. Freshly arrived on campus from his home in Southern California, Newton headed out the door for class. He steeled himself against a brutal north wind. He made it about 200 feet. "You've got to be kidding me," he thought. Then he turned around, went back to Harper and climbed back under the covers.

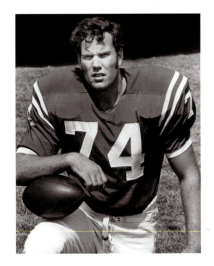

Bob Newton

Newton had to question his own sanity. What the heck am I doing out here on these frozen Plains? The answer to that question, as with so many others, gets back to that 1968 season and Bob Devaney's desperation to turn things around.

Recruiting, of course, is the lifeblood of college football. Players are only in your program, at best, for four or five years. You have to keep the talent coming. And Devaney usually could count on reeling in a load of new talent every year. As one writer once put it, Devaney had a knack for "accumulating large, capable football players by the cattle-car lot."

When it came to recruiting, the Huskers were without doubt handicapped by the state's small population. But Nebraska also had one huge advantage compared to most other schools in the country, and it came down to the resources the university was willing to put into football.

Today, the NCAA allows big-time football schools no more than 85 total scholarships. But during Devaney's time, the NCAA set no limits, leaving such rules to the conferences. When it came to football, the Big Eight was all in, with league schools allowing 45 new scholarships every year and no limit on the total number. That contrasted with the Big Ten, which allowed schools only 30 new football scholarships a year. Southwest Conference schools were allowed no more than 100 total scholarships. It wouldn't be unusual during Devaney's time for NU to have upwards of 150 scholarship football players between the varsity and freshman teams. Many other Big Eight schools were right there or close to it. While perhaps excessive, the Nebraska system certainly could be defended as a more humane one. Coaches at schools with strict limits tended to run off players who didn't pan out. Sometimes the coaches would even subject young men to torturous physical drills to try to force them to quit. With Devaney, pretty much the only way to lose your scholarship was to flunk out, cause trouble or quit.

Still, there's no doubt that such scholarship numbers added up to a huge advantage for Nebraska and the Big Eight. Nebraska's largely unfettered ability to hand out grants in aid was surely one of the reasons Devaney never lost a game to a Big Ten school in his career, going 11-0.

Bob Newton (74) gets sideline instruction from assistant coach Carl Selmer.

Devaney used that advantage, turning Big Ten country into arguably his most important recruiting ground outside Nebraska. Each year Devaney pulled loads of players out of Michigan, Ohio, western Pennsylvania and other Rust Belt states. That was the area he was most familiar with from his days recruiting at Michigan State. And it was flush with guys who could play. Devaney knew places like Fond du Lac, Ypsilanti and Uniontown about as well as he did McCook, Hastings and Kearney.

Four of Alabama's five starting offensive linemen for the 1967 Sugar Bowl weighed less than 200 pounds.

Devaney's 1968 varsity team had a total of 32 players from Michigan, Pennsylvania, Wisconsin and Illinois, not that far below the 46 who came from Nebraska. By blending Nebraska kids with others from the Big Ten's footprint, Devaney could count on having the talent to win in the Big Eight.

However, despite that inherent advantage and Devaney's history of recruiting success, he and his coaches later would admit that during the mid-1960s their recruiting efforts slipped. Complacency that set in during the string of conference championships helped lead to a void of talent and speed at several positions during 1967 and 1968. And the lapse came just as other Big Eight schools like Kansas, Kansas State and Missouri were stepping up their recruiting game.

Now the results were clearly showing up on the field. As the 1968 season wound down, Devaney told his coaches they were going to have to hit the recruiting trail hard in the coming months. The most crucial and pressing need was finding some offensive linemen. The void in that particular area wasn't just the result of complacency, but due to a tactical mistake Devaney had made two years earlier.

After both the 1965 and 1966 seasons, Devaney's Huskers lost bowl games to Bear Bryant's Alabama teams. The second of those games hadn't even been close, Bama crushing the Huskers in the Sugar Bowl 34-7. And the Tide did it with one of the smallest offensive lines in all of college football.

Bryant had taken a bunch of fullbacks and linebackers and turned them into linemen. They averaged about 5-11 and no more than 190 to 200 pounds, but they played like little gremlins. They got off the ball quickly and tied up Nebraska's bigger, more lumbering linemen, allowing the Alabama running backs to scoot right by.

Devaney started to think little crab-like blockers might be just what his program needed to get to the next level, so he started recruiting smaller linemen. He also ordered the linemen already in his program to cut back on the steak and potatoes and run off excess weight. By the fall of 1967, the Husker line featured four guys who weighed between 201 and 215 pounds and a fifth who had dropped his weight from 275 to 248. The 1968 line was even smaller, averaging about 210 across the board. Nebraska newspapers around that time featured a number of optimistic stories touting the tonnage the line had shed.

But the trimmed-down Huskers got pushed all over the field. In the 1968 loss to bottom-feeding K-State, the offense had managed just 78 yards on the ground. The line was so overmatched against Oklahoma two weeks later that a wiseacre in a letter to The World-Herald suggested that Nebraska's quarterbacks should have just signaled for a fair catch on each snap. As Devaney later put it, "I went out and looked for small, quick kids like Bryant had — and got small, slow ones instead." Jokes aside, it's not exactly clear why it didn't work the same way it did for Bryant. It's possible the smaller linemen weren't a good fit for Nebraska's style of offense or the play in the rugged Big Eight.

Regardless, Nebraska needed help, and fast. And since freshmen by NCAA rule weren't eligible to suit up with the varsity — a rule that didn't change until 1972 — Devaney wasn't going to get immediate help from some high school stud. The only real choice was to scour the junior college ranks looking for guys who could step in and play right away. And so in late 1968, Tom Osborne suggested to Devaney that they might try recruiting California, the state with the nation's most extensive system of junior colleges.

Recruiting California at the time was considered a bit of a gamble, Osborne later would recall. The conventional wisdom was that you couldn't get guys from warmer climes to stick around for a Midwest winter. Once the snow started flying, they'd be gone. It sounds surprising now, but in 1968, Nebraska actually had just one player from west of Nebraska on its entire roster, and he came from Wyoming. And the school had only one player from south of Kansas, a lineman from Arkansas. But given the need, Devaney figured it was worth taking the chance. Go west, young man, he told Osborne.

Bob Newton, right, was with the first-team offense as fall practice began.

IN SEARCH OF HELP

Recruiting at the time was not nearly as sophisticated as it is today. There were no scouting services, star ratings or websites with videos of players in action. Osborne went to meet with the coaches of some of the better junior college programs and asked them to recommend players from their teams and their opponents. Then he asked the coaches to set him up with some game film and a projector so he could have a look for himself. That led Osborne to Bob Newton.

Newton had turned from a gangly kid coming out of high school to a solid force on the offensive line at Cerritos Junior College in Norwalk, California. He still wasn't highly recruited, but several other schools saw potential in him, including Oklahoma and UCLA. He was preparing for his season-ending banquet when Osborne first called to ask if he could stop by. Soon Newton was greeted at the front door of his apartment by a tall and slender redhead.

Osborne told Newton about the school and that the team was looking to build up its offensive line. And he mentioned that Newton could have a look at the team for himself, with the Huskers scheduled to play on national TV against Oklahoma the next week. "Wow, they do need some help," Newton thought when he tuned in.

Bob Terrio

A couple of weeks later, Devaney himself came out to Norwalk and charmed Newton's dad with his sense of humor. Despite the Huskers' huge need on the line, Devaney didn't offer a lot of promises or hype. It wasn't his style to tell a kid he was going to make him an All-American. But Devaney told Newton that if he worked hard, the coaches thought he could one day contribute to the program.

In December, Newton flew into Lincoln along with two other junior college recruits from the Golden State: Bob Terrio, a fullback from Fullerton; and Dale Didur, an end from Long Beach. Back then, the jets parked on the tarmac in Lincoln, requiring a walk of some 100 yards to the terminal. The Californians recalled wearing T-shirts as they stepped off the plane into single-digit temperatures. As they moved briskly to the terminal, Osborne could see the wheels spinning in their heads. Indeed, Terrio later would recall thinking, "It's too damn cold for California boys." Nonetheless, they all had a good visit, struck by Devaney's grandfatherly charm and Osborne's low-key sincerity.

Newton was slow to commit, though. He was holding out hope for an offer from a school right down the road from Cerritos: USC. Not only were the Trojans the nation's top team in 1968, but their star offensive lineman was a fellow Cerritos product, future NFL Hall of Famer Ron Yary.

A USC coach had told Newton weeks earlier they were interested and would be getting back to him, but since then he'd heard nothing. So before committing anywhere else, he called the USC football offices. "Who is this again?" Newton was asked. He was quickly shoved aside. At that point, Newton was ready to commit — to San Diego State — figuring he'd stay in comfortable Southern California, close to his family. He told Osborne as much. Later in his coaching career, Osborne would have accepted that answer. He didn't believe in continuing to harangue kids once they had made a decision. But he and the Huskers were desperate, so he begged for one more chance to meet with Newton.

The lineman relented to the visit and then surprised even himself by accepting Nebraska's scholarship offer. One of Osborne's big selling points: In each of the next two seasons, Nebraska would be playing USC.

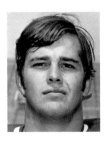

Keith Wortman

In the end, Terrio and Didur also signed with the Huskers. And in the process, the players opened up a key new recruiting ground for Nebraska.

The next year, Osborne and Devaney went west again to pull four more players out of junior colleges, including three more offensive linemen: guard Dick Rupert from Los Angeles; guard Keith Wortman from Whittier; and tackle Carl Johnson from Phoenix Junior College in Arizona. Osborne was able to grab Wortman away from USC, repeatedly flying west and pointing out to the lineman that McKay had been taking him for granted. "How many times has Coach McKay been here to see you?" Osborne would ask.

Together the recruits ultimately would resolve the Huskers' offensive line woes. Newton was a starter by the end of the 1969 season and by 1970 a consensus All-American. Rupert as a first-year Husker would join Newton as a starter on the 1970 line. Then Rupert, Wortman and Johnson claimed three of the five spots on the 1971 starting line. In all, five of 22 starters on the 1971 Huskers were plucked by Osborne out of West Coast junior colleges. It was a truly Golden haul — one that would provide a solid foundation for the great Husker teams to come.

From that point on, big names from California high schools and junior colleges would annually dot Nebraska's roster — players like Vince Ferragamo, Steve Taylor, Lawrence Phillips, Brenden Stai, Michael Booker, Ralph Brown, Marlon Lucky and Taylor Martinez.

California wasn't the only critical new recruiting territory that Nebraska opened in 1969. While Devaney sent Osborne west, he dispatched Monte Kiffin east to New Jersey.

Devaney always had recruited western Pennsylvania's steel and coal country hard, an extension of his recruiting the Big Ten region. But his eastern reach pretty much stopped there. Nebraska at the time didn't have a single player on its roster from the northeastern United States.

Penn State each year got the pick of players out of Jersey. But the school couldn't take them all. Devaney recalled that the bustling, congested streets of northern New Jersey had been a productive area for him when he was coaching at Wyoming. Back then, he always had a coach meet those big-city boys at the airport in Laramie to make sure they didn't turn around and get right back on the plane once they got a look at the place. Devaney told Kiffin they might discover some gems if they got into New Jersey now. That proved an understatement.

Kiffin just days later found himself sitting down to dinner at a Howard Johnson's just off the New Jersey Turnpike with a pair of high school prospects: Daryl White, an offensive lineman out of East Orange, and Rich Glover, a defensive lineman from Jersey City.

A New Jersey recruit's high school coach recommended that Monte Kiffin look at other players from the state. Kiffin spotted Rich Glover on film from another school and offered a scholarship to the future Outland Trophy winner.

Johnny Rodgers

Daryl White

Willie Harper

Joe Blahak

Both ultimately signed with Nebraska and were All-Americans their junior and senior years. In time, this new recruiting pipeline would bring to Lincoln some of the greatest players in Nebraska history — names like Heisman Trophy winner Mike Rozier, Irving Fryar, Barron Miles and Jason and Christian Peter.

The movement into California and New Jersey represented the first significant expansion of Nebraska's recruiting territory since Devaney's first year in Lincoln. And it became a precursor to the truly national recruiting strategy that Tom Osborne would employ at Nebraska beginning in the 1970s.

Nebraska would make some other recruiting scores in the class of 1969. It always was a goal to lock in the best in-state kids, the ones who grew up with a passion for Big Red football. In February, Devaney sat down at a steakhouse in Omaha and signed his top Nebraska target, an elusive flyer from Technical High School named John Rodgers.

When it comes to recruiting, college coaches trade on the futures market. You never know how an 18-year-old is going to pan out four years later. That was even more true in 1969, when most athletes played multiple sports in high school, had done little in the way of weightlifting and were yet untrained in the finer points of the game. But in the end, the 1969 recruiting class would go down as surely one of the greatest ever at Nebraska. Players who would join Terrio, Newton, Rodgers, Glover and White in the marquee class included Willie Harper, John Dutton, Joe Blahak and Monte Johnson — all building blocks of future Husker greatness.

It was the junior college transfer Newton, however, who would make the most immediate impact. He was able to enroll right after signing in December. So he and Terrio packed all their stuff and big bodies into a little red VW bug in January 1969 and drove shoulder-to-shoulder cross-country to Lincoln. It was a wild trip. And despite the initial shock of that first Nebraska winter, Newton did survive and stick around.

Indeed, spring ultimately did come to Lincoln, bringing to an end what Devaney later would call "the longest winter I ever spent." The snow melted. The winds stopped howling from the north. Young women again started walking campus in shorts and miniskirts. And the Huskers returned to the practice field, the start of 1969 spring ball.

Newton was out there with his new, beefier teammates on the offensive line. He was raw and unpolished — "not that good," a teammate would put it years later. But ultimately through hard work in the weight room and on the field, he'd emerge by fall as an impact player.

Kiffin and Osborne were out there, too. This spring practice session was absolutely critical as they introduced their units to the new formations and plays they had worked up over the winter. There was a huge learning curve ahead for everyone, including the coaches. This wasn't going to be easy.

As the players absorbed the new playbook, they moved around the field with a new spring in their step. They were in the best shape of their lives after all the off-season conditioning. Mike Green, a former left halfback from Omaha now learning the fullback position in Osborne's new I-formation attack, felt so fresh and strong that he wished the Huskers could start playing the 1969 slate right then.

Of course, every college football team is optimistic in the spring. However, it seemed that Devaney and his team had true reason to look forward to better times ahead. With the longer vision of hindsight, Devaney and the Huskers would years later look back on the lost seasons of 1967 and 1968 and come to see them in a whole new light.

Had it not been for the disappointing years and the critical changes they spawned within the coaching staff, the Huskers' schemes, strength and conditioning and recruiting, the era of greatness that lay ahead for Devaney and Nebraska might never have come to pass.

The World-Herald reported in the fall of 1969 that the freshman football team had some unusually large players, including 6-foot-7 John Dutton, at left, and 6-6 Monte Johnson, right, both of whom went on to long pro careers. In between them are 6-2 Joe Henderson and 6-4 Frank McKinley.

Super Sophs

ON PICTURE DAY AS THE CORNHUSKERS KICKED OFF their 1969 fall camp, quarterbacks Van Brownson and Jerry Tagge stood on the grass inside Memorial Stadium doing the bidding of a World-Herald photographer. Picture-day shooters notoriously had players strike all manner of contrived poses. Diving for an imaginary fumble. Stiff-arming a phantom tackler.

But the pose this photographer had the two fresh-faced sophomores strike was as unique as it was contrived. Both clutched in their hands the same football, as if they were in tandem turning to hand it off to an on-rushing Nebraska I-back.

More than 40 years later, the picture would stand as a remarkable image — a visual, moment-in-time metaphor for the experience the two touted signal-callers would share during coming autumns in Lincoln. These two varsity newcomers would come about as close to actually sharing the football as any two starting quarterbacks could.

In Brownson, from rural Shenandoah, Iowa, and Tagge, from blue-collar Green Bay, Wisconsin, the Huskers had a pair of gifted and promising quarterbacks. Both possessed strong arms, strong wills and potential without limit. The reality in football, though, is that there is only one ball, and only one quarterback could lead the Nebraska huddle when the starting offense trotted out to the field.

By the time the quarterbacks were photographed that day in their crisp scarlet and cream jerseys bearing numerals 12 and 14, they already had battled in practice for more than a year for the chance to be "the man." Still, it would be another two years before either would lock down the job that both coveted madly.

There's a football coaching adage that if you have two starting quarterbacks, you really don't have any. Two quarterbacks usually means indecision, disruption, mediocrity, lost games and shortened coaching careers — a subject that surely would have been a little touchy for Bob Devaney in the fall of 1969. But that football chestnut wouldn't hold true at all in Nebraska during this era. Not with Jerry Tagge and Van Brownson.

Over the coming years, the Huskers would win — and in the end win big — as each regularly took snaps with the team's fortunes in his hands. Week after week and score after score. Cheer upon cheer and win upon win. Van or Jerry, Jerry or Van. It didn't really seem to make much difference.

By the time their college journeys would end, though, one of the young quarterbacks would be destined for Nebraska immortality. Even Husker fans generations later would know the name and recognize his image, heroically reaching to extend a football over the goal line. The other was fated to more footnote status, a fragile body and his own youthful indiscretions conspiring to dash his dreams.

"It's way, way too early to tell what we'll do this fall."

— **Devaney, assessing his quarterbacks in the spring**

Jerry Tagge (14) congratulates Van Brownson (12) after a touchdown pass against Oklahoma State in 1969.

That time, however, remained years off, beyond the horizon. During this moment in time, as two young, earnest quarterbacks posed in Memorial Stadium grasping that single pigskin, each had every possibility for football glory still well within his reach.

In the fall of 1969, Bob Devaney was set to kick off arguably his most pivotal season as coach at Nebraska. And he would be doing so having to put his faith in a quarterback with no previous varsity experience.

Leading the Husker varsity was pretty heady stuff for any 19-year-old who the previous year played for the Husker freshman team, going up against the likes of McCook Junior College. In fact, the preseason prognosticators were saying Nebraska was going into the season with "a quarterback problem." But Devaney was hopeful. He knew that in Brownson and Tagge, this Nebraska team had more raw talent at the quarterback position than any in his previous seven years in Lincoln.

Van Brownson had grown up in Shenandoah, a nearly straight 80-mile shot east of Lincoln on Highway 2. Even decades later, he still was considered one of the finest all-around athletes ever to come out of the state of Iowa.

Standing 6-foot-2 and weighing 176 pounds, he lettered in five sports in high school — football, basketball, track, baseball and golf. He remains one of only a handful of athletes in Iowa to be named first-team all-state in both football and basketball during both his junior and senior years. The World-Herald in 1968 tabbed him as Southwest Iowa's Athlete of the Year. By his senior year he'd picked up so many trophies, his bedroom looked like Aladdin's cave.

On the football field, Brownson was both a strong, accurate thrower and a nifty runner. He'd first burst onto the scene as a high school sophomore in 1965 when his coach inserted him late in the first half of the Mustangs' third game. Brownson threw for three touchdowns and ran 70 yards for another that night. By the end of the season, the 16-year-old became the first sophomore ever voted by coaches to The World-Herald's All-Southwest Iowa team.

National recruiters were on to him by the time he was a junior. And by the end of his senior year, he had thrown for 53 touchdowns and rushed for 17 more, racked up miles of yardage through the air, and averaged 6.6 yards each time he ran the ball.

Brownson averaged 25.5 points and 16 rebounds a game in basketball as a senior at Shenandoah.

Forty major schools wanted Brownson, including Duke and Kentucky in basketball. Nebraska was one of five schools to offer him scholarships in both football and basketball.

The Huskers, though, had a bit of an inside track when it came to landing the young talent. Van had been born in Lincoln, where his dad worked for the regional distributor of Ford brand tractors and farm implements. The family had moved to Iowa soon after, when his dad took over a dealership of his own in Shenandoah.

Devaney made his final recruiting pitch to Van's parents one day in Lincoln while their son was away golfing, convincing them that the proximity of Lincoln and quality of the program made Nebraska the right place for their son. Devaney himself came to Shenandoah for the signing, Van becoming the most highly touted recruit in Devaney's 1968 class. Devaney would say later that he had never recruited an athlete harder. A big reason for that was Devaney's decision, after the 1967 season, to find a different kind of quarterback.

The Husker signal-caller that year, Frank Patrick, was a classic drop-back passer who stood tall in the pocket at 6-foot-7. He had a strong arm, actually leading the conference in passing. But he wasn't much of a runner. And looking around the Big Eight, Devaney was seeing that the trend was moving toward quarterbacks who could both run and throw. The epitome was Kansas' Bobby Douglass, who would make all-conference in both 1967 and 1968, beating Devaney's Huskers both years. Kansas coach Pepper Rodgers swore by such dual-threat guys, saying any team that didn't have one was playing 10 against 11. Douglass helped convince Devaney, too.

"Today, it seems the teams scoring a lot of points in college football have a quarterback who runs as well as passes," Devaney said. "We have not had the real great quarterback who can do all the things of a Douglass."

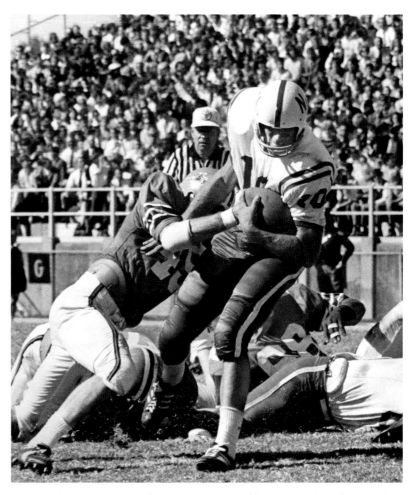

Frank Patrick, the starting quarterback in 1967 and part of '68, was moved to tight end in '69.

So in his 1968 recruiting class, Devaney brought in no fewer than seven scholarship quarterbacks. Yes, seven. All had been stars on their high school teams. And they all started out their careers in Lincoln at the quarterback position, even if only for a few days.

Noting the uniqueness of the situation, The World-Herald had all seven line up for a photo at the start of fall camp that year. At Nebraska back then, freshman ball was a big deal. Unlike most coaches, Devaney didn't use his freshmen as practice-time cannon fodder for the varsity. They practiced separately, spending weeks getting tutored in the Huskers' way of doing things. Then late in the fall, they played an abbreviated four-game schedule against junior colleges and other schools' freshman teams.

Freshman quarterbacks in 1968, from left, Jeff Kinney of McCook, Max Linder of Plattsmouth, Mike McGuire of Bellevue, Chuck Osberg of Omaha, Brownson, Tagge and Skip Klutka of New Brighton, Pennsylvania.

With non-scholarship walk-ons joining the 45 scholarship freshmen, there were 60 to 70 new players out on the field, three-deep at almost every position. Roughly half would wash out before their sophomore year, although many continued as students. Less than two dozen would see meaningful varsity action by the time they were seniors, and still fewer would become starters. It was all a numbers game, particularly with this big batch of quarterbacks.

Freshman coaches sorting out the new quarterbacks didn't have them throw the ball. Instead, they were lined up to run 40-yard dashes. Those results established the initial pecking order among the candidates and showed the premium coaches were putting on quarterbacks who could run the ball.

Jeff Kinney may well have been the fastest, but he was such an impressive runner that coaches soon moved him to running back. Max Linder was right up there, too, a rocket who had been the top high school athlete in Nebraska the previous year. But Linder would battle a back injury that eventually helped derail his Husker career.

Brownson didn't quite have the top-end speed of some of the others, but he was plenty fast. And he packaged that speed with remarkable quickness and elusiveness. It seemed he instinctively could avoid contact and slip tackles. He was a slick ball-handler, too.

And of the quarterback competitors, arguably nobody threw a prettier ball than Brownson. They were glorious spirals, flying with the nose of the ball slightly elevated to give the receiver lots of ball to latch onto. Those assets helped him emerge from the pack to become the starter that fall for the Husker "yearlings," the horse-racing term Nebraska scribes often applied to the NU freshman team.

Brownson would have the finest season ever by a freshman quarterback at Nebraska. While the Husker varsity was stumbling to its second straight 6-4 finish that fall, Brownson led the freshmen to a 4-0 mark, setting NU frosh records for completions, passing yards and total offense. "I never thought of myself as being better than any other," he recalled years later. "I felt fortunate just to get the chance to get on the field and help the team."

In the spring of 1969, Brownson was immediately tabbed by the press as the top contender to unseat Patrick, who was going into his senior year. Brownson ended up missing considerable time that spring due to a shoulder injury and was unable to play in the spring game. Still, by the end of drills in May, Devaney had Patrick taking reps at tight end, the position he'd move to permanently in the fall. Hastening that move was not only Brownson's obvious talent but the sudden emergence of a second sophomore quarterback: Jerry Tagge.

Tagge wasn't listed on the first depth chart in the spring of 1969, but a World-Herald story noted that he was "an apparent hard worker during the offseason."

Like Brownson, Tagge was a Nebraska native who spent most of his childhood in another state. He lived in Lincoln and Omaha until age 4 before his dad was transferred to a job in Green Bay. Tagge grew up just a mile from Lambeau Field, home of the NFL's famed Packers, who at the time were in the midst of a 1960s dynasty under legendary coach Vince Lombardi. Tagge idolized Packers quarterback Bart Starr and even worked on Sundays selling popcorn and Coke at Lambeau.

A standout in football, basketball, baseball and hockey, Tagge soon made a name for himself on the athletic fields at nearby Fisk Park. He was always bigger than most kids and as a high school senior stood 6-1 and a sturdy 220 pounds — bigger than most of the offensive linemen blocking for him. But Tagge combined that size with natural athletic ability. The big man set the conference scoring record as a center on Green Bay West's basketball team but also had such good dribbling skills that he brought the ball up the floor. On the gridiron, he was a sprint-out quarterback with a live arm and great instincts for what to do with the ball. West, which actually played its home games at Lambeau, lost only one game in the two years Tagge started at quarterback.

Tagge finished his high school career as an All-American in football and had 42 scholarship offers and a pro baseball contract on the table. By then, Devaney already had established a recruiting pipeline into Green Bay West. In fact, over a two-year period, he would lure West's entire four-man 1966 backfield — Dennis Gutzman and Jim Anderson in 1967 and then Tagge and Dave Mason in 1968. Tagge's thought was that they'd all go down to Lincoln and pretty much duplicate all their success from high school.

But Tagge soon found it was not that easy. He arrived at fall camp to hear one of the coaches call out, "All quarterbacks over here." Quarterbacks? He was shocked by the numbers, having no idea he was facing so much competition. And if speed was going to be a key factor in separating the candidates, Tagge never would measure up. He would recall finishing last in that initial 40-yard dash. Even he would later admit he didn't look like a quarterback on film back then, moving sluggishly around the backfield. Show the film in slow motion, and it looked like he was hardly moving at all.

SUPER SOPHS

Because of Tagge's size and relative lack of speed, the freshman team's coaches tried him at linebacker and tight end in addition to quarterback. Tagge even did some long snapping as a center.

That fall turned out just miserable for Tagge. It didn't help that he sprained his ankle jumping over a tackling dummy while practicing with the defense. The worst part of all was standing on the sideline and watching Brownson throw four touchdown passes to Mason, Tagge's old high school buddy. Tagge instead shared backup duties with Chuck Osberg, attempting 22 passes and completing just nine.

To top it off, Tagge's grades were bad, the quarterback later recalling that he carried three F's and a D during the first semester. Devaney, noting the D, said, "You obviously are concentrating way too much on one subject." Tagge was ordered to attend Tom Osborne's 6 a.m. study hall sessions, purgatory for players struggling to stay eligible.

At the end of that fall, Tagge's confidence was shot. He went back to Green Bay over winter break and moped around, feeling depressed. He told his old high school basketball coach he might not even go back to Lincoln for the spring semester. "Jerry, they gave you a scholarship," his coach told him. "If nothing else, go back, get your degree and get on with your life."

Tagge did return to Lincoln. Osborne, who around that time was being handed the reins of the NU offense, also helped talk Tagge off the ledge. He saw potential in the raw quarterback and urged him to keep working. All the advice would pay dividends for Tagge in the spring. That's when he suddenly began a surprising rise up the Husker depth chart.

Tagge was barely on the press' radar when 1969 spring practice opened. He wasn't listed on the four-man depth chart and was the last of seven potential quarterbacks reeled off by The World-Herald in its spring football preview. Tagge wasn't much on Devaney's radar, either — at least as a quarterback. Devaney later admitted that he gave a lot of thought going into that spring of moving the burly quarterback to center. As Tagge put it years later, "Devaney was high on Van Brownson."

But spring practice often is a time when coaches find out who their real football players are. And Husker coaches soon would find they had one in Tagge. By the first scrimmage two weeks into spring, the sophomore-to-be had moved up to the fourth team, praised by Devaney for showing marked improvement. The coach was beginning to find there was perhaps more to Tagge than met the eye.

"The way he's running, we'll have to look at him at one of the running back spots if he isn't one of the first two quarterbacks," Devaney said of Tagge (14) after watching the quarterback in spring practice.

Tagge had been working hard during offseason conditioning to improve his quickness and agility. And while he still wasn't going to dazzle anyone with his running, he was surprisingly smooth, not even looking like he was putting out much effort. He ran with power, too, able to take on a linebacker and still make yardage. Tagge didn't always throw the prettiest ball, but he'd put it where it needed to be.

After Tagge excelled again in the second scrimmage, throwing for a pair of scores, he moved up to No. 2. He was cited by coaches as a potential gamer, a player who would show up on Saturdays. "Tagge has become a good quarterback," Devaney said after a breakout May scrimmage. "He's made some bonehead plays, but he runs his unit. He's big and tough and passes well."

In the annual Red-White spring game, Tagge fared the best among all the quarterbacks. And with Brownson hurt, Tagge had an opportunity to seize the No. 1 job. But in addition to leading his unit to a score, he also threw an early interception that was returned for a score, a big no-no in Devaney's book. "I did some foolish things," Tagge said afterward.

Still, the spring had dispelled Tagge's personal doubts. He had firmly established himself as a contender to start for the 1969 Huskers.

Come fall, Brownson's shoulder was healthy again. He, Tagge and junior Tony Dvorsak all showed the kind of confidence you expect from your quarterback. But they also all had a new offense to grasp. As drills progressed, NU coaches weren't particularly happy with how any of them were executing it. In one early scrimmage, the indecisive quarterbacks combined to be dumped behind the line 13 times. Devaney spent the whole preseason waiting for one to assert himself. It didn't happen. "We've got to find a quarterback who can lead and get the job done," he lamented to reporters one day after practice.

Brownson and Tagge went into the final week that fall in a dead heat. In the last scrimmage, Brownson led what Devaney considered to be the day's best-executed drive, a

A Brownson fumble — possibly caused by a face-mask violation that wasn't called — ended Nebraska's first series against USC.

13-play march that went nearly the full length of the field. In that same scrimmage, Tagge suffered an ankle injury that left him hobbled. That, almost by default, gave the nod to Brownson. He would make the start in the Husker opener.

It was a big spot for any young quarterback. And it was made even more monumental by the opponent the Huskers would face that day in September 1969. As Brownson took the field in Memorial Stadium — a hopeful and energized home crowd of some 67,000 looking on — lined up across the field in their classic white, gold and maroon jerseys were none other than the mighty Trojans of USC.

Deep down, Brownson and his teammates had to wonder: Are we really ready to take the field against one of the best teams in college football? Preseason prognosticators ranked Southern Cal fifth in the country. The Huskers were picked fifth in the Big Eight. As Brownson warmed up on the field that afternoon, he looked calm, but the butterflies in his stomach were the size of raptors.

But this was a moment Brownson had been dreaming of since the day he committed to the Huskers. The first time he led the Huskers onto the field was an experience he'd never forget. All the red in the stands shone so brightly in the midday sun, it was almost blinding.

Not surprisingly, though, Brownson and the Husker offense got off to a sluggish start, helping the Trojans jump out to a quick 14-0 lead.

The blame was hardly all on Brownson's shoulders. Joe Orduna, the Huskers' leading rusher the two previous seasons and the featured back in the new I-formation offense, was leaning against crutches on the sidelines. The senior from Omaha Central had suffered a season-ending knee injury during a preseason scrimmage just two weeks earlier — a huge blow to the team. He was this team's only established offensive star.

The offensive line also was nearly all new. In an effort to find something that worked up front, Devaney had four players lined up at new positions and another new starter manning the other spot. That makeshift unit was going up against a massive Trojan defensive line that writers would dub "The Wild Bunch." They frequently had Brownson running for his life.

But the Huskers did finally get some things going in the second quarter. Wingback Larry Frost, whose son Scott nearly three decades later would quarterback Nebraska to a national championship, broke away for a 36-yard run to put NU in business. From there, Brownson ran it in from the 2 for his first touchdown as a Husker. NU trailed just 14-7.

Though the Huskers subsequently were down 21-7 at the half, Brownson was at times showing flashes of brilliance. He completed most of his passes and created some buzz in the crowd with his scrambling ability and nifty ball-handling.

Wingback Larry Frost (28) turns the corner on a 36-yard run to the USC 3-yard line.

On one early play, Brownson found himself face-to-face with a Trojan defender. He used a pump fake to get around him, cut clear across the field and broke loose for a 14-yard gain. It was a razzle-dazzle play so unlike any ever seen from a Husker quarterback, The World-Herald deemed it worthy of showing off to readers two days later in a frame-by-frame photo montage.

Jeff Kinney

Devaney still was going with Brownson late in the third quarter even after the Trojans went up 28-7. But then Tody Smith, the massive brother of Baltimore Colts star defensive end Bubba Smith, whacked Brownson in the shin. The sophomore limped off. And Jerry Tagge hobbled on for the first time in his Husker career. Despite his bum ankle, he was feeling no pain as he led the Huskers into the huddle, adrenaline surging through his body.

He immediately sparked a rally. Taking over at midfield, the 19-year-old drove the Huskers to a quick score. The touchdown came on a short run by I-back Kinney, the sophomore forced to step up in his first varsity game because of Orduna's injury. After a successful NU onside kick, Tagge got the Huskers moving again.

He passed 15 yards to Frost, in the process taking a lick that sent him to the sidelines briefly in favor of Dvorsak. Tagge returned and, sore ankle and all, kept the ball on an option, eluded a linebacker and scored from the 2.

It was suddenly 28-21 with 3:40 left. A team that had started off tentatively and unsure of itself was gaining some confidence. You could feel it. The Sea of Red in Lincoln was roiling with excitement.

The crowd got even louder when the Blackshirts made a stop, giving the Huskers one last chance. But then Tagge dropped back deep in Husker territory and made his first big mistake. His misfired pass was speared by a Trojan defender at midfield and returned to the NU 23. That set up USC for a clinching field goal. The final was 31-21 Trojans.

Afterward, Devaney praised his team. Sure, they'd made too many mistakes to win. The Blackshirts twice had gotten beat on long passes, both of them on a new play the Trojans had never shown before. But when the Huskers fell behind 28-7, they could have folded and didn't. And they weren't outclassed by a very good team, one that would go undefeated, finish No. 3 in the country and win the Rose Bowl. This game felt a lot better than that last one in Norman in 1968. The Huskers could take some good things away from it.

Devaney also liked what he'd seen from those fuzzy-cheeked newcomers, Brownson, Tagge and Kinney. The three sophomores each had scored one of Nebraska's touchdowns, offering a first glimpse at futures filled with promise. By the end of the season, these three 1968 recruits would be dubbed Nebraska's "Super Sophs." Their arrival in 1969 was well-timed for Devaney.

Both young quarterbacks had played pretty well for the first time out. They took command in the huddle, completed most of their throws and showed the ability to call plays and move the team.

If Brownson and Tagge were going to continue to share the ball like this, Devaney decided, it wasn't a bad problem for a coach to have.

> "I can't find fault with our young players. They made mistakes that veteran players might have made also.
> … I don't like to lose, but in looking for something encouraging, I was glad the way this team came back."
>
> **—Bob Devaney after a 31-21 loss to USC**

Teetering on the Brink

IT WAS DESPERATION TIME FOR BOB DEVANEY and the Huskers. They trailed Kansas 17-14 in Lincoln with less than two minutes to play. And they now faced a do-or-die fourth and 16 from deep in their own territory.

Tight end Jim McFarland was the leading receiver returning in 1969, but a leg injury slowed the junior from North Platte early in the season.

Jerry Tagge dropped back and instantly was flushed from the pocket by the Jayhawk pass rush. Scrambling to keep Husker hopes alive, the young quarterback heaved a long ball in the general direction of tight end Jim McFarland.

As McFarland tried to run under the pass, it became abundantly clear to him — and soon to everyone else in Memorial Stadium — that the ball had been badly overthrown. Devaney himself later admitted it: McFarland couldn't have caught that ball if he'd been standing on a ladder.

At that moment, it seemed much more than a football game hung in the air with that errant throw. It's quite possible Devaney's entire career hung in the balance.

A loss to the Jayhawks in this October 18 game would drop Nebraska to 2-3 and, most critically, 0-2 in the Big Eight. Just two weeks into league play, the Huskers already would be out of the hunt. What's more, such a start could prove a big blow to the psyche of this young and fragile team. The entire season could go spinning into an abyss. If that should happen, it could very well be the color pink would join red in the palette of Nebraska football — the shade of the paper slips Devaney and his staff could be handed at season's end. "It was teetering on the brink a little bit," Tom Osborne would recall years later.

But as dire as prospects appeared when that ball was soaring high above McFarland's head, it soon would become clear that the football gods had other plans for Devaney and Nebraska. While McFarland indeed would fail to catch the ball, the Huskers instead would catch a break. This play wasn't just going to be the unlikely turning point in a wild football game. It arguably would mark the turning point of Devaney's entire career.

So how did the Huskers get to this critical juncture early in the 1969 season?

Memorial Stadium rocked at the end of the 1969 Kansas game.

NEBRASKA HAD FOLLOWED THAT RESPECTABLE LOSS to USC with a pair of nice nonconference wins. The Huskers shut out Texas A&M 14-0 on a September day so hot in Lincoln that the Huskers changed out of their sweat-soaked jerseys at halftime. They then traveled north and gave Devaney another Big Ten pelt, overwhelming Minnesota's Gophers 42-14. Along the way, Van Brownson and Jerry Tagge continued their close and spirited battle for quarterback duties. Brownson started against the Aggies and got off to a sterling start, completing five of six passes for 55 yards and a touchdown. But then he got hurt again, suffering a twisted knee. In relief, Tagge completed 12 of 18 and led the Huskers to their other score that day. That helped earn Tagge his first college start the next week against the Gophers.

All Tagge did in Minneapolis was set a Nebraska record for total offense, completing 15 of 23 passes for 219 yards and running for another 82. He also had a light-bulb moment during the game. Osborne had noted during film study that the Gopher safety would tip off when he was going to blitz. "Jerry, do not miss this," Osborne had told him.

Sure enough, during the game, Tagge saw the safety cheating up. He made his first audible call, sending Larry Frost on a post and hitting him for a 38-yard touchdown. Tagge would remember it later as a big shot to his confidence. "I can lead this team," he thought.

In fact, it was a breakout game for Osborne's new offense. Nebraska's 587 total yards against Minnesota were the second most in school history. The new attack obviously was showing much promise and versatility. But with the young people running it, it was at times a bit of a high-wire act.

Against Minnesota, I-back Jeff Kinney harkened back to his high school quarterbacking days by throwing a 12-yard halfback pass to Guy Ingles for NU's first score. Minutes later, Kinney misheard a call in the huddle and mistakenly thought he was supposed to chuck the ball again. Rearing back and suddenly finding no one even going out for a pass, Kinney improvised and lobbed a pass back toward Tagge. A Gopher picked it off and took it 99 yards the other way for a touchdown.

"I'm two for two as a passer," Kinney told Devaney on the sideline once the game was well in hand. He took a lot of ribbing for that play. But with two rushing touchdowns, the sophomore from McCook also seized control of the starting I-back job.

Tagge's 301 total yards against Minnesota — 219 passing and 82 running — broke the school record of 264 set by John Bordogna in 1951 and tied by Frank Patrick in 1967.

The win in Minneapolis had happy Huskers chanting "We want Missouri!" in the locker room. They felt they were ready for their shot at the conference rival that had beaten them the previous two seasons. But the Huskers went to Columbia and on a chilly, muddy day took a 17-7 beating from the No. 7 Tigers. Missouri always was the hardest-hitting team on the Nebraska schedule. Win or lose, you never felt good after playing the Tigers. But this team could do a lot more than just hit you.

The Tigers scored two minutes into the game on a long bomb to receiver Mel Gray, the Big Eight's fastest runner and a future NFL star. The Tigers then stacked up the NU run game, holding the Huskers to a feeble 36 yards on 38 attempts. As a result, Nebraska logged passing numbers you would not have expected to see in college football until some future high-flying era. Tagge and Brownson put the ball in the air a combined 42 times.

Tagge again started the game, but his critical fumble deep in Nebraska territory just before the half helped the Tigers take a 14-0 lead. He threw a long touchdown pass to Kinney early in the third that raised hopes. But when the Huskers later stalled, Devaney turned to Brownson for a spark.

It didn't come. In fact, both quarterbacks' play showed the growing pains of the new offense. When calling an audible at the line, Brownson checked into a handoff to the I-back. There were many problems with the call, not the least of which was the fact that there was no I-back in the backfield at the time. The Huskers were in the spread.

Fullback Mike Green, the lone back in the spread, was unsure whether to take the ball or not. He and Brownson bobbled the exchange, and the lost fumble killed one of Nebraska's last hopes. Brownson also threw two interceptions during the final period, the third and fourth turnovers of the game for NU's young quarterbacks.

Missouri, which held Nebraska to 36 yards rushing, stops Husker fullback Mike Green short of a first down in the third quarter.

It wasn't a bad loss. Missouri had a heck of a team, the preseason Big Eight favorite that would play in the Orange Bowl at the end of the season. And Devaney thought the Huskers had been hurt by some bad officiating. At one point, he had yelled at a ref, "They're not going to take you to Miami with them!"

But given how badly the Huskers had wanted this game, the loss was deflating. Devaney tried to prop up his team afterward, worried the loss could cause a lingering emotional hangover. "When you get to the point that you give up, they might as well bury you in the ground," he told his team. "I don't believe there's anybody on this team ready to be buried."

BUT THAT'S JUST WHAT KANSAS WAS AIMING TO DO when it came to Lincoln the next week. The Jayhawks, now led by powerhouse running back John Riggins, had beaten the Huskers the previous two years and had shared the 1968 Big Eight title. For the 2-2 Huskers, this was suddenly a season on the brink.

While Devaney knew that preparation was what won games come Saturday, like any true Irishman he also was more than a little superstitious. Years earlier, a guy who found a penny on the street gave it to Devaney for good luck before the Gotham Bowl. After the Huskers won that game, NU coaches made a habit of picking up and collecting stray coins, amassing a lucky treasure trove that they kept in the coaching offices.

Before this game against Kansas, sports information director Don Bryant was in the coaches' locker room when he pulled his keys out of his pocket. A red rabbit's foot, one that had been given to him by some Boy Scouts, fell to the floor. After spotting it, Devaney asked if he could rub it. "We need all the luck we can get," he said.

Don Bryant

It seemed early on against the Jayhawks that luck indeed was with the Huskers. Kicker Paul Rogers boomed a pair of long field goals, including a school- and Big Eight-record 55-yarder. Then Kinney showed his versatility, scoring on a short plunge and catching a pass from Tagge for the two-point conversion. It was 14-0 Nebraska early in the second quarter.

From there, things turned sour. A Jayhawk field goal just seconds into the fourth quarter gave KU a 17-14 lead. Minutes later, the Huskers muffed a punt, setting up Kansas at the NU 24. Only some Blackshirt heroics kept the game within reach. Al Larson, who had fumbled the punt, teamed with Ken Geddes to make a critical third-down tackle, and then the whole defense threw up a wall to stop KU on fourth. It gave the Huskers the ball on their own 12 with just minutes left.

Tagge, who for the first time quarterbacked Nebraska the entire game, got the Husker drive started with a 15-yard pass to Kinney. But after a sack, the Huskers found themselves facing fourth and 16 from their own 31. That's when all kinds of mayhem broke out.

On the snap, KU's defensive end broke loose and quickly was in Tagge's face. The quarterback retreated and was able to step out of the Jayhawk's diving tackle attempt, but the timing of the play had completely broken down.

Touching a lucky horseshoe has been part of the Huskers' tradition "for as long as anyone can remember," the university says.

Devaney congratulates Paul Rogers (30) after his record 55-yard field goal.

Official Glenn Bowles signals interference, as McFarland gets back on his feet and KU's Emery Hicks protests.

Tagge ran toward the east sideline, where Devaney and the rest of the Huskers were standing, with two other Jayhawk defenders in hot pursuit. Tagge finally ran out of real estate and, just as he was decked, unloaded the ball nearly 50 yards downfield for McFarland.

The senior tight end, son of the yardmaster of Union Pacific Railroad's sprawling car-sorting yards in North Platte, originally had come to Lincoln on a baseball scholarship. He'd been offered a pro baseball contract, too. But after Devaney told McFarland he could walk on to the football team in addition to playing baseball, he passed up the pro offer and went to Lincoln. The baseball thing didn't work out at NU, the pitcher wild and unable to find the plate.

He had some down moments in football, too, including that memorable day two years earlier when Devaney's pep talk had picked him up. He became a starter as a junior in 1968. Now a senior in Osborne's new offense, he was emerging as an all-Big Eight tight end. At 6-4, 223 pounds, he was a big target with good hands, a reason he would go on to play six years in the NFL.

On this play out of the spread, listed in Osborne's playbook as "79 Two Minute Pass," McFarland was the primary receiver. He ran a hook route down the hash and curled in just beyond the first-down sticks. But after seeing Tagge in trouble, McFarland raised his hand to get the quarterback's attention and raced deep downfield toward the goal line. McFarland suddenly saw Tagge's pass hanging in the air. He also saw he had no hope of catching it.

Fortunately for Devaney and Nebraska, McFarland didn't just look on helplessly as the ball sailed over his head. On the spur of the moment, McFarland dove headlong into the nearest Jayhawk, cornerback Mark Geraghty, in a desperate move intended to draw a pass interference call. Both players ended up in a heap on the grass right near the Husker bench. The ball landed nearly 15 yards behind them.

Immediately, Monte Kiffin ran off the NU sideline toward game official Glenn Bowles, pointing at the tangle of bodies and screaming. "Interference!" McFarland got up and also pleaded for a call.

All eyes on him, Bowles reached into his back pocket and threw the yellow flag.

If the same play happened today, there almost surely would have been no flag. For pass interference to be called, the pass has to be catchable. But there was no such standard in the pass-interference rule back then. The only question was whether the defender had interfered with the receiver. On that count, McFarland's acting job had been Oscar-worthy.

The pass-interference rule in college also later would be changed to make the penalty a 15-yarder. But the penalty at this time, like the current NFL rule, called for the ball to be placed at the spot of the foul. In this case, that was the Kansas 32.

The craziness didn't end there. KU's Emery Hicks, the team's middle guard and captain, rushed over to Bowles and used some choice words disputing the call. Another 15 yards were tacked on for unsportsmanlike conduct.

The end result: On a play that should have dashed Husker hopes, NU instead picked up a net of 52 yards, all the way to the Kansas 17. You'd have to go back to the 1862 Homestead Act to find a bigger grab of free land in Nebraska. The crowd of 66,667 in Lincoln roared.

It took four plays for Tagge to calmly complete the unlikely comeback. He converted a key third and three from the 10 by gaining four yards over right tackle. That caused more Jayhawk frustration to spill out, with KU's Jim Hatcher giving receiver Guy Ingles a forearm shiver to the head. That penalty put the ball at the 3. On the next play, Kinney followed the block of fullback Dan Schneiss into the end zone. With 1:22 left, Nebraska led 21-17.

The Blackshirts held on from there, but even then it was a bit of an adventure. KU's quarterback got loose on the game's final play, running downfield nearly 30 yards before being hauled down at the Husker 18.

Tagge threw for 260 yards against Kansas, but his most-remembered pass of the game was an incompletion.

Afterward the Jayhawks and Coach Pepper Rodgers were fuming. When a sportswriter opened Rodgers' postgame press conference with a "tough game to lose" comment, Rodgers answered with an obscenity. "Let's see you print that!" he howled. He later screamed "No comment!" to a question about the interference call.

An assistant coach took that inopportune moment to hand Rodgers his post-game sack lunch. After some more strong language, Rodgers balled up the lunch and hurled it with a thud against the locker room wall. "How about that?" he shouted. "There's your story: Rodgers throws sandwich against wall with vengeance — and by the way, it was beef!"

Rodgers definitely had a beef. And he probably would have been even more upset if he'd known some of the historical significance of this game. The loss didn't just end KU's two-game winning streak over the Huskers. Counting this one, the Huskers would go on to defeat their rivals from the south an astonishing 36 years in a row.

The Huskers had been lucky, and they knew it. Dana Stephenson, captain of the NU defense, declared the Cornhuskers "the luckiest people alive." McFarland initially disputed the notion. "I don't know if you'd call it luck," he told reporters afterward. But the Husker hero couldn't keep a straight face, breaking into a big grin. "Well," he corrected himself, "yes, you would."

McFarland acknowledged he couldn't have caught the ball but still defended the ref's call. It would be years before he'd publicly admit it: He was the one who initiated the contact with the KU defender.

Devaney didn't talk much about luck immediately afterward, lauding the fight in his team. In fact, he told the Huskers in the locker room they'd learned a lesson that day. "Never give up," he told them. "Never give up."

Adrian Fiala

But Devaney knew there was as much luck as pluck in this comeback. He years later said it was hard to predict how that season would have turned out had Nebraska not caught that break and fallen to 2-3. "If we'd lost that game, we might have had a bad year," he said.

He wasn't the only one to ponder the possibilities years later. Adrian Fiala, a linebacker on the field that day who later served as a longtime Husker football broadcaster, couldn't help wondering how the play could have altered the course of Husker history to come. "Frankly, that play today is no call," he said. "If we lose that game, and the heat goes from simmer to high, and Bob gets run out of town, what would that have done to Nebraska's fortunes?"

The witty Devaney later would joke about the break he caught, referring to the ref who made the call as his brother-in-law. And he and Don Bryant also shared a good laugh about the rabbit's foot. This game would mark the start of a new pregame ritual for Devaney. For the rest of his time on the Nebraska sideline, he'd seek out Bryant and rub that rabbit's foot.

They didn't realize it that day, but it would be quite a while before the luck in that old rabbit's foot would run out.

Jeff Kinney followed the block of Dan Schneiss (22) for the game-winning touchdown against Kansas.

The Quarterback Shuffle

NEBRASKA'S TEAM BUSES WERE BOARDING outside Schulte Field House for the three-hour drive down U.S. Highway 77 to Manhattan, Kansas, the home of Kansas State University. Tom Osborne already was in his seat near the front of the bus when Van Brownson climbed aboard and headed up the aisle.

The coach looked at the Huskers' quarterback. Brownson's brown locks were growing shaggier by the day, sideburns sprouting below his ears. The young coach made an observation that cracked up everyone seated at the front of the bus. "Van," Osborne said, "you look like Peter Fonda."

Indeed, his teammates later agreed, you could see a lot of Fonda in Brownson. The son of Omaha native and acting legend Henry Fonda, Peter Fonda had become an icon to their 1960s generation months earlier with his portrayal of the searching young Wyatt in the motorcycle epic "Easy Rider." He was cool and freewheeling, and the chicks dug him. In November 1969, just about every young guy in America wanted to be like Peter Fonda. But Brownson, who just happened to possess his own movie-star good looks, could pull that off better than most.

It was a light moment between the de-facto offensive coordinator and the young man who was slated to serve as the Huskers' backup quarterback against Kansas State the next day. Jerry Tagge had been working with the No. 1 offense all week and would be getting the start against the Wildcats. But Brownson knew he had to be ready, because you never knew who would end up quarterbacking the Huskers. In the season's previous eight games, Bob Devaney already had changed his starting quarterback three times.

Nebraska players throughout 1969 had been going to battle each week in helmets with football-shaped stickers on the front commemorating the 100th season for college football. The oddly placed, eye-shaped stickers, planted in the middle of the Huskers' foreheads, made them look like a bunch of cyclopses. But lately, the Huskers actually had started playing like a team of monsters. Since that close shave against Kansas, the Huskers had ripped off wins over Oklahoma State, Colorado and Iowa State — all with little luck involved.

Trainer George Sullivan wraps Van Brownson's injured elbow.

An Oklahoma State defender struggles to pull down Tagge during the 13-3 Husker victory In Lincoln.

Speaking of monsters, Monte Kiffin's new Monster defense was leading the way. In fact, ever since the opener against USC, the Blackshirts were keeping the Huskers in every game. The young defensive coordinator had learned a lesson against the Trojans, when the Huskers twice were beaten on long passes and surrendered those 31 points.

"Listen, you two young pups," Devaney told Kiffin and Warren Powers after the game. "I don't ever want to see our corners get beat like that again." The next week, Kiffin had the cornerbacks playing so deep, you couldn't even see them on the game film. Now the Blackshirts were really digging in, holding those last three opponents to a combined 13 points.

The defense was a senior-laden unit, and it was quickly taking on Kiffin's infectious energy and enthusiasm. Nobody all season had been able to block nose guard Ken Geddes, a Florida native who had first come to Nebraska when sent to the famous Boys Town home for delinquent youth just west of Omaha. He actually had been an all-conference linebacker the previous season for the Huskers before Kiffin asked him to man the middle of the defensive line. Now he was on his way to making all-conference at his new position, too.

Jerry Murtaugh, Geddes' replacement at linebacker, was racking up tackles on a pace that would set the Nebraska single-season record. And defensive back Dana Stephenson, a gambler with a penchant for playing off his receivers and then pouncing at the last second, also was having an all-conference campaign. He picked off a school-record three passes against Colorado and would finish the year with NU records for interceptions in a season and career.

Progress was slower on offense, though. Everyone still was working to grasp the details of Osborne's new system, particularly the quarterbacks. Things just weren't quite clicking. Not once since the KU game had the Huskers managed to score three touchdowns in a game.

But when the players were able to execute the new offense, it was proving a remarkably effective scheme. Guy Ingles, a junior wide receiver for the Huskers, later would recall being struck with a realization amid the Husker win streak: We might not win every game, he thought, but we are never going to be outcoached.

Colorado quarterback Jim Bratten fumbles under pressure from Nebraska's Al Larson (20), Mike Wynn (90), Bob LIggett (71) and Dave Walline (76). The Buffs had eight turnovers in their 20-7 loss to Nebraska in Lincoln.

Both Tagge and Brownson were getting their chances to lead the offense. Neither had been able to assert himself as clearly the more capable. But it was becoming clear that each brought unique strengths to the huddle.

Brownson had shown himself to be the more exciting runner, while Tagge seemed to have the edge as a thrower. The knock on Brownson was that he was a little quick to give up on his receivers and take off running. Tagge's biggest weakness was his speed, or lack thereof.

But regardless of who started, Devaney had shown no hesitation in switching between the two if the offense wasn't moving the ball. Sometimes a change at quarterback could give the Husker offense a spark or throw a confusing change of pace at a defense. It seemed to be working, particularly in these last three weeks.

After the win over Kansas, Tagge had made his fourth consecutive start against Oklahoma State. But with the Huskers clinging to a 7-3 lead in the second half and looking lackluster offensively, Devaney called on Brownson.

It was the Iowan's first appearance since the Missouri game, and Brownson quickly rewarded Devaney's move. Again flashing his ball skills, Brownson dropped back to pass, faked a throw to the sidelines, and then laid out a beautiful 47-yard bomb to Ingles. For Ingles, a junior out of Omaha, the catch highlighted a career day in which he hauled in five passes for a school-record 163 yards.

Most importantly, the Huskers' 13-3 victory over OSU came on the same day that Big Eight favorites Oklahoma and Missouri both were upset. All of a sudden, the Huskers found themselves in a three-way tie with them atop the league. "Definitely," Devaney said enthusiastically when asked if his team now was back in the conference race.

With his performance against OSU, the starting job once again was Brownson's, and he was electric in running the option in the following week's 20-7 win over Colorado.

Devaney called Guy Ingles' second-quarter reception of a Tagge pass in the victory over Oklahoma State "the darnedest catch I've ever seen." Ingles leaped for the ball and gathered it in before hitting the turf and tumbling over.

"The 101st means more right now," Devaney said after getting a cake for his 100th win.

Brownson started again the next week against Iowa State, scoring on a run and hitting McFarland on a key 69-yard pass play. But this time Devaney called on Tagge to relieve Brownson in the third quarter with NU up just 7-3.

The steady Tagge completed nine straight passes at one point and connected with Mike Green for the clinching score in the 17-3 win — the 100th victory of Devaney's career.

As was Devaney's rule, whoever best moved the team would get the next start. That meant Tagge would get the call for that week's game against Kansas State.

Amid all the twists and turns, the two quarterbacks tried to take their daily battle for playing time in stride.

Both would admit they badly wanted to be out on the field. It was not an easy spot for any 19-year-old. "I'm going to try to hang in there," Tagge told a reporter at one point that fall.

But if there was any animosity or jealousy between the quarterbacks, they kept it well-concealed. Both would say years later there truly was no bad blood between them — a notion supported by teammates. "There was never ill feelings between Van and Jerry," Dave Morock recalled.

While the two quarterbacks didn't exactly pal around together, they got along quite well. They really had to. They were assigned to room together when on the road. And they spent their lunches together every day in Selleck Quadrangle getting drilled by Osborne on the week's offensive game plan.

Every day at noon, the coach would set up a chalkboard in the corner to go over which plays they should call in each situation. And for each play, they'd go over every blocking assignment, every receiving route, every dump-down option and every audible that could be called against every possible defensive look they'd see. It was exhausting. But such study was critical.

Osborne later in the week would give the quarterbacks a six-page written test. You had to have it down if you had any hope to play on Saturday. In this way, both on and off the field, the two quarterbacks pushed each other to get better. And that no doubt made the Huskers better.

The other Husker players didn't seem bothered by the uncertainty at quarterback. They had confidence in both. Years later, Ingles recalled thinking how great it was that NU had two solid quarterbacks. "The coaches will figure it out," he thought at the time.

But it would be inaccurate to say there was no tension in Lincoln over Nebraska's quarterback situation. Players would say years later that Brownson's father complained to Devaney more than once about his son's playing time, much to Van's embarrassment. Like any parent, he wanted to see his son succeed. But that's a line you don't cross, particularly in college athletics.

Others griped on Brownson's behalf, too. When Brownson's injury-plagued spring had left him No. 3 on the opening depth chart that fall, the Shenandoah Sentinel newspaper in his hometown called it "unimaginable" and "hard to swallow." The paper also said there had been "speculation in some quarters that if Brownson does get beat out, he might leave Nebraska in favor of some other football school that is short on quarterbacks."

The small-town paper quoted Brownson as saying that if he lost the job fair and square, he'd most likely stay to try to crack the lineup. "But if I got beat out and then didn't get a good chance to prove myself in game situations, then I might think about leaving."

Asked by World-Herald sports editor Wally Provost whether he was worried about the battle for the quarterback job, Brownson replied, "Yes, I worry a little. That's good for everybody."

Brownson pitches to fullback Dan Schneiss against Iowa State. He gave way to Tagge in the second half. "I wouldn't say either (quarterback) was great," Devaney said afterward.

THE QUARTERBACK SHUFFLE

Amid the quarterback battle, Tagge at one point made an amusing observation when a World-Herald writer asked what it was like to compete for the job. "It's like fighting over the same girl," Tagge said.

"Yeah," Brownson chimed in, "except I would win the girl every time."

As teammates would say years later, Brownson wasn't just bragging. With deep blue eyes, that athletic build and those shaggy good looks, Brownson got the girls. He had a well-earned reputation as a ladies' man. "The girls loved Van," Jerry Murtaugh recalled years later. "Every woman on campus flocked to him."

But that wasn't the only reputation Brownson was establishing for himself off the field in Lincoln. Brownson also was widely known on campus as a guy who liked to party. And that ultimately would create another factor that was quietly playing into Nebraska's quarterback competition — a very private one that neither Brownson nor his teammates would mention publicly until years later. Brownson by this time was developing a serious drinking problem. As Brownson himself put it when broaching the subject in a 2014 interview: "Let's put it this way: I enjoyed the other aspects of college life other than athletics."

To be sure, with the kind of roll the Huskers were on now late in the 1969 season, just about every guy on the team was having the time of his life. College is a time to enjoy new freedoms and branch out socially. And college life was even better if you were a member of a Nebraska football team. Back then, students were much more engaged with the games and the team than they are today. Students sat right behind the Husker bench and cared about what happened on Saturday. Players were recognized and revered on campus. And they indeed got lots of attention from the girls.

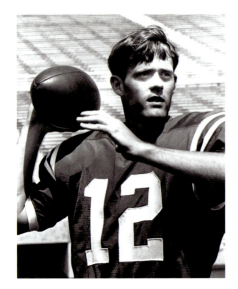

"The pressure from the competition makes you do better," Brownson said.

Saturday nights after the games were the best, filled with parties, drinking and music. But few on the team were enjoying themselves as much as the fun-loving, hard-charging Brownson.

"Van was a partyer, and he liked the ladies," recalled his teammate and friend Adrian Fiala. "And if you go to parties and like the ladies, guess what else is involved — and it's not root beer."

Brownson later would say his partying and drinking were rather innocently rooted in his freshman year in Lincoln. Though standing tall and confident on a football field, Brownson was by nature quiet and shy. That made all the notoriety that came with being a quarterback on the Nebraska football team difficult to deal with at first. He soon found an escape in beer, which as a member of a fraternity he never had trouble obtaining. He hadn't drunk alcohol in high school but found in Lincoln that drinking helped him break out of his shell.

From those simple beginnings, Brownson and teammates later would acknowledge, his partying lifestyle ultimately got out of hand. It wasn't confined to just the weekends. And it often kept him out late into the night. "I drink quite a bit," Brownson would say in a revealing 1972 interview with Sports Illustrated, one where he truly let his hair down. "I wonder sometimes how many brain cells all that beer has killed."

It's hard to gauge today how much burning the candle at both ends affected Brownson's performance as he battled Tagge for the quarterback job. But it surely didn't help. (Tagge, for the record, liked to drink beer and chase women, too, though on that score he and teammates would concede that he was not in Brownson's league.)

Also unclear is whether Devaney or the other coaches had caught on by this point to the developing situation with their young quarterback. But clearly it was not a major concern. Because the coaches continued to trust Brownson in tight spots. As it turned out, they would do so again during the key Big Eight game against Kansas State.

In Manhattan, this already had been a football season like no other. Weeks earlier, the Wildcats had pulled off one of their most memorable upsets ever, laying the wood to Oklahoma, 59-21. They'd gained their first national ranking in years. Now at 5-3, they had very real hopes for a bowl, which would be a first in school history. And with a win over Nebraska, K-State would spoil any hopes their longtime Big Eight rivals had for a conference title or bowl trip.

The man behind this sudden outburst of Purple Pride was Vince Gibson, a defensive-minded coach who had come to Kansas' Flint Hills from Tennessee in 1967. The hiring was part of a huge commitment K-State had made to finally get out of the Big Eight's cellar. Campus leaders built a brand-new football stadium with carpeted locker rooms. And they funded a new athletic dorm more swanky and well-appointed than any Nebraska had.

Nebraska middle guard Ken Geddes (37) turned back a Kansas State drive in the second quarter with an interception.

If all that didn't make KSU inviting enough, some 60 attractive young women known officially on campus as "Gibson Girls" used their feminine charms to help the coach woo recruits. They'd escort the players on their campus visits and even correspond with them after they went home. The Gibson Girls were considered so integral to what the school was trying to do, they even got their own spread in the campus yearbook.

"We gonna win" was Gibson's message, and it was proving effective. Whether attracted by the girls, the dorms or the bright lights of the town that locals called the Little Apple, highly touted quarterback Lynn Dickey had been lured to Manhattan two years earlier. He had keyed the 12-0 win in Lincoln the year before. Now he was set to lead the Big Eight's top-ranked offense to another conquest of Nebraska.

More than 30,000 passionate purple fans were among the 40,000 who packed KSU's new stadium. Dickey almost immediately brought them to their feet. During the first quarter, he engineered an 80-yard drive against the Blackshirts to put the Wildcats up 7-0. At the same time, Nebraska's offense was floundering against a fired-up KSU defense. Jerry Tagge connected on just five of 16 passes.

After the Wildcats forced another punt late in the first half, the new stadium was a cauldron of sound. North-central Kansas was suddenly an alien land no Husker team had ventured into before, a treacherous place where season hopes go to die. Devaney talked it over with Osborne and backs coach Mike Corgan, who gave Brownson the word: Get ready. You're going in.

Just after halftime, Brownson finally got some things going for Nebraska, leading the Huskers on a drive to a field goal. Then in the fourth quarter, he and hard-headed backup fullback Dan Schneiss went to work. Brownson read the defense, called an audible at the line and then pitched to Schneiss, who rambled 34 yards to the Wildcat 14 with the help of several great blocks from the offensive line.

The makeshift unit was really coming together late in the season, particularly with the recent ascension of junior college transfer Bob Newton.

Then on the next play, Brownson threw to Schneiss for another first down at the K-State 2. Two plays later, Brownson launched his lanky frame over the goal-line from the 1. The Huskers had claimed their first lead at 10-7.

The Blackshirts, who had held the Wildcats scoreless since the first quarter, would have to thwart several more thrusts. The last was a particular heart-stopper. Stephenson brought down a Wildcat receiver just 6 yards from the Husker goal line. Time expired as the frenzied Cats scrambled vainly to get off one more play.

The NU celebration at the final gun was as raucous as any ever seen on an opponent's field. Kiffin leaped high and landed in the arms of his Blackshirts and then started rolling around on the ground. And many of the estimated 9,000 red-clad fans who had made the trek south spilled onto the grass.

While Kiffin and the players were energized by the thrilling finish, for Devaney it had been one of the most nerve-wracking victories of his career. Dogfights like this one really wore on him. This whole season — hell, the last two years — had been draining. He didn't know how much more of this he could take.

So as the Husker buses bumped their way north on the two-lane highways between Manhattan and Lincoln, Devaney suddenly had the notion of retirement on his mind. He pulled a trusted aide aside to share some thoughts on the program's future — a conversation whose contents wouldn't be divulged for two more years.

In his own seat on the bus, Brownson was feeling pretty upbeat about his own future. After sparking the second-half rally, he knew he most likely had reclaimed the starting quarterback job from Tagge. It would be the fourth change since Brownson had first been named starter for the Southern Cal opener, and the third change in four weeks.

Brownson's start the following Saturday would present an even bigger opportunity for the rising sophomore: a showdown against archrival Oklahoma, with a Big Eight championship on the line.

> "If you think this was something, wait till next week."
>
> — Linebacker Adrian Fiala, looking ahead to Oklahoma after the Kansas State game

Dan Schneiss, left, and Jim McFarland celebrate on the field with Husker fans after the victory over Kansas State in Manhattan.

Norman Conquest

BOB DEVANEY AND CHUCK FAIRBANKS were renewing old acquaintances during a pregame chat when the Oklahoma head coach introduced Devaney to some Sooner players standing nearby. It was a nice gesture from a rival that in the past had not proven a very hospitable host to Devaney and the Huskers. In spite of some great years at Nebraska, Devaney was 0-4 in his previous trips to Norman.

Of course, that included the 47-0 shellacking on this same field the previous year. That one still was fresh in everyone's minds — including the young Sooners now standing on the field by Devaney. "Now, boys, you embarrassed us on television last year," Devaney told them. "So please go easy on us. We are still not very good."

Call it a quirk of Big Eight scheduling. Call it fate. But for whatever reason, the Huskers in 1969 found themselves for the second straight year playing Oklahoma on its home field in Norman.

During that amiable pregame meeting, the Sooner players and Devaney shared a chuckle over his words. At the same time, the coach's remarks certainly did nothing to diminish the confidence the Sooner players were bringing into this game November 22. With losses to three ranked teams, including eventual national champ Texas, the talented Sooners had underachieved some this season. But they also had the nation's best running back in Steve Owens, the bruiser who had rushed for 172 yards and those five touchdowns against the Huskers the year before.

However, whether it was Devaney's intent or not, the Sooner players who heard the coach's words that day within a few hours would get the feeling they had just been suckered. Because this one in the end wouldn't turn out anything like the game played on the same field 12 months earlier.

It's hard to say today whether Devaney was just having fun with the Sooner players or whether he was setting them up for a fall. Either way, he did know this for sure: There was a lot of fight in this Husker football team.

Many of his current Huskers had been on the same field the previous year, and even when they were getting the hell beat out of them, they did not quit. Rather than dreading a return to Norman, they actually relished the opportunity to get another shot at the Sooners on their home field.

Steve Owens, who would win the 1969 Heisman Trophy, rushed for an NCAA record 3,867 yards in his three seaons at Oklahoma.

With 10 tackles against Oklahoma, Jerry Murtaugh broke Wayne Meylan's 1966 record for tackles in a season.

Typical of the players' attitude going into the game was that of Mike Green, the offensive captain. He went to Devaney that week and told him to break with tradition and not show the team any of the game film from the previous year. "Coach, we don't need to see that game," he told Devaney.

Green, out of Omaha's Tech High, had been an important and inspirational leader for the Huskers this season as they rallied from their 2-2 start. And he was part of a big and highly motivated group of Husker seniors — guys like Jim McFarland, Adrian Fiala, Dana Stephenson, Larry Frost, Sherwin Jarmon, Al Larson, Bob Liggett and Ken Geddes. Those seniors had been determined from the start of the season not to become the first varsity class under Devaney to fail to win a conference title or to go to a bowl. Even after the loss to Missouri, they had insisted that the Big Eight still was there for the taking.

Mike Green

Since that time, the Huskers had played some of the most courageous football of any team Devaney had coached. Now both those goals were within their grasp. A win over OU would give Nebraska a share of the Big Eight title with Missouri.

Also driving Green, Devaney and all the Huskers that day was a belief that they had a big score to settle. It wasn't just the 47-0, though that's obviously quite a big score. It was the fact that Sooner coaches had kept Owens on the field until near the very end of that romp.

Devaney always believed Fairbanks privately held a grudge against him that dated back nearly two decades, to when he had been Fairbanks' position coach at Michigan State. Devaney suspected Fairbanks blamed him for his lack of playing time in East Lansing. Regardless of the motive, Devaney and the Huskers certainly had taken note of the way the Sooners had run it up. "I didn't think that was a bit funny," Devaney recalled years later.

Green and the other seniors also badly wanted this one for their coach. They had appreciated how Devaney had shouldered the public blame after last year's embarrassment. Now it would be great to be the first NU team to give him a win in Norman.

Devaney, in the end, agreed with Green when it came to last year's film. They wouldn't show it. To the coach, Green's attitude was just another sign his team was ready to play.

As determined as the Huskers were, the game actually started out much like a ghastly repeat of 1968. Kicking with a 30-mph wind behind their backs, the Sooners pinned the Huskers back at the 20 and then swarmed over Van Brownson on third down for a 10-yard loss. Dan Schneiss' punt went up into that howling wind, stalled, dropped like a stone and then actually rolled backward. The Huskers downed it at their own 18.

It took the Sooners just one play to cash in. Talented sophomore quarterback Jack Mildren faked an option pitch to Owens, who was engulfed by a keyed-up Husker defense. Mildren waltzed into the end zone untouched.

Only one minute, 27 seconds into the game, Oklahoma already led 7-0. As Devaney stood on the sidelines, he'd later say, all of a sudden 47-0 didn't look so bad. Hundreds of thousands of Husker fans listening on the radio in Nebraska at the moment surely were dreading another Sooner onslaught.

But the rough start seemed to hardly faze this Husker team. On NU's next possession, Brownson marched his team 96 yards into the teeth of that wind. And from that point on, it was all Nebraska. Three-hundred sixty-four days after the 47-0 embarrassment, on the very same field, the Huskers would completely turn the tables on the Sooners.

The Blackshirts blanketed Owens, holding him to just 71 yards on 21 carries. It ended a streak of 19 games in which Owens had gained at least 100 yards. He also was held out of the end zone, the first time that had happened in 16 games. The hard-charging Owens still would go on to win the Heisman Trophy a month later. But this one would not look good on his résumé. "Stevie, how's your day going?" Husker linebacker Jerry Murtaugh recalled asking at one point after bringing Owens to the turf. For the Blackshirts, this was glorious payback.

Nebraska's Ken Geddes (37), Jerry Murtaugh (42) and Sherwin Jarmon (81) are on the scene as Oklahoma's Steve Owens fumbles.

And as a World-Herald scribe would write, it was impossible to tell the Heisman candidate in this game without a program. Because Owens was completely outplayed by Husker I-back Jeff Kinney. On this day, the sophomore would have his first truly great game as a Husker. He provided a preview of the fierce, determined competitor that a rapt nationwide audience would see the next time these same two teams got together in Norman. While few outside of Nebraska now knew who he was, Husker fans already were finding a lot to like about Jeff Kinney.

KINNEY HAD COME TO LINCOLN IN 1968 from his native McCook, an agricultural hub in southwest Nebraska's verdant Republican River valley. The son of a railroad brakeman, he'd grown up an outdoorsy kid, hunting amid the stubble of cornfields and fishing for bass and crappie at nearby lakes. Sometimes Kinney's parents would drop him and a buddy off at a lake with their fishing poles and a tent and come back to fetch them two days later. He also became a huge Cornhusker football fan, listening to games on the radio and then looking over all the photos the next morning in the Sunday World-Herald, a paper that circulated to every corner of the state.

Jeff Kinney starred in football and basketball at McCook and qualified for the state track meet in the high jump.

Before long, the football, track and basketball star had a scholarship offer from his beloved Huskers. But Kinney's mom really liked the Kansas State coaches, and Vince Gibson came close to luring him to the Wildcats. On his campus visit in Manhattan, Kinney was wowed by all the new facilities. Then a fetching young Gibson Girl escorted him to the top of a campus overlook. Together, Kinney and the Wildcat temptress stared out over the boundless horizons of north-central Kansas. "Nothing happened obviously but 'Come to Kansas State and you never know what might happen,' I guess," he recalled years later with a chuckle.

Tom Osborne, his main Nebraska recruiter, appealed to some of the young man's other urges: He took Kinney fishing. In the end, Osborne's low-key approach and the home-state Cornhuskers won out, and Kinney eventually signed his letter of intent in front of Devaney. For a Nebraska kid, it was like being in the audience of the president.

Once in Lincoln, the 6-foot-1, 196-pound kid presented an intriguing offensive weapon for Husker coaches. He had so many skills and attributes, they didn't know where to put him. Having been a high school quarterback, he was a capable thrower, and he might have played there as a freshman were it not for Brownson. He also was a tremendously strong runner. He didn't have top-end speed for a running back, but he was fast enough. He had great balance, hard to knock off his feet. And he had terrific hands. He was smart, too, possessing a quarterback's understanding of what a defense was trying to do. He was really a complete player.

In the end, he played mostly at halfback as a Husker freshman. Then in an effort to get him on the field, NU coaches moved him to wingback in the spring of 1969. KInney was starry eyed that fall on picture day, the first time he put on a varsity uniform. Gazing with pride upon his scarlet No. 35 jersey, he said, "I have a lot to live up to."

He'd get a chance to do that sooner than he thought. Two weeks later, Joe Orduna went down with his knee injury. Husker coaches the very next day moved Kinney to I-back. He got just eight carries in the opener against USC, but within two weeks he had unseated junior Frank Vactor, who had started against the Trojans. Now nearing the end of a breakout sophomore year, Kinney was earning comparisons to Bobby Reynolds, the Husker sensation who earned All-America honors as a sophomore in 1950. Kinney became Nebraska's first player since Reynolds to score touchdowns in his first five games as a Husker.

Kinney from the start had shown tremendous ability to run through contact. He was just a load to bring down. And he was one player who didn't necessarily care for Devaney's rule of not hitting in practice once the season started, feeling like the contact made him stronger.

That attitude quickly made him a favorite of Husker running backs coach Corgan. A former World War II merchant marine who had played at Notre Dame, Corgan was well-known for his hard-nosed mentality — as well as the sometimes questionable drills he used to toughen up his backs.

Green recalled that Corgan once had his backs practice goal-line plunges by having them dive over a pile of tackling dummies. "Cut that crap out!" Green recalled Devaney saying. "You're killing my backs!" He also put his charges through a one-on-one drill called "backs on ends" that sent the players charging into each other full-blast.

Corgan also regularly sent his backs running through a six-armed contraption that was supposed to test their ability to hang onto the ball. He'd set the springs on that thing so tight you could hardly get through it without disabling a limb. Corgan wanted his backs to go into contact like men. Despite such torture, Kinney and the backs loved playing for the colorful Corgan.

They didn't always understand him, though.

"He used to tell us, 'You couldn't knock a whore off a pisspot,' " Kinney recalled years later. "I still don't know what that means."

But what really made Kinney the perfect fit for Osborne's new I and spread offense was his ability to catch the ball out of the backfield. Nebraska's only score against Missouri had come when the sophomore snared a breathtaking bomb, one of a school-record 44 catches he would make on the year.

As the season went along, the 19-year-old's growth paralleled that of the new offense. He started picking up on the nuances, reading blocks and knowing which way to cut.

Each week, he played a little faster and looser, less worried about making a mistake. By season's end, the sophomore would lead the Huskers in rushing, receptions and scoring.

The football field wasn't the only place that Kinney was quickly growing up. In the winter of his freshman year, he'd learned that Becky, his sweetheart since their high school days in McCook, was pregnant. One day he had to tell Corgan why he'd missed off-season conditioning the day before: He had to attend a wedding — his own.

Then just two days before the Kansas State game, Becky had given birth to Jeffrey Scott. It was tough balancing fatherhood and marriage with all the demands of school and football. Kinney didn't feel he was equipped for it. But thanks to supportive parents and coaches, he and Becky made a go of it, ultimately raising three kids together. As Oklahoma's Sooners would soon find out, this serious sophomore didn't shrink from anything.

> "As the season progressed, I didn't worry about this team. They seemed to have the kind of confidence you don't get instilled from just talking to them."
>
> **— Devaney after defeating Oklahoma in 1969**

KINNEY SCORED ON A 3-YARD PLUNGE late in the first quarter to give Nebraska its first lead over the Sooners. Then in a 12-minute span of the second half, Kinney scored a touchdown about every way you can. He ran one in from 11 yards. He threw a 7-yard pass to Guy Ingles for another score. And then he caught a 6-yard pass from Brownson. For the day, Kinney logged 35 carries for 127 yards while catching three passes for 26 more, accounting for four touchdowns.

Kinney was not the only Nebraska runner to outshine Owens that day. Brownson ran for 82 yards on just 11 carries. A big chunk of them came on a single scramble that displayed the kind of crazy-legged escapability that had been making him a fan favorite all year.

On the very first drive after OU took the 7-0 lead, Brownson rolled to his left from the Husker 30 and nearly got sandwiched by two Sooner defenders. He ended up eluding both, retreating backward 15 yards. Then he zigged to the right hashmark before zagging back to the left, avoiding two more Sooner tacklers. He spun out of the clutches of a fifth Sooner before finally being dragged down. The scramble had gained 38 yards, but it probably covered 100.

When the play was over, Devaney called a timeout. Brownson figured he was going to get chewed out. Corgan hated it when runners pussy-footed around instead of planting their foot in the ground and getting upfield. But after reaching the sideline Brownson soon found otherwise.

"I didn't want anything," Devaney told him.

Kinney barrels over the goal line for the first of three touchdowns against Oklahoma.

"I just thought you'd be tired after all that running." They shared a laugh. Before long, the entire game became a laugher for the Huskers.

Once Kinney's scoring pass — a perfect strike to Brownson — put the Huskers up by 30 early in the fourth quarter, Devaney started taking out his starters. Ingles wasn't happy about being pulled, wanting to run up the score the same way the Sooners had the year before. But he soon stopped complaining. Tagge and the second team went in and drove right down the field for another score.

The final: Nebraska 44, Oklahoma 14 — a remarkable reversal of the previous year's outcome. "It is pretty amazing when you think about it," Osborne recalled years later, "to lose by 40-some points one year and to win by almost the same margin the next year, on the same field." Not only was it Devaney's first win over Oklahoma in Norman, it was Nebraska's biggest victory over its most fierce rival in more than 40 years. Afterward, Fairbanks offered testament to the turnaround Devaney had engineered over the past year. "Bob Devaney has forgotten more football than a lot of us may ever know," he said.

Devaney and the Huskers retired to the locker room to celebrate their Big Eight championship, the team's first since 1966. Kiffin was going nuts, shouting and slapping everyone on the back. Devaney met up with Green. "I'm glad we didn't show that damn film," he told the senior. Then Green and the rest of the happy Huskers hauled Devaney into the showers for a celebratory dousing, that era's version of the Gatorade bath.

The Huskers' season wasn't over yet, though. For the first time in three years, NU was going bowling, their bowl game draw having been set five days earlier.

Back then, Alabama coach Bear Bryant usually controlled the bowl lineup. He'd decide where to take his team and arrange an invitation to the opponent he wanted to play. The other bowl games — there were only 11 at the time — would fall into place from there.

After both the 1965 and 1966 seasons, Bryant had talked Devaney into taking on his Crimson Tide in bowls, first in the Orange Bowl and then the Sugar Bowl. Devaney came away thinking he'd been outcoached by Bryant, with the Bear springing several trick plays on the Huskers. Devaney also later decided he'd been snookered by Bryant. Bear only called him, Devaney decided, when he knew he had a better team.

Devaney wasn't surprised the day after Nebraska beat Kansas State when he got another call from Bryant. The Alabama coach suggested that their teams get together again and have some more bowl-trip fun. "Which bowl do you have in mind, Bear?" Devaney later recalled asking Bryant.

"We were thinking about the Liberty Bowl," Bryant said.

"Gee, that sounds great," Devaney replied. The next day, he signed up his Huskers to play Georgia in the Sun Bowl.

Starting offensive tackle Paul Topliff takes a seat in the fourth quarter with a safe lead over Oklahoma. "The offensive line was the most beautiful thing in the world," Mike Green said after the game.

Black and White

IN THE HUDDLE, VAN BROWNSON called for an I-back sweep, one of the most brutally simple plays in the Husker playbook. The quarterback handed off to Jeff Kinney, who followed fullback Mike Green into the hole. Green mashed a Georgia linebacker, and the powerful Kinney delivered some punishing blows of his own before he was hauled down in the secondary. "Call that play again," Green recalled telling Brownson after the Huskers returned to the huddle.

Green was fired up. And Kinney was, too. And for good reason. This Georgia team across the line from them during the December 20, 1969, Sun Bowl game in El Paso, Texas, represented one of the last bastions of the nation's shameful segregated past. The Bulldogs were an all-white outfit, and they had come into this game talking trash in a condescending "we're-gonna-whup-you-boys" Southern drawl. Green, Kinney and other Huskers would recall the N-word and racist innuendo thrown across the line at Nebraska's black players that day.

"There were some things said that got us riled up," Kinney recalled years later. Which was why Kinney, who was white, and Green, who was black, were taking great pleasure in pounding the ball right down the Bulldogs' throats. As offensive lineman Wally Winter would put it years later, "We just kicked the hell out of them — and had fun doing it."

> "I knew Georgia didn't have a chance. Nobody would have had a chance against us today."
>
> — Nebraska defensive back Dana Stephenson

By the time of the 1969 Sun Bowl game, a full five years had passed since President Lyndon Johnson signed the Civil Rights Act of 1964, a law outlawing racial discrimination in all its ugly forms, including school segregation. But apparently the University of Georgia had not yet received that memo. In fact, the majority of football teams in the Southeastern Conference at that time remained all white.

Nebraska would likewise play against an all-white Louisiana State team in a bowl the following season. And after the 1971 season, the Huskers played an Alabama team suiting up its first two black players, only one of them a starter. It would not be until 1972 that final SEC holdouts LSU and Ole Miss saw their first black players take the field.

By 1969, the nation was fast changing on issues of race. But it also was a turbulent time, with rising militant attitudes among blacks over the pace of change and rioting in the wake of the 1968 assassination of Martin Luther King Jr. Parts of north Omaha, the heart of Nebraska's black community, burned in 1968 when a visit by segregationist presidential candidate George Wallace sparked a riot and again in 1969 after a white police officer shot and killed a 14-year-old black girl.

However, Husker players would recall that the University of Nebraska, and the Nebraska football team in particular, at the time were models of racial harmony. And the tone for that was set by Bob Devaney, a coach with a well-earned reputation for being colorblind.

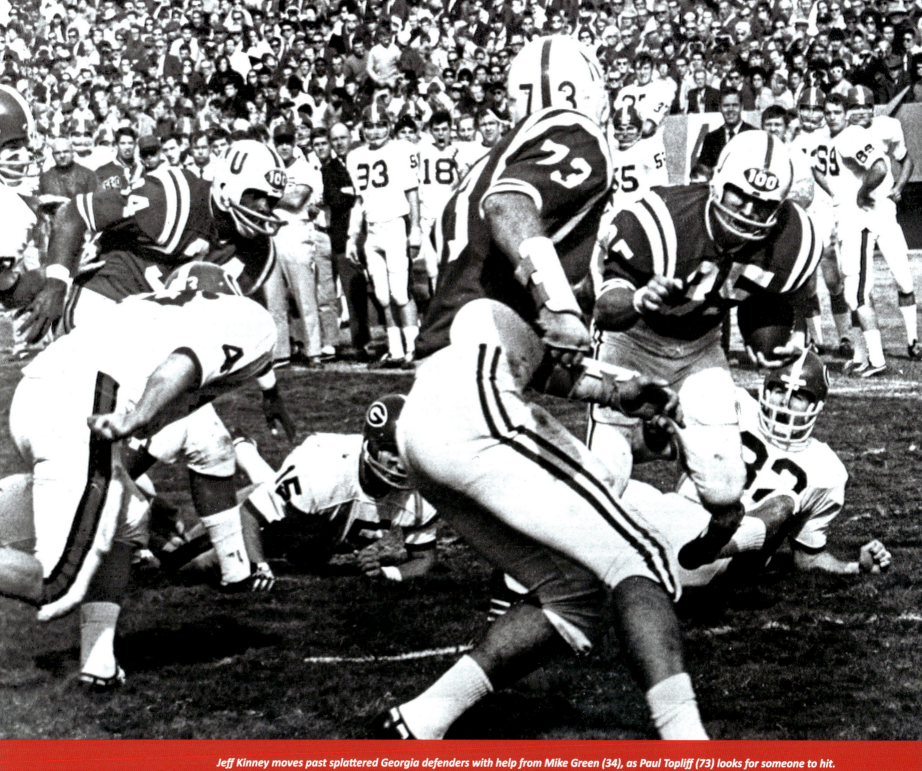
Jeff Kinney moves past splattered Georgia defenders with help from Mike Green (34), as Paul Topliff (73) looks for someone to hit.

Devaney always had been comfortable around black people, perhaps because of his days at the foundry in Michigan, where he sweat side by side with black co-workers. He had gotten his first experience recruiting and coaching black players at Michigan State, which had had tremendous success recruiting black players from the South.

At a banquet after the 1969 season, Devaney called Ken Geddes the best all-around athlete he had coached.

Devaney's first family baby-sitter in East Lansing had been a black player he coached. He subsequently recruited the first black players ever to play at Wyoming, proclaiming to wary administrators that race "doesn't make a damn bit of difference."

By the time Devaney got to Lincoln, the school could point to a long, mostly laudable history of welcoming black athletes to campus. George Flippin, a standout on the 1892 Nebraska football team, was only the fifth black athlete in the nation to play at a predominantly white school. Missouri forfeited a game against NU before it would take the field against this man with brown skin. In 1908, Nebraska became the first predominantly white school to suit up a black basketball player.

However, once Nebraska joined the Big Six Conference, the precursor of the Big Eight, for nearly half a century it recruited no black athletes. NU was said to have been unwilling to buck league schools like Oklahoma and Missouri that refused to play teams with black players. It took lowly Kansas State to break the conference color line in 1949, and by 1951 Nebraska followed suit.

Devaney inherited several black starters on the Nebraska roster when he arrived in 1962, and he continued to recruit heavily in inner-city neighborhoods. "Bob didn't care what ethnicity you had," Tom Osborne recalled. "He only cared if you could play football."

On this 1969 team, four of the five starters on the defensive line were black, as was fullback Green. There were numerous other blacks playing key backup roles.

Devaney earlier that spring had also added former Husker Thunder Thornton to his coaching staff, among the first black assistant coaches in the Big Eight. "To me, being a black player for Bob Devaney was no different than being a white player," nose guard Ken Geddes recalled. "He treated everyone equally."

The coach also had a history of standing up for his black players. In his early years at Nebraska, he ran into restaurants and hotels that were reluctant to serve his players. When Devaney brought his team to Miami in 1964 to play an all-white Auburn team in the Orange Bowl, the manager of the Huskers' hotel asked Devaney if he would keep his black players out of the lobby and swimming pool. "Hell, no, we're not going to do that," Devaney told him. He did accede to the Orange Bowl's request that he not bring black players to the post-game banquet, a decision he later regretted.

Some years later, both Devaney and Osborne fought local politics in Lincoln to open up off-campus housing to blacks.

It wasn't just Devaney who was welcoming to black players. Bob Brown, who played on Devaney's first team, recalled that students, teachers and the university community embraced them. Just like the white players, black players were treated like celebrities on campus. A downside in Lincoln was that there were few blacks in the student body who weren't athletes, making the campus environment somewhat isolating.

Bob Brown

Many of the black athletes dated white women, something they said was never frowned upon by Devaney or fellow students. The people who most often seemed to have trouble accepting it were the girls' parents. Culturally, the state still was in transition when it came to interracial relationships. It had not been until 1963 — Devaney's second year — that Nebraska repealed its long-standing law prohibiting marriage or intimate relations between people of different races.

It was not uncommon at the time for conflicts over race and discrimination to lead to strife within college football programs. Just months earlier, 16 black players had boycotted the first spring practice at the University of Iowa and were dismissed from the team.

Then 14 black players were kicked off the Wyoming football team in October 1969. Their offense: wearing black armbands to the coach's office before a game against Brigham Young University, a protest against a then-existing Mormon Church policy barring blacks from the priesthood. The coach reportedly told the players if they didn't like it at Wyoming, they should go to a black college like Morgan State or Grambling.

Such open conflict between player and coach wasn't likely at Nebraska. Because when issues did arise, black players always knew they had Devaney's ear.

During 1968, the Huskers' black running backs met with Devaney and objected to the fact many of them were stacked at the same position in the Huskers' three-back system. If there was any tension in the meeting, Devaney immediately broke it up. With a grin, the coach told one of the complaining players who was down on the depth chart, "Maybe you're just not as good as you think you are." They all laughed about that. But Devaney also listened to the concerns and offered any of them the chance to switch to one of the other running back spots.

Within the team, black and white players alike say the Husker locker room was a true brotherhood. The fact that Green could be elected offensive captain of the predominantly white team speaks volumes about the level of respect between white and black players.

Johnny Rodgers and others later would recall that there was one white player on the team — a prominent one they declined to name publicly — who was well-known for racist attitudes. But they said it didn't prove disruptive. Players from the era couldn't recall a single incident of racial disunity or strife, on or off the field. "Everyone on the team was the same color," recalled Jeff Hughes, a white reserve I-back on the 1969 Huskers.

Sometimes players teased each other about their cultural differences, the blacks calling the white players "Caucs," short for Caucasians, and the whites calling the black players "Groids," short for negroids.

The black and white players didn't all socialize together, many tending to hang out in familiar surroundings with guys of the same color. And there was some self-segregation that took place at mealtime, with blacks and whites sitting at separate tables. At one point in the next two years, Monte Kiffin challenged the team to put a stop to it, standing in the middle of the dining room and declaring, "That's the last of this."

Regardless, black or white, players say they always freely befriended and socialized with anyone they chose to. Race simply was not an issue. "I had white friends I hung out with, and we partied and stuff," Geddes recalled. "I hung out with who I wanted to hang out with."

This much is certain: Come game day, red was the only color that mattered. Black or white, the Huskers went to battle for each other on the field. That's why during this 1969 game against Georgia, none of the Huskers would stand back and take any static from a race-baiting Bulldog.

As it was, the Huskers didn't really need any extra motivation going into the Sun Bowl. They were excited to be playing in the school's first bowl game in three years. Moreover, the players felt they still had something to prove. They thought they'd deserved a spot in a far more prestigious bowl, hurt by those two early-season setbacks and the fact that Notre Dame this year had decided to end its 50-year policy of declining bowl invitations.

> "We don't hardly get any free time."
>
> **— A Husker starter complaining anonymously to a World-Herald reporter before the Sun Bowl**

By the end of the regular season, Devaney and his Huskers believed they were among the very best teams in the country. They were playing like it and actually had hoped for a bid to the Cotton Bowl and a shot at No. 1, undefeated Texas.

But the rest of the country had no such regard for Nebraska, which was ranked only 14th in the polls. When the bowl lineups came out, the Huskers had tumbled all the way down to El Paso, a barren outpost not particularly known for its bowl pageantry. As a further sign of disrespect, they were matched up against an unranked Georgia team that limped in with a 5-4-1 record. The Bulldogs were a team in the wrong place at the wrong time. "I don't know if Georgia knew what they were in for," monster back Dave Morock recalled.

Not that it was all business for the Huskers in El Paso. They had a blast. El Paso was right across the Rio Grande from Juarez, Mexico, and most Huskers crossed the river in search of south-of-the-border fun.

Some found a little too much. Two or three days before the game, a large group of players went to a bar in Juarez to hear a band. A disturbance broke out, and several drunken players ended up locked in a Mexican jail. "It was quite a night," recalled linebacker Adrian Fiala, who was not among the wild bunch. Other players pooled their bowl per-diem spending money to raise the $500 cash to bail out their teammates. Lots of guys ended up missing curfew, and Devaney blew up when he found out. He immediately went to the offenders' rooms to bawl them out.

The players, most of whom were starters, feared they'd be suspended for the game. In the end, one reserve player who drunkenly mouthed off to Devaney was sent back to Lincoln, never to wear a Husker uniform again. The others received a battery of punishments that included a lot of extra running, but they all got to play.

Brownson wasn't involved in the Juarez incident. But he did spend some time in Mexico and found himself in hot water when he overslept and missed the team bus. He hitched a ride and still made it to practice on time, but he also feared he'd be held out of the game. When Devaney said a bus was leaving at 2, that meant you'd better be ready to go at 1:45. Like the others, Corgan just made Brownson run extra sprints after practice.

"We're not going to have a quarterback," Green told a teammate as he watched Brownson huffing and puffing on the field. "Corgan's going to kill that guy." Come game day, though, none of the Huskers' extracurricular hijinks would prove a major distraction.

The tension between the Nebraska and Georgia players actually had started to rise before the game at a joint team barbecue. A Georgia player got up to speak and referred to the "boys" from

Brownson started the game, throwing for one touchdown and running for another.

up north. Many Huskers felt the condescending words were particularly aimed at Nebraska's black players.

The Huskers ended up choosing Bob Liggett, a senior defensive tackle from western Pennsylvania, to speak for them. Fiala said they most likely did so not only because Liggett was black and an imposing 6-foot-3, 250 pounds, but because they knew he wouldn't lose his cool.

Liggett offered thanks and other pleasantries for the El Paso hosts. Then he stared for several seconds in the direction of the Georgia players. There was no bluster. He simply told the Bulldogs the Huskers were going to show them "where it's at." The Nebraska players erupted.

"And then," Fiala recalled, "we went out and kicked their asses."

Bob Liggett

Paul Rogers shows off his record-setting right foot.

Early on, the Huskers literally kicked the Bulldogs, with placekicker Paul Rogers doing the honors. It's hard to believe today, but back then, Devaney and most college coaches didn't go out to recruit kicking specialists. They'd get their players together in camp and have open tryouts to see who could punt, kick field goals and kick off. Sometimes the job would go to a lineman.

Rogers, out of Rock Rapids, Iowa, had been recruited to Nebraska as a fullback in 1967, and he'd log a few carries during his Husker career. But he'd make his real mark as the placekicker for the Huskers from 1968 to 1970.

While soccer-style kicking was just beginning to take hold in football, Rogers booted with an old-school straight-on toe. In fact, he was having nothing of the new-fangled style. He said he about pulled a leg muscle when he experimented with kicking soccer style. He later would be quoted as saying he thought the soccer-style kicking fad was on the way out.

Fortunately for Nebraska, Rogers' kicks were a lot more accurate than his predictions. He rarely missed extra points. And while he missed his share of field goals, he also made many of the longest and biggest in school history. That included a desperation, school-record 51-yarder that lifted Nebraska to a 13-10 win over Wyoming in 1968. Devaney told Rogers he may have saved his job with that one.

Rogers broke his own school record with the 55-yarder he booted against KU weeks earlier — a mark that would stand for four decades. By the time he left Nebraska, Rogers would own all the kicking records.

One of Rogers' records was set in the Sun Bowl. Four times in the first half alone, the Nebraska offense bogged down in Georgia territory. And four times Rogers booted the ball through the uprights. They weren't gimmes, either, covering 50, 32, 42 and 37 yards. In between those kicks, Kinney ripped off an 11-yard TD run, staking Nebraska to a 18-0 halftime lead.

The Huskers poured it on from there. Brownson ran for a touchdown and passed to Green for another, a sweet moment for the black Husker captain. And just days after Corgan made the quarterback do all that extra running, Brownson delighted the coach with a hit he delivered on a run.

Corgan always told his backs that even though they were carrying the ball, they were the ones who should be distributing the bruises. He preached getting your pads low, finding a nice soft spot on the defender, then lifting up on contact. Brownson did just that and demolished a Bulldog. Corgan bear-hugged Brownson when he got to the sidelines, lifting the quarterback off the ground. "That's the way to deliver a blow!" Corgan chortled.

The defense frolicked, too, picking off six Georgia passes. At the end of the third quarter, Fiala was on the sidelines drinking a margarita with some of his fraternity brothers. The final was 45-6. It was Georgia's worst loss in almost two decades. It still ranks today among the most lopsided victories in Nebraska bowl history.

> "I'm not taking anything away from the Southeastern Conference. But I have to say Nebraska is as good or better than any team we played. I just couldn't believe men that big ... could move like they did. They were quick for such big men."
>
> — **Georgia defensive tackle Steve Greer**

Tagge rushed for 37 yards and passed for 53 in a backup role.

At the end of the season, the NU offense was hitting its stride. The 45 points here had followed the 44 rolled up against Oklahoma, the most points scored by NU in back-to-back games in 19 years. It took most of the season, but the Osborne offense was now racking up points like a pinball machine.

After the game, defensive captain Dana Stephenson presented Devaney the game ball, calling him "the greatest coach in the nation." Devaney spoke with pride of the team, calling it perhaps his best ever.

Devaney wouldn't have said it, but this also was surely the best coaching job of his career. It wasn't just that he'd taken a team picked fifth in the league to a Big Eight title and bowl win. It was the way he'd done it: Overcoming the crippling preseason loss of his offensive star, Joe Orduna. Keeping the team moving forward after a rough start. And judiciously managing an unsettled situation with two rookie quarterbacks.

With the 9-2 finish, conference title and No. 11 final poll ranking, the Huskers had returned to the standard of success Devaney had set during his first five years in Lincoln. However, on that happy day in El Paso, even the coach himself wouldn't have had an inkling of the big things that were building in Lincoln.

With this amazing bounce-back season, Devaney's program was now on a trajectory that would take it to heights even Nebraska's most hopeful fans could not imagine.

Nebraska center Glenn Patterson liked the Sun Bowl so much, he took a picture of some of the 7,000 Husker fans who traveled to El Paso for the game.

Dawn of a New Age

IN MAY OF 1970, angst over President Richard Nixon's Vietnam policies and the killing of four students at Kent State University by Ohio National Guardsmen boiled over into the first significant war protests on the University of Nebraska campus. Hundreds of student protesters occupied the campus military sciences building. Five days later, some 4,000 students, faculty members and others rallied on a campus green. Daisies were handed out in what organizers called "a beautiful nonviolent rally for love and peace."

Just four blocks away from the peace rally, there was a much larger gathering of Nebraskans, attracted to a display of controlled violence. The Cornhuskers' annual Red-White spring game drew some 13,000 fans to Memorial Stadium. The somewhat ironic concurrence of the events had been noted by several speakers at the peace rally. "This is where the real scene is," one speaker declared. "Over there is the freaky stuff."

It's unclear what specific freaky things in Memorial Stadium that peacenik was referring to. But looking back, you could make a pretty good case that it might well have been Johnny Rodgers. Freaky, after all, was the word that best described the 19-year-old's athletic talent — gifts that were on full display that day as he made his public debut with the Husker varsity.

The Age of Aquarius was slow to arrive in Lincoln, Nebraska. As the counterculture movement swept across America in the late 1960s, those rebellious winds of change tended to blow as wispy breezes in Nebraska's capital city. Lincoln was a deeply religious city, set in its ways and not prone to excess. It wasn't until 1966 that its voters decided that the sale of liquor by the drink would not doom the masses. And Nebraska as a whole was a bedrock conservative state.

But as the calendar turned to 1970 and the start of the next American decade, a new culture clearly was emerging on the Lincoln campus, one that was extramural in its outlook and self-consciously nonconformist.

T-shirts and bell-bottom jeans gained uniform status on campus, and students were letting their hair down. Women turned away from the puffy perfect bouffants of the previous decade toward a longer, free-flowing look. For men, locks that covered the ears and swept the forehead, combined with long, slick sideburns, fast were becoming the norm.

Nebraska's football players were not immune to these fashion trends. The photos in the media guides of the day offer evidence of the mops increasingly hidden beneath those helmets. Devaney had no prohibitions on long hair, though if it did start reaching toward your shoulders or you were growing some kind of crazy facial hair, the coaches were likely to needle you until you got it trimmed.

> "There are a few students and faculty members who embarrassed us, but the thing that really stood out was that ... the responsible student leadership took charge."
>
> — NU Chancellor D.B. "Woody" Varner, responding to calls for a strike after the shootings of students at Kent State

Fans greeted Johnny Rodgers and Bob Devaney when the Huskers returned to Lincoln after the tie with USC in Los Angeles in 1970.

Dave Morock recalled the previous year when he showed up for the first bowl practice with a Fu Manchu mustache. "You know, Dave, we're going to the Sun Bowl," Devaney told him, "and we'd like to take you with us." Morock shaved the next day. Players had no real problem with how Devaney drew that line. At a time of a growing generation gap between adults and America's restless youth, this old cat was with it. He mostly let you do your thing.

The rising anti-establishment feelings on the Lincoln campus became obvious to all in the spring of 1970, when long-simmering anti-war rumblings boiled over into the first real acts of civil disobedience. The May 4 shooting deaths of students at Kent State sparked an immediate reaction.

That night, some 2,000 young men and women occupied the NU military building, though with a live band playing, it had more the look and feel of an all-nighter than a subversive act. Then on Saturday, May 9, came the daisy-laden rally on a campus athletic field. "It's about time Nebraska woke up and joined the rest of the nation," one speaker said. "What the nation needs is new vision, not your damn football players on Saturday afternoon."

There were thousands of Nebraskans at Memorial Stadium at that moment who would have quibbled with that statement. Many of them attended the Red-White game intent on seeing one player in particular. And Johnny Rodgers, freshly up from the freshman team, fast made an impression.

Van Brownson looks for a receiver in Nebraska's 1970 spring game, the last time the Huskers competed on grass at Memorial Stadium.

The rookie blazed downfield during the game-like scrimmage to snare a 29-yard pass from Jerry Tagge. Moments later, he leaped high to grab an 11-yard pass. Rodgers also ripped off two shifty punt returns totaling 43 yards. And he did it all despite a wet, muddy track — clear justification for Devaney's decision to spend $321,685 before the fall to replace Memorial Stadium's grass field with artificial turf.

AstroTurf was installed in Memorial Stadium in the summer of 1970 at a cost of $321,685. University officials said no tax money was involved.

Husker fans that day learned very quickly: When Rodgers stands back alone waiting for a kick, you need to get out of your seat, because it's likely that something spectacular is about to happen.

He showed tremendous speed, the reason fans soon would be calling him "Johnny the Jet." And he was ridiculously elusive. He seemed able to move his body in two or three directions at once. His ability to stop, go and change speeds left his pursuers looking like they were groping for a light switch in the dark.

In the larger picture, Rodgers possessed difference-making talent — and for the Huskers, transformative talent. As with all those other changes that had emerged on the University of Nebraska campus that spring, it indeed appeared that a new age was born.

It was the dawning of the age of Johnny R. Superstar — a time that forever would alter the image and culture of Nebraska football and take it to heights never seen before.

During the Rodgers era, while many across the country were flashing two-finger peace signs, Nebraskans would take to another popular hand gesture: proudly holding aloft single index fingers. Tom Osborne summed it up simply four decades later: "Johnny changed us from a good team to a national championship team."

Bob Gibson

Bob Boozer

JOHNNY RODGERS GREW UP IN OMAHA'S GHETTO, the neighborhood just north of downtown that was the center of the city's sizable African-American community. People from outside Nebraska might have been surprised in the 1960s to find a community of some 34,000 blacks in what was widely seen as a rural farm state.

As in other Midwest cities, Omaha's blacks had been lured from the Deep South over the first half of the 20th century by the promise of good jobs. In Omaha, they found that work in the city's thriving meat-packing industry. South Omaha for years was home to the nation's largest livestock market, with beef cattle and swine coming into the city daily by the trainload. It turned Omaha into America's butcher shop. All of the nation's major meat producers had significant slaughter and cold-packing operations in the city.

The work was hard and raw, but the pay was good. The packing plants gave thousands of low-skilled Omaha workers — black and white — the chance for a middle-class life. The paychecks those black packinghouse workers brought home helped support a bustling retail community on the near north side that employed hundreds of other blacks. Life in north Omaha was still no picnic, with high levels of poverty, hunger and deprivation. But compared to a lot of places, it was a relative mecca for a time.

The only thing Omaha seemed to churn out in greater abundance than beef at that time was great black athletes. Even before Rodgers came along, ponder this: What other city in a mere decade's time could claim to have produced a Hall of Fame major league baseball pitcher (Bob Gibson) and a Hall of Fame NFL running back (Gale Sayers), not to mention pro football's first black quarterback (Marlin Briscoe) and an Olympic and NBA champion basketball player (Bob Boozer)? Many other Omaha blacks during that time went on to star in high school, college and even the pro ranks. Rodgers would become the heir to that line of greatness.

But the north Omaha of Rodgers' 1960s youth also was rapidly changing in ways that would prove disastrous. The deindustrialization that pummeled most of America's inner cities at that time hit north Omaha hard. The packing industry left for places where it didn't have to pay union wages. All of Omaha's big plants shut down, one by one, costing the city some 10,000 jobs.

Rage and unrest on the north side peaked in 1968, when the rioting that earlier had hit other major cities burst out in Omaha. Frustrated blacks took to the streets demanding "jobs, jobs, jobs."

Much of the north Omaha business district burned to the ground and was looted, and was not rebuilt. It was an economic calamity from which north Omaha never has recovered.

The north Omaha streets where Rodgers grew up became rife with poverty, drugs, dropouts, crime and violence. The seemingly hopeless life of the ghetto can swallow the promise of youth. Kids often become ensnared in a cycle of poverty, breakdown of families and lack of opportunity, running the streets — and into trouble.

The lure of street life pulled hard on Johnny Rodgers. At age 13, he accidentally shot a kid in the stomach. At 14, he was stabbed in a fight. That same year he ran away for months to Detroit. By age 16, he had fathered boys with two different girls. Here was a kid clearly lacking in direction. Much could be traced to his home life.

Rodgers had been born into abject poverty to a 14-year-old single mom. He wouldn't meet his dad until he was 17. For the first five years of his life, he lived in a house his grandfather had built in the Bottoms, a rundown part of east Omaha within the Missouri River's floodplain. The family had no running water, indoor plumbing or electricity. His grandmother would read to him by candlelight. Rodgers suffered from severe asthma, and one time was wheezing so badly his mom ran with him to the bus stop to get him to the hospital. He thought he was going to die.

Another distinct early memory was being about 5 years old and stressing over whether to make a dash for the outhouse, some 50 yards away. The source of his anxiety was a mean red rooster that would chase him whenever he stepped into the yard. When Rodgers later thought about his style of running on punt returns, he believed the roots of his flashy moves may have been dodging that nasty bird.

Around the time Rodgers started school, his grandfather got a job with Cudahy, a major Omaha packer. That allowed his family to move out of the Bottoms to a house at 27th and Pinkney, the heart of north Omaha. His mother subsequently married a construction worker.

But while the financial picture had brightened, Rodgers' family situation did not. He and his stepdad didn't get along. Sometimes his mother and stepfather would fight, and Rodgers would intervene and "get jacked," he said. Rodgers often took shelter at his grandparents' house. Other times he just took off.

Rodgers would roam the streets, hooking up with girls and shooting craps to hustle for money. At 14, he fathered his first child. The girl's mother fired a shot at him when he said he wouldn't marry the girl. But he rather enjoyed his risky lifestyle.

For fun, he and his friends would shoot each other with BB guns. The real trick was to catch a BB in your hand.

Gale Sayers

Marlin Briscoe

DAWN OF A NEW AGE   109

Once when he was 13, he and his best friend skipped school, the buddy bringing over a real handgun he'd taken from his aunt. They thought it wasn't loaded. While Rodgers was on the phone with a girl, the friend was brandishing the gun, aiming at him and pulling the trigger. Rodgers said he got mad, grabbed the gun and pulled the trigger, aghast to see he'd shot his friend in the stomach. Rodgers was afraid he'd killed him. Luckily, the boy made a full recovery and told the police it had been an accident. It was the only time as a young kid that Rodgers would have contact with police, though hardly the last time he'd be in trouble. "There was trouble all over," he said years later. "You can't get away from trouble."

Around age 14, Rodgers and an older boy ran off to Detroit in a 1951 Chevy. Rodgers saw a pretty girl in an ice cream parlor there and followed her outside. He was suddenly jumped by a boy wielding a knife. Before the youth could stab him, the pretty girl pulled out a razor and cut his attacker. Such was life on the edge. Rodgers escaped unscathed — that time.

Juvenile authorities ultimately caught up to him and brought him back to Omaha, with an agreement that he'd move in with his grandparents. It made for a more stable home life, but he'd recall it in some ways as "jumping from the frying pan into the fire."

To get from his grandparents' house to Horace Mann Junior High, he had to cross Lake Street and go through a rough neighborhood that was considered the territory of a street gang. Rodgers was no gang member, he said, but the gangsters still didn't like him setting foot on their turf. It made getting to and from school a daily adventure.

Rodgers learned that if he kept his eyes open and walked in the middle of the street, he was OK. Given a head start and his speed, there was no way they could catch him. But at other times he had no choice but to stand his ground and fight. Though always small for his age, Rodgers wasn't afraid to fight. He'd later have the scars to prove it.

One time he was surrounded by the south-of-Lake gang and fought his way out by swinging a dog chain. Another time the gang cornered him outside a north Omaha rec center. One of the toughs, a 250-pound kid Rodgers knew as "Bear," plunged a knife into the back of his shoulder. It left a two-inch scar. Rodgers insisted years later he never was an instigator, only fighting in self-defense. "I didn't start fights," he said. "But I seldom lost fights."

To hear the stories now, it's easy to believe Rodgers could have ended up dead or in prison, the fate that would befall many boys he grew up with. But ghetto life, just like the many would-be tacklers he'd see later on the football field, would not be able to knock the legs out from under Johnny Rodgers. Sports would prove his salvation.

In his grade school years, Rodgers lived near Kountze Park, where during the late 1950s and early 1960s the pantheon of great black athletes in Omaha would gather to play football, basketball and baseball. Gale Sayers and his brothers would be there, along with Briscoe and future Huskers like Mike Green, Joe Orduna and Dick Davis. Rodgers was eight years younger than Sayers, but the older boys let him play. The speedy little guy flashed natural athletic ability.

"I used to go out every Friday, Saturday and Sunday, and I'd fight every Friday, Saturday and Sunday."

— **Johnny Rodgers, looking back on his youth**

Rodgers made his first mark in organized sports, believe it or not, as a tumbler. As a third-grader at Lothrop Elementary, he performed with the school's tumbling team at places like the Crossroads Mall. For the grand finale, the other boys would form a pyramid, and the young Rodgers would fly over the top with a complete 360-degree flip.

Later at the Eugene Eppley Boys Club and north Omaha YMCA, he'd excel in team sports. Just show him how, and he could do it. He'd prove talented enough to set a national Junior Olympic record in the triple jump and to later be drafted by baseball's Los Angeles Dodgers. On a football field, though, Rodgers was particularly special.

Rodgers put on pads for the first time with a Boys Club team that competed in Omaha's midget league. Playing quarterback, the 13-year-old Rodgers took a team that had finished last in the city league the previous year to the 1964 championship game.

"Johnny had a lot of things to learn," recalled Don Benning, one of his early coaches and mentors. "We tried to help him in regards to what's right, what's wrong and what was ahead of him." Rodgers' youthful teammates became his gang.

Rodgers saw a future for himself as a pro athlete, telling his mom he was going to make $100,000 some day. She told him to quit such crazy talk. In fact, Rodgers said she and his stepfather originally didn't give him much encouragement in athletics, telling him he needed to get a job and support the family.

The coaches at Omaha's Technical High School knew little about Rodgers, good or bad, when he came out for football as a sophomore in the fall of 1966. But even before the team completed its first round of calisthenics, coach Dick Christie knew the muscular new kid was bound for the varsity. He was able to do twice as many pushups as everyone else.

The first time Rodgers carried the ball in a varsity game that fall, he went 60 yards for a touchdown. To watch guys try to tackle him was almost comical. This, after all, was a kid who had grown up dodging fists and knives, not to mention an angry rooster. And as a receiver, Rodgers had no match. When you've snagged BB's out of the air, grabbing a football is nothing.

Rodgers with Tech High football coach Dick Christie. "In high school, he accepted any discipline he had coming," Christie said. "There was never an argument."

DAWN OF A NEW AGE

Rodgers ran for more than 1,100 yards in nine games in his senior season at Omaha Tech. "The best thing I can say about him is his leadership as captain both on and off the field," said coach Christie. "He set high standards for the others with training rules and hard work in practice."

"Football comes easy," he said in a 1969 interview. "I don't think about running. I just get the ball and go. When you're about to make a cut or go around someone who's a few feet away, you don't have time to think. You just move out."

He made it look easy, too. By his senior year, the high school All-American was rewriting the record book in Omaha's Metro Conference, setting new marks for career touchdowns, career touchdown receptions and longest touchdown run.

Despite the obvious talent, it was the character of the kid that stood out most to Christie. Even though football was a breeze for Rodgers, he still worked harder than anyone else on the team. He stood only 5-foot-9 and weighed 155 pounds, but the street-tough kid craved contact and begged the coaches to scrimmage. And he'd do anything for his school, a true competitor who would rush from his baseball game to get in a few jumps at the track meet that was going on at the same time.

Such character strengths, when combined with his rough background, made Rodgers something of a paradox in the halls of Tech. Christie hounded him to stay on top of his schoolwork. And the coach later would say he frequently took knives off Rodgers. The boy would protest. "How am I going to get home?"

But Tech coaches and administrators regularly proclaimed Rodgers a standout student and citizen. Rodgers possessed superior intelligence and was quick-thinking and streetwise. He was a good-natured kid whose sincerity and charm endeared him to teachers. He didn't skip class or shirk responsibility. The coach believed Rodgers was a black "Jack Armstrong," the fictional All-American boy, possessing every quality you'd want in a son.

While at first an average student at Tech, Rodgers eventually graduated in 1969 in the top third of his class and was voted senior class president and prom king. His stated goal — if pro football didn't work out, of course — was to teach English.

He was honored that spring as The World-Herald's high school athlete of the year. The paper's story pictured a clean-cut young man lying in the grass, and it extolled his virtues, not offering a whiff of his troubled past. It all sounded too good to be true — and to some degree, it was.

Still, Rodgers had clearly overcome a lot. By then, four of Rodgers' teammates on that rags-to-riches Boys Club midget football team already were in jail. Even before Rodgers played his first varsity down as a Husker, he was being touted in north Omaha as a beacon for all youth. A poster that would hang in the Boys Club in the summer of 1970 read, "John Rodgers says you can do it, too — stay in school."

Rodgers seemed bound from ghetto to glory. He became the most highly recruited high school athlete coming out of Omaha in years. Not surprisingly, Bob Devaney and Cletus Fischer, who recruited Omaha for the Huskers, regularly cruised the 50 miles down the new concrete ribbon of Interstate 80 to Tech's games. Devaney eventually took over Rodgers' recruitment personally, considering him one of the finest athletes in the country.

Rodgers, though, had more than 20 college offers. And were it not for geometry, he might have ended up in Los Angeles at Southern Cal. Rodgers didn't particularly care for Nebraska's harsh winters. And USC was a national power that churned out NFL stars, a school Rodgers figured would give him more exposure to the pro scouts. That was the path to get him that $100,000. "I had no interest in talking to Bob," Rodgers later would say of the man who became his mentor. "Nebraska wasn't on my radar at all."

Rodgers starred in football, basketball and baseball at Omaha Tech High. He also registered the state's best mark in the triple jump as a part-time member of the track team.

DAWN OF A NEW AGE 113

Rodgers said he considered going to USC to escape Nebraska's winters. "I don't like our cold weather here," he said. "It makes me sick sometimes."

But USC reneged on its offer. Coaches discovered that Rodgers lacked a geometry credit that the school required for admission. He was crushed. In the end, Charles Washington, a north Omaha activist and newspaperman, helped convince him that Lincoln was where he needed to be. Washington months earlier had arranged the first meeting between Rodgers and Devaney. The Huskers were in the midst of their second straight 6-4 season, but Rodgers recalled that Devaney told him he could help turn things around.

Rodgers could see Nebraska really wanted him — more than USC did. And he also saw Devaney as a fatherly figure, one he got the sense would be in his corner. In February 1969, a bespectacled Rodgers sat down with Devaney for dinner in Omaha and signed his Big Eight letter of intent. "John will fit into our program as a halfback," Devaney told the papers that day, the first public comments he'd make about Rodgers. "He is a real fine runner, and I'd like to take advantage of that."

Rodgers for his part told the paper he'd decided that he might just as well write a new Nebraska success story. "I felt I had made it so far in Nebraska, I'd better stay here."

Heading to Lincoln the following fall, Rodgers played wingback for coach Jim Ross' freshman team and led the squad in just about every offensive category. And it took him only a handful of practices with the varsity in the spring of 1970 to move up to the No. 1 unit. He'd confirm that status with his breakout showing in the Red-White game. Rodgers was just a perfect fit for the wide-open offense the Huskers had unveiled the previous year.

Teammates later would recall that the newcomer was confident while not crossing the line into cockiness. Rodgers modestly fit in among his new teammates, saying little and not making any waves or attracting attention to himself. "He wasn't J.R. Superstar or Johnny the Jet," Morock later recalled. "He was just Johnny Rodgers."

Along with his obvious athleticism, he also impressed teammates with his toughness. "You hit him, and he got right back up," recalled Jerry Murtaugh, a hard-hitting linebacker going into his senior season. "You could tell he was a tough little kid." Rodgers worked hard, too, staying late after practice to catch pass after pass from Brownson and Tagge or Osborne, his position coach.

Buzz surrounded Rodgers in Lincoln going into the fall of 1970, his debut the most anticipated of any player in the Devaney era. Husker coaches walked around with knowing smiles. Even the young Tagge knew remarkable talent when he saw it. In an interview during fall camp, he proclaimed Rodgers "the greatest offensive weapon they've ever had around here." A World-Herald columnist warned fans before the opener that they'd be wise to stand up when Rodgers got the ball in his hands. "To be truthful, he hasn't been overrated," Conde Sargent wrote. "He's for real. Watch him."

Some 66,103 fans took that advice during the Huskers' season opener September 12, 1970. There was a familiar feel of electricity in the air in Memorial Stadium, which on a fall Saturday always was a special place. But there was change in the air, too.

The new vacuumable fake-grass field stood as a symbol for the way college football was changing. It was leaving behind the days of sis-boom-bah, letter sweaters and big megaphones and becoming big business. Wake Forest, the opponent that day, was a late addition to the Nebraska schedule, a match made possible when the NCAA decided to allow schools to schedule 11 regular-season games instead of 10. College athletic departments were chasing dollars, a pursuit that would become never-ending.

THE HUSKERS ALSO WERE TAKING to that new carpet wearing helmets with single red N logos on the sides, as opposed to the NU logos they had sported since 1967. Going into the fall, equipment manager Gib Babcock discovered that he didn't have enough U decals to go around. So he simply went with the N.

The oversight would prove a mixed blessing. It would lead to jokes at Nebraska's expense: "What's the N stand for? … Nowledge." But it also marked the launch of one of the most iconic helmet logos in all of college football — as luck would have it, just when the Huskers were about to crash the national stage in a big way. Before long, every sports fan in the country would recognize that N.

No doubt, expectations already were rising everywhere for these Huskers. After a two-year lapse, NU once again was starting the season in the Top 10, coming in at No. 9 in the Associated Press preseason poll of sportswriters. And it was hard to imagine what kind of defense it would take to stop the Husker attack.

Nebraska returned both outstanding young quarterbacks in juniors Tagge and Brownson. Fellow junior Jeff Kinney now was paired at I-back with senior Orduna, back from the knee surgery that had sidelined him the previous season. Add to that offensive mix Rodgers, who spoke confidently at the season's start about the offense's capability. "We're going to score a lot of points, so it'll take a lot of points to beat us," he said. "And other teams aren't about to do that."

Rodgers debuted for Nebraska against Wake Forest. "Rodgers handled the ball only six times, but the pell-mell little guy had the crowd on its feet on each of his possessions — even when he was banged down after a 3-yard reception of a pass," The World-Herald reported.

Now weighing a solid 170 pounds, Rodgers cantered onto the field for the first time against Wake Forest like a thoroughbred headed to post. Sure enough, it wouldn't take long for the rookie to get the fans out of their seats. With the Huskers down 3-0 in the first quarter, they ran a play that would become a Husker staple in the Rodgers era. On the snap, Tagge, Orduna and his fullback went left as if going that way on the option. But instead, Rodgers came in from his left side wingback spot and took an inside handoff from Tagge on a counter going right.

It was the 23 Counter Trap, an inside reverse the Huskers called their "Scissors play." The name came from the way the backfield was going in two different directions, but it also would become appropriate because of the way Rodgers used the play to cut up defenses. It was an early example of the creative ways Osborne and Devaney would use to get the ball into Rodgers' hands.

On this initial scissors play, despite the deception involved, Rodgers found himself facing a wall of Wake Forest defenders. But with a quick move of his hips, Rodgers sidestepped the defensive end and, in the words of Husker radio play-by-play man Lyell Bremser, "left that fella standing there counting his change." It was the first of many colorful calls Bremser would make to describe Rodgers' on-field artistry over the next three years. It was about as effortless an 8-yard gain as you'd ever see. Soon after that play, Orduna scored the touchdown that put the Huskers ahead for good.

Early in the second half, Tagge called for a bomb, sending Rodgers on a fly pattern straight down the field. Rodgers turned into a red streak. Maybe it was that springy new AstroTurf carpet, but it was hard to imagine anyone ever running faster on the floor of Memorial Stadium. By the time the blazing Rodgers ran under Tagge's perfect heave, he already was 15 yards beyond the nearest defender.

That electric 61-yard touchdown was the play of the day in Nebraska's workmanlike 36-12 takedown of the Demon Deacons, a team that would go on to win the Atlantic Coast Conference championship that season. The World-Herald noted that Rodgers had fans getting out of their seats all six times he touched the ball — even when he was brought down after a 3-yard pass reception. The dynamo rushed for 33 yards on three carries and took the only kick he fielded 37 yards. His first college action left Rodgers beaming on the sideline.

Afterward, everyone from Devaney to the Wake Forest coaches and players were talking about Rodgers. Sporting a medium-length Afro hairdo and a thin mustache, Rodgers spoke to reporters about the bomb play, admitting that it actually was the second time Tagge had called it. "I messed up the first one," he said candidly. "Tagge had a few words for me on the sideline after that one. I didn't miss the second chance."

It wouldn't be the last time at Nebraska that Rodgers would find himself benefiting from a second chance. But for Rodgers and the Huskers, the 1970 season was off and rolling. It was the perfect start to Nebraska football's new age.

Lyell Bremser of Omaha radio station KFAB broadcast Nebraska football games for 45 years, but the sound of his voice is most associated with his excited calls of Johnny Rodgers' big plays. Bremser wasn't certain where he picked up his popular expression "Man, woman and child!" but thought it might have been from an uncle who was prone to such outbursts.

Devaney's Problem Child

JERRY MURTAUGH STOOD INTENTLY at his linebacker position just behind the line, his eyes locked on USC quarterback Jimmy Jones. At the snap, Jones turned and gave the ball to I-back Clarence Davis, a breakaway threat who was among the nation's leading rushers the previous year. The offside guard and tackle pulled, and along with the fullback, formed an imposing entourage for the Trojan back to follow around the right end.

Murtaugh recognized the play right away as "Student Body Right," the signature play of coach John McKay's powerful I-formation offense. It was the play that made Heisman winners out of Mike Garrett and O.J. Simpson. It also was the play that just the previous week had helped the Trojans roll up 485 yards on the ground against Bear Bryant's Crimson Tide in Birmingham. McKay had a stable of Trojan horses he would run at you, and he'd pummel you with Student Body Right (or Left) until you proved you could stop it. Now with all those lead blockers in front of Davis, it seemed the entire USC student body was bearing down on the Husker defense.

But if Murtaugh had proved anything during his two previous seasons with the Husker varsity, it was that it was hard to keep him away from the football. Sure enough, Nebraska's mean tackling machine stepped over a block and with a dive took Davis down by the ankles. The public address announcer in the hallowed Los Angeles Memorial Coliseum was getting used to calling out No. 42's name. On this spectacular night for football in Southern California, Murtaugh would rack up a staggering 25 tackles.

On September 19, in just their second game of the 1970 season, Nebraska's ninth-ranked Cornhuskers faced a challenging test against the third-rated Trojans of USC. Southern Cal was arguably the pre-eminent program in college football at the time. The men of Troy were riding a 22-game unbeaten streak and had two recent national titles under their belt. They came in as whopping 13-point favorites over Nebraska.

A major factor in that point spread, and the main reason few people outside Nebraska thought the Huskers could win this game, was uncertainty about the Blackshirts. For all the attention to Nebraska's constellation of stars on offense, the Huskers in 1970 returned only Murtaugh and two other starters on defense. With experience on defense as "short as a coed's skirt," as one scribe termed it, there were major questions all around.

Jerry Murtaugh

Devaney gives Murtaugh instructions on the sideline during a 1969 victory over Texas A&M. Defensive coordinator Monte Kiffin listens in.

Four of the five Blackshirts up front were new. There was no size at all at nose guard. And two of those D-line starters, as well as one of the cornerbacks, were sophomores. This was one of the greenest groups of Blackshirts Devaney had ever fielded. "We're not sure whether we can find the answers," Devaney told the Big Eight's Skywriters, an annual preseason tour of sportswriters to all the Big Eight campuses.

But from the start of the 1970 season, Jerry Murtaugh was having none of such doubtful talk. The strong-jawed senior from Omaha with thick wavy hair and long sideburns never accepted that this was a rebuilding year for the Blackshirts. "The defense isn't down," he confidently told reporters after a preseason practice. And while he hadn't said it publicly — at least not yet — he saw no reason why the Cornhuskers wouldn't go out this year and win the school's first national championship.

There would come a day when the Cornhuskers would start every year with the expectation of competing for a national championship. But up to this time, such talk was pretty rare around Lincoln.

Each year under Devaney, the Cornhuskers opened the year with two goals: win a Big Eight title, and land in a major bowl. That's what Devaney always talked about in recruiting. Jerry Tagge, Jeff Kinney and others later would say that when they came to Lincoln, Big Eight titles and big-time bowls were the stuff of their dreams. Even before this season, when Van Brownson and Tagge were asked about their goals, both said they wanted to play in a top-tier bowl. National titles simply weren't mentioned.

And while the Huskers under Devaney had become a frequent Top 10 team, they had only once — in 1965 — ever been a serious part of the national championship discussion. In an era when the best teams rarely matched up at the end of the season due to bowl tie-ins, national titles often were seen as more theoretical than real. The media often put the word "mythical" in front of any national title reference.

The national pundits didn't have the Huskers in the championship conversation this year, either. Much of the talk of title contenders at the start of this 1970 college football season centered on USC, Ohio State, Texas and Notre Dame, four traditional powers that had resided at the top of the polls throughout the 1960s.

The Blackshirts take a seat on the Memorial Stadium turf for a lecture from Devaney.

But years later Devaney would say the players on his 1970 team were quietly aspiring for more. Behind the scenes, they were determined not just to rule the Big Eight but to be the No. 1 team in the country. "We believed we really were the best team," Johnny Rodgers said later of the team's preseason attitude. "We were going to bring it on." Recalled Dave Morock: "We knew we had a good football team and a bunch of guys who wanted to prove it." And players would recall that one of the prime voices behind that belief, and one of the leaders relentlessly pushing them toward the goal, was Jerry Murtaugh. He was convinced that the Huskers were going to win it all.

Of course, all teams start their seasons with ambitious goals. You have to go out on the field and prove it. Murtaugh figured Nebraska now had a great opportunity to do just that. If the Huskers truly were going to be a title contender, there was no better way to launch the bid than flying out to L.A. and knocking off USC's mighty Trojans. In fact, talking to a reporter when the skywriters came to Lincoln before the season, Murtaugh had boldly predicted that the Huskers were "going to beat the hell out of USC."

That statement was bound to cause Murtaugh some problems. Devaney always warned players about inflammatory talk. The story making the rounds at that time was that Kinney had to pull Murtaugh away from the skywriters, telling him, "You just look pretty, and let me do the talking." The two tried to explain the statement away, saying Murtaugh was just joking around, but it was too late. Murtaugh's words were sure to end up on the bulletin board in the USC locker room.

Devaney was livid when he heard about it, but that wasn't unusual. The coach always struggled to control Murtaugh, a player who was constantly in the doghouse. To hear the stories years later, you'd wonder how Murtaugh survived four years in Lincoln. But if you saw him on a football field, you'd understand why Devaney continued to trot him out every Saturday. On the field, Murtaugh was a holy terror, one of the nastiest players ever to put on a Cornhusker uniform.

Murtaugh grew up in Omaha's working-class Benson neighborhood, part of a big family of roughnecks. There were five Murtaugh boys, known as talented wrestlers and, in less formal settings, unmatched street fighters. Everyone in northeast Omaha feared the Murtaugh brothers. The dread extended beyond the boys in the Murtaugh family. Jerry Murtaugh said the true reason he grew up so tough can be traced to his five sisters, who were all "meaner than hell."

As a high school senior, Murtaugh was all-state in football and won a state wrestling title at 180 pounds, completing an undefeated season with three straight pins at the state meet.

The Murtaughs became the winningest family in the history of Nebraska high school wrestling, with Jerry and two brothers winning state titles. As a 180-pound senior at North High in 1967, Jerry Murtaugh never lost a match, pinning all three of his opponents at the state meet. While Murtaugh didn't earn as much acclaim in football, he was a smart and extremely aggressive linebacker. Both Nebraska and Oklahoma could see in this athletic grappler big potential to hogtie opposing ball carriers.

He later would say the two schools engaged in quite a recruiting battle over his services. Boosters from Oklahoma, he said, offered him under-the-table inducements: a car, cash, clothes and airline tickets. Though such bounty clearly would have been illegal under NCAA rules, Murtaugh was ready to gladly accept it all. But he said Devaney got wind of the booster offer and issued a warning: If word that you took that stuff gets out, you'll be ineligible. And if you have any hopes of playing pro ball, those dreams are gone. Murtaugh said Devaney eventually won him over and did so offering nothing beyond the standard tuition, room, board and $15-a-month laundry money.

Incidentally, lest anyone thinks Nebraska was completely above such shenanigans, Murtaugh years later said he did know of Husker players in the Devaney era who received bonuses outside the lines from boosters. And other players from the era give the impression that things weren't squeaky clean in Devaney's program. Johnny Rodgers says he regularly scalped his complimentary tickets for well over face value, something he said was known to Devaney. Other players speak of businesses that gave them free meals, even free kegs of beer.

Tom Osborne, who would develop a reputation during his own head coaching days for scrupulously following the rules, in a 2014 interview said he had no direct knowledge of any such abuses. He said Devaney never suggested that Osborne offer a player anything under the table. As for the activities of NU boosters, Osborne acknowledged that he was concerned enough about things he heard about a couple of them during Devaney's day that he told them to stay away from his team when he took over the program in 1973.

The ticket selling was difficult to police and eventually became so widespread in college football that the NCAA switched to a pass-gate system, under which players listed who would be using their complimentary seats, taking the actual tickets out of the players' hands. Osborne wasn't surprised to hear that Rodgers had scalped his. "Johnny was very entrepreneurial," he said. "There was a lot of scalping that went on at that time."

Once in Lincoln, Murtaugh's relationship with Devaney quickly turned rocky. While most of the Husker players of that era later would speak glowingly of Devaney, Murtaugh was not among them. "We never saw eye to eye in the four years I was there," he said. "We never liked each other."

Murtaugh also admitted that their sour relationship had a lot to do with the fact that he was a renegade and a boozer, incapable of staying out of the bars. Murtaugh was sure to be around whenever players retired to the Diamond Bar and Grill, a downtown watering hole that was favored among NU athletes. He even sneaked out of the on-campus hotel where the Huskers stayed the night before games to hit the bars. He liked his beer. "I was in the midst of it, always," Murtaugh recalled. "And once in a while I'd get out there, and all hell would break loose."

The trouble Murtaugh landed in was never anything huge, the worst being a handful of alcohol-fueled brawls. The knucklehead showed up for the spring game his freshman year with his eye swollen shut after he'd blocked a punch with his face. Murtaugh's transgressions weren't the kind that would get his name in the papers. Most such incidents tended to be handled quietly between Devaney and Lincoln's police, outside of public notice.

NU linebacker Jerry Murtaugh (42) takes aim at Kansas running back John Riggins (32), as defensive end Mike Wynn (90) takes on a blocker.

But the sheer volume of trouble Murtaugh found set him apart. Given his reputation, it's surprising he hadn't been among the players arrested in Juarez the previous year during the Sun Bowl trip. He wasn't far from that affair, though, collecting the bail money that night.

Devaney's typical punishment when players ran afoul of team rules was to send them running up the Memorial Stadium stairs. During his time in Lincoln, Murtaugh knew the view from the top of the stadium better than anyone. Teammates said he probably set some kind of record for the steps coaches made him run. "He was a wild man back in the day," recalled Wally Winter, Murtaugh's close friend and drinking buddy. "He didn't listen to a lot of authority."

Wally Winter

At times, Murtaugh's insubordination showed up on the field, too. He years later told the story of a preseason practice his senior year. The Huskers were doing a noncontact drill, running through the motions of plays. He thought Tagge was showing up the defense, and he didn't really like the quarterback anyway. So when Tagge carried the ball on the option, Murtaugh drilled him.

Devaney went nuts, screaming at both Murtaugh and John Melton, who as Murtaugh's position coach had the impossible job of keeping him in line. "Can't you control that SOB?!" Devaney yelled. Just to prove that Melton couldn't, Murtaugh went ahead and dropped Tagge on the next play, too. Devaney, now totally beside himself, again stepped in — and fired Melton on the spot.

Things eventually got smoothed over. With his job back, Melton that night phoned his obstinate linebacker at home to tell him things had been resolved. "You've got to learn to control yourself," Melton said. But Murtaugh never did. He thought the whole episode was funnier than hell.

Not everyone from the era recalls that story, though they say it certainly fits with the Murtaugh they remember. "There's not a whole lot of embellishment in that," recalled Morock. "Jerry would hit you just for fun."

Husker opponents couldn't control Murtaugh, either. Which was one reason that Melton, despite all the grief, treated Murtaugh like his own son. He was a reliable anchor in the middle of the Husker defense who racked up tackles like no one who ever before had worn a Nebraska uniform.

"Your job is not hard," Melton used to tell Murtaugh. "Just go get the football." Indeed, Murtaugh was the epitome of a player with a nose for the ball. The solid 6-foot-3, 212-pounder wasn't the fastest runner. But he seemed to instinctively sniff out plays. He didn't stay blocked, and when he got to the ball carrier, he arrived in bad humor. He delivered the punishment. Teammates wondered whether he even felt pain. Some longtime Husker football observers considered him the most ferocious hitter in Lincoln since 1940s legend Tom "Train Wreck" Novak.

Assistant coach John Melton with linebacker Barry Alvarez in 1967.

Murtaugh forced his way onto the field early as a sophomore and soon grabbed a Blackshirt. The newcomer led the team in tackles that year, averaging nearly 10 a game. He topped that as a junior, earning all-Big Eight honors and setting a single-season Husker record for tackles with 126. He saved his best game for last that year, in the bowl against Georgia, logging 15 tackles, knocking down two passes, recovering a fumble and returning an interception 31 yards. He shrugged off the accolades. "Hey, I'm supposed to make tackles," he said.

He was a preseason All-American as a senior, an honor he would live up to. He also would be voted by Big Eight coaches as the league's player of the year — even beating out all the league's offensive stars for the honor. And he'd finish his career as the Huskers' all-time leading tackler, a record that would stand until linebacker Barrett Ruud broke it in 2004. Given all that, is there any wonder why Devaney never sat his problem child for even one game? The coach later would say — perhaps begrudgingly, given their poor relationship — that Murtaugh was the best linebacker he ever coached.

No matter what Devaney thought about Murtaugh's antics, teammates didn't seem bothered. In the ultimate sign of respect, they voted the player they called "Rat" co-captain of this 1970 team. He was the kind of competitor you wanted as a teammate. "I'm sure glad he's on our team," Brownson said that fall. As Tagge would put it years later: "People on the team liked him because he was crazy. He was mean, nasty and intimidating."

Murtaugh wasn't a particularly vocal leader, ruling over teammates mostly through fear. He was in total command of the defensive huddle, most other players afraid to say anything. He did not tolerate mistakes. Teammates later would say that one of the reasons the Huskers played so well in 1970 was that they feared what Murtaugh might do if they lost a game.

Murtaugh made it abundantly clear going into the big game against USC: Losing is not an option.

The Los Angeles Coliseum for a night game was one of the great atmospheres in all of college football. Huge crowds under bright lights. Balmy weather. The classic Trojan mascot roaming the sideline astride a white horse. While standing in the tunnel before the game, the Nebraska players heard a deafening rumble and roar as the Trojans took the field. Then the Huskers started out into the lights and were startled by another huge roar. They looked up into the stands to see as many as 20,000 Husker fans among the 73,760 spectators surrounding the field.

Jerry Tagge started against USC and threw for 140 yards.

Nebraska rooters, the players knew, were famous for the way they supported their Huskers home and away. That kind of support at Kansas in 1970 would lead KU's Pepper Rodgers to say to Devaney, "Sometime I'd like to play you guys at home." It really was no different on the Pacific Coast, home to a large and organized group of expatriates called "Californians for Nebraska." This night, NU and USC would play a game worthy of the great atmosphere — one that, had it been televised, would have gone down as a college football classic.

The biggest drama going into the game for Nebraska was over who would start at quarterback. Both Brownson and Tagge were making visits to the campus medical clinic during game week. Brownson had not played a down against Wake Forest after injuring his elbow in the preseason. Tagge took a helmet to the thigh and ruptured a blood vessel during another preseason scrimmage and later aggravated it against Wake Forest. He didn't practice that week before heading out to Los Angeles. Devaney even had Kinney taking snaps at quarterback in case of emergency. "I was ready," Kinney later recalled. "But I don't think Bob Devaney was." In the end, the still-hobbled Tagge was the game-time pick as starter.

Dan Schneiss

Given the uncertainty at quarterback, Nebraska initially put the load on Joe Orduna and his surgically repaired knee. The senior toted the ball eight times for 43 yards on the Huskers' first drive, a deep incursion into USC territory. The march came to a sudden halt when Orduna lost a fumble near the Trojan goal line. Still, the success on the ground fired up the Nebraska crowd and showed everyone in the Coliseum that the Huskers had come to play.

Husker Dan Schneiss, the offensive captain, typified Nebraska's physical attitude early on. The hard-nosed Wisconsin native and fellow fullback Jim Carstens drew the assignment of blocking Greg Slough, the Trojans' preseason All-America linebacker. Schneiss returned to the Nebraska sideline after one early drive with blood all over his white road jersey.

"Are you all right?" Carstens asked.

Schneiss pointed to the blood on his shirt. "You mean this? That belongs to Greg Slough."

Murtaugh and the Blackshirts, meanwhile, were showing as much respect for the USC attack as Murtaugh typically did for authority, shutting down the Trojans on their first five possessions. Murtaugh forced a fumble and Columbus, Nebraska, native Bill Kosch picked off a pass.

Going into the game, Husker coaches had made plans to pull out all the stops on offense. Early in the second quarter, Osborne pulled the first of several trick plays out of his bag, and it went for a touchdown. Out of the spread, Tagge pitched to the bloodied Schneiss. He ran around the right end before rearing back and surprising the Trojans with a perfect pass. Guy Ingles, who had been born in Los Angeles and moved to Omaha as a kid, caught it near the goal line and tumbled into the end zone for a 17-yard touchdown. Nebraska led 7-0, putting a charge into the Husker partisans.

Two possessions later, Trojan Ron Ayala intercepted a Tagge pass and returned it to the Nebraska 26 to set up the Trojans to tie the score. But Tagge helped put the Huskers on top again in the final minute before halftime. Under pressure at the USC 42, Tagge fired off a wounded duck that just reached Rodgers at the USC 15. One play later, Tagge found Rodgers again flaring out of the backfield. The wingback, waving furiously for the ball, made the reception and slipped a tackle to complete a 15-yard score and put Nebraska up 14-7 at the half.

Joe Orduna ran for 135 yards against USC and was named the game's outstanding offensive player by the press in attendance.

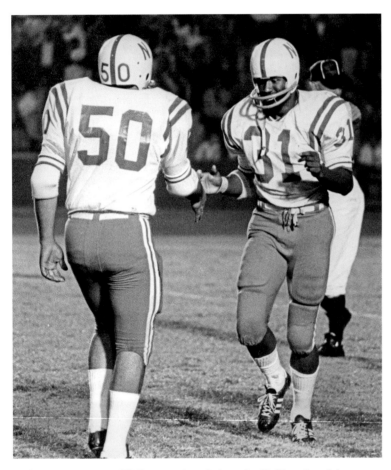

Backup center Doug Jamail (50) congratulates Orduna after his 67-yard touchdown run against USC.

It's possible that at that point McKay was regretting the snub of Rodgers over the geometry credit. Because the Husker wingback was on the field giving lessons in the subject, making cuts at angles the Trojans likely hadn't seen before. His 30-yard punt return set up Nebraska's first score. For the game he would pile up 188 yards receiving, rushing and returning kicks.

Rodgers wasn't the only Husker who had been especially looking forward to this contest. Bob Newton, the starting left tackle, didn't forget how USC ignored him coming out of Cerritos, just a 20-minute freeway ride from the Coliseum. He had been quoted in the papers that week saying the Trojans had essentially "laughed at" him in recruiting. After the Wake Forest game the previous week, Newton quickly had shed his gear and headed straight to the Husker weight room to get ready for USC. His dominant blocking on this night — before a big section of family and friends — helped spring Orduna for 135 yards. At one point, Newton recalled looking from the huddle over at McKay on the sideline and thinking, "You know what? You could have had me."

Nebraska started the second half driving impressively to a first down at the USC 25. A sack set back the Huskers, and Ayala picked off Tagge for a second time to end the threat. The Trojans again made the Huskers pay for the turnover, sustaining a long drive for a touchdown that tied the game at 14.

Orduna, the Bible-quoting son of an Omaha preacher who always said a little prayer on his way to the huddle, less than a minute later had Husker fans screaming, "Hallelujah!" Taking an off-tackle pitch at the Husker 33, he followed a great block by Schneiss and blasted through a hole. Newton pulled to the outside on the play, laid out and chopped down defensive end Tody Smith like a giant redwood. Smith scrambled back up but could reach only in vain as Orduna cut back against the grain and ran right by him. Now in the clear, the high-stepping Orduna outran four USC defenders into the end zone. Nebraska suddenly led 21-14 late in the third period, sending another surge through that huge Husker rooting section.

Seconds later, Nebraska had a chance to perhaps put away USC, when fast-rising sophomore tackle Larry Jacobson forced and recovered a fumble at the Trojan 15. The Huskers soon after were setting up for a 22-yard field goal, roughly the equivalent of an extra point kick. But the snap from center skimmed on the grass and was momentarily bobbled by the holder, throwing off Paul Rogers' timing. His kick barely missed wide right.

For the third time, the Trojans made Nebraska pay for a critical mistake, driving deep into Nebraska territory. Facing a crucial third down inside the 10, the Trojan quarterback handed off to Davis, who found a gap in the line. Murtaugh was a half step slow getting to the hole, his dive coming up just short. Davis scooted into the end zone, and the extra point kick tied the game at 21 with eight minutes left.

After the ensuing kickoff, the Trojans made short work of the Husker offense and, for the first time all night, had the upper hand. They had the ball with good field position at their own 42. Most importantly, they had all the momentum. The Coliseum crowd could sense the swing.

Three hard runs netted the Trojans 9 yards, setting up fourth and 1 near midfield with three minutes to play. McKay kept his offense on the field. He was going for it. And he had his quarterback turn and hand the ball to the running back most likely to get that yard: fullback Sam "Bam" Cunningham.

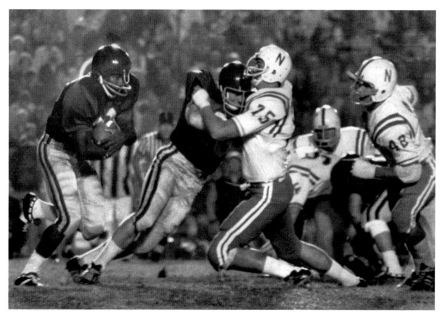

Nebraska defensive tackle Larry Jacobson (75) takes on a blocker, as Murtaugh (42) takes aim at a Trojan runner.

A bruising 210-pound sophomore, Cunningham had left his mark — lots of them, actually — on the Bama defense the week before, ripping off 135 yards and two touchdowns on just a dozen carries. In the mythology of college football, that game has gone down as the day Bear Bryant became convinced that he needed to start recruiting black football players. But as good as Cunningham was — a future NFL standout — on this night in Los Angeles the Trojan battering ram met his match.

Cunningham charged into a gap in the line and was met headlong by Murtaugh. The sound of clashing pads rang through the Coliseum. And the Husker stopped Cunningham cold. The officials didn't even bother to measure to see if he'd gotten the yard. It was the last of Murtaugh's 25 tackles on the night, and it ended the last serious threat by either team. The clock ran out on the 21-21 final.

Neither team had much enthusiasm for the sister-kissing result. The Huskers walked off dejectedly, one player slamming a helmet to the turf. Morock recalled giving a dirty look to one fan afterward who told him "nice game." Even comedian Bill Cosby barely drew a smile when he cracked jokes during a congratulatory visit to the Husker locker room, the celebrity USC fan in jest challenging Rodgers and Orduna to "step outside."

Devaney was disappointed, too. As always, he had gone in expecting to win. He'd been publicly quoted that week saying, "If you don't figure to win, you should just stay home and save the expense." Afterward, he lingered on the field longer than normal and later chewed out some assistants, feeling that mistakes — particularly five turnovers — had doomed Nebraska's hopes. The Huskers should have put this team away. "We are too proud to be tying this team," one Husker coach recalled him saying. "We have to have a stronger belief in ourselves."

> "They say a tie is just like kissing your sister. So you guys go ahead and kiss your sister. It was a great tie, a great game."
>
> — Comedian Bill Cosby in the Husker locker room after the tie with USC

This was one of those rare cases where Devaney and Murtaugh actually agreed on something. The linebacker also was upset by the mistakes, particularly his own. Even with all the tackles he racked up, he beat himself up for coming just short of nabbing Davis on the final touchdown. "What you make really doesn't count," he said afterward. "It's the ones I missed."

However, the Huskers' efforts had clearly earned them some respect. As Murtaugh dressed after the game, he was told that someone wanted to speak to him. Out in the concourse he found Trojans Davis and Slough, who wanted to congratulate the Huskers. "You guys are good," Murtaugh recalled one of them saying. The Trojans particularly complimented the Huskers' physical play. In many ways, Murtaugh had been right — the Huskers did beat the hell out of the Trojans. They just didn't win.

As down as the Huskers were with a tie, most fans were ecstatic to have seen their team travel out to California and go toe-to-toe with one of college football's best. They showed their appreciation the next day when some 500 well-wishers came out to greet the Husker plane at Lincoln's airport. Such support eventually would help the Huskers see that tie in a new light.

In fact, months later, when all the bowl results were in, that tie for Devaney and the Huskers would make all the difference in the world.

Devaney signs an autograph after the team arrived back in Lincoln from Los Angeles. A crowd of about 500 greeted the Huskers.

The Jerry and Van Show

STEVE RUNTY WAS THE THIRD-STRING QUARTERBACK on the 1970 Huskers, right behind Van Brownson and Jerry Tagge on the depth chart. And since Runty wore uniform No. 13, he found himself lockering between No. 12 and No. 14. That gave him a unique vantage point to watch the weekly battle for playing time between Nebraska's dueling, dual quarterbacks.

Steve Runty

There were times Runty would be sitting with Tagge when Devaney came by. "Tags, you had a great practice. I look forward to big things Saturday," Devaney would say. "You're our man." But another time Runty could be sitting with Brownson and hear the same speech from the head coach. "Van, you're our man."

"It was hilarious," Runty recalled.

Amusing as it was, there probably was nothing deceitful in Devaney's dealings with his quarterbacks. It was natural for the head coach to offer encouragement to both. And during 1970, just as in 1969, on any given week Van or Jerry could indeed be the man. The starting quarterback job over the course of the season once again would change hands more than once.

Devaney was making it plenty confusing for the kids playing quarterback in Nebraska's sandlots. Should they pretend to be Van Brownson or Jerry Tagge? In fact, Husker fans as a whole were split. The general consensus was that the steady Tagge was a better thrower, while the dynamic Brownson dazzled with his running and scrambling. But both were more than capable. "They were both professional-grade quarterbacks," Runty said. "The team knew you could flip a coin, put one in, and we weren't going to drop off."

Without a doubt, Brownson had gained a toehold on the job with the two big wins finishing out 1969. But over the course of that season, he and Tagge had shared the job on a remarkably equal basis. Brownson had started six times, Tagge five. Brownson had run or passed for 10 touchdowns to Tagge's seven. Brownson had produced the two most impressive wins and had thrown only four interceptions to Tagge's eight. But Tagge had set single-season school records by running up more than 1,500 yards in total offense and completing 57.1 percent of his passes. He also set a team record by at one point completing 88 passes without an interception. Both quarterbacks still had a lot of football in front of them, with two years of eligibility left.

Brownson came out of 1969 confident, but by no means did he believe he had the job sewn up. He knew that Tagge was capable and that Devaney would go with the one he felt gave Nebraska the best chance to win. Tagge, for his own part, was in a much better place than a year earlier, when he'd had those thoughts of quitting the team. He had proved to everyone he could play in Lincoln. He felt part of this team. And he continued to work hard in the offseason, even shedding five pounds down to 215 to further increase his mobility. He was ready to make another run at the job.

Brownson and Tagge both said they had difficulty with friends and family members putting down the other.

During 1970 spring ball, the quarterbacks picked up where they left off in the fall, with both playing at a high level. In the first scrimmage, they put on two of the best passing performances ever seen in a Husker spring drill. Brownson, running with the No. 1 unit, completed 19 of 26 passes for a touchdown and 131 yards. Tagge, leading the 2s, completed 11 of 17 for a touchdown and 222 yards. Tagge wasn't going anywhere. In fact, he climbed to No. 1 after that scrimmage. The next time out, Brownson had practice observers raving about a wild fourth-down scramble for a touchdown after all his receivers had been covered. When the next depth chart came out, he was No. 1 again. And so it went. Not surprisingly, the two quarterbacks went into the fall as co-No. 1s, Devaney declaring the race nearly dead even.

Both wanted the job as badly as ever. Their battle was a natural subject of fascination in the press. They sat down for a lengthy piece in The World-Herald's Sunday magazine, the paper dubbing their rivalry "The Jerry and Van Show." Both made it clear in their comments throughout the season that their rivalry was a friendly one.

> "Brownson is the biggest question mark. He's up on what we're going to do because he attends quarterback meetings, but he's rusty on execution."
>
> — Devaney on Brownson's injury before the 1970 season opener against Wake Forest

At times, the two good-naturedly ribbed each other. "Van is the only friend I have (who) I hate," Tagge deadpanned during one interview that fall. "I say a lot of things about Van, and I try to never say anything nice about him."

And both accepted that they would have to work and perform well all season if either expected to seize and keep the job. "If you falter at all, you know the other guy is coming in," Brownson said later in the season. "It's friendly competition. And it's good for the team."

As fall camp began, Brownson loved the feel of the new Memorial Stadium AstroTurf. He felt fast, and it was easy to make cuts. Schools and pro teams were switching to artificial turf because of the difficulty in maintaining grass fields during the wear and tear of a long football season.

But one of the criticisms of artificial surfaces already bubbling up nationally was that they caused injuries. Players got "turf burns" sliding on the surface. Some believed the more solid footing put more stress on joints, producing more ankle and knee injuries. Within a year, a House subcommittee in Washington would hold a hearing looking into the matter. And though there was padding under the carpet, beneath that was a layer of concrete. Landing on the turf could deliver a jolt.

Brownson soon would suffer one of the first significant injuries whose roots could be traced to Nebraska's new carpet. In a preseason scrimmage, he was tackled and bounced hard on the turf. His right elbow immediately swelled up, a bubble the size of a golf ball forming on the end. It was bursitis — a rupture in a sac of fluid that allows smooth movement of the elbow joint when the arm is flexed. To make matters worse, the injury became infected and inflamed.

For the next several weeks, his elbow had to be regularly drained of fluid. The first time, he would have strangled the team physician were it not for the two trainers holding him down. It was the most intense pain Brownson had ever experienced. And while he could play with the injury, he didn't feel he could get any zing on his passes.

Tagge looks down the field for Johnny Rodgers, who pulls in a 43-yard touchdown pass in the second quarter of a 28-0 rout of Army.

The elbow kept him out of the opener against Wake Forest and the big battle in Los Angeles. Tagge, essentially handed the starting job, took advantage of the opportunity with solid play, though he did throw three interceptions against USC. Nebraska returned from L.A. to defeat Army 28-0 in Lincoln. The Cadets held the Huskers to a single touchdown in the first half, which seemed to bode well for national security but didn't say a lot about the NU offense. Tagge came on strong as the game wore on, though. He threw two touchdown passes to Rodgers, one a 43-yarder on which he hit the speedster in stride.

But Brownson was the quarterback who drew the biggest buzz from the crowd that day when he saw his first action of the season in the fourth quarter. He again showed why he was a nightmare for both defenses and radio play-by-play men, with nifty moves on the option that made it hard to tell who had the ball. He had some nice scrambles and, despite his bad elbow, threw for a touchdown, too. He was the quarterback who got the headline in the next day's World-Herald: "Brownson Shifty in NU Return." But Tagge did nothing to lose his hold on the job, and he led Nebraska capably the next week in its 35-10 win over Minnesota.

Tagge had taken Nebraska through the nonconference schedule 3-0-1 and now was ready for one of the most anticipated games on the Husker schedule: Missouri. Nebraska had not beaten the Tigers since 1966, and the two teams had played on even terms since Devaney arrived in Lincoln. With the thumping in Columbia the previous year, some thought the Tigers were in the Huskers' heads. In fact, the Huskers had voted Missouri — not Oklahoma — their biggest rival when The World-Herald asked their preference before the season.

As usual, it was the hardest-hitting game on Nebraska's schedule. This year, one hit in particular by a Husker would alter the course of the contest. Missouri boasted the nation's leading rusher in Joe Moore, a 205-pound tank. Early in the game, Missouri ran a trap play on Husker defensive tackle Dave Walline. The guard in front of Walline let him go, with the idea he would be blind-sided by another pulling lineman. But Walline anticipated the snap and got off so quickly that the blocker couldn't get around to him in time. Walline demolished Moore, not only sending the senior to the sidelines with a separated shoulder but ending his college career.

Nebraska tackle Dave Walline (76) throws Missouri's Joe Moore to the turf.

Tagge led Nebraska on an 80-yard scoring drive in the first half. But the Huskers mustered little after that, stymied by the blitzing Tigers. With a struggling Tagge completing only 4 of 13 passes for 22 yards, the teams went into the half tied at 7. In shades of 1969, Devaney decided it was time for a change and brought in Brownson for the second half.

A Missouri turnover — one of six picked up by the opportunistic Blackshirts — set up a drive that Brownson capped with a 1-yard sneak. That score proved the game-winner in the 21-7 Husker victory. Brownson afterward took no credit, saying the rugged Missouri defense had a lot to do with the struggles the Huskers had while Tagge was in the game. "It wasn't because one quarterback was in there," he said.

Still, following Devaney's precedent, the guy who showed the best would earn the next start. With the season reaching its midpoint, Brownson once again was Nebraska's quarterback. He took full advantage the next week against KU, producing one of the most sensational games running and throwing ever by a Nebraska quarterback. Brownson shined the brightest at a critical moment in the first half.

NU had led 10-0 and seemed to be cruising along. But then a 96-yard kickoff return for a touchdown ignited the Jayhawks. They recovered the ensuing onside kick and scored again. Then they forced a punt and went down for another quick touchdown. The seven-minute, 20-point eruption had Devaney scratching his head and Kiffin looking a little stunned. Kansas kicked deep and forced Nebraska to start on its 20. Jayhawk fans were now in a tizzy.

That's when Tom Osborne decided it was time for Nebraska to go for a gut-punch of its own. On the phone with Brownson from the press box just before the Huskers

Assistant Monte Kiffin and Devaney were feeling the heat after Kansas ran off 20 straight points in Lawrence.

took the field, he called for a bomb on first down. Rodgers was to run a crossing route while Guy Ingles would go straight for the goalposts. "If the safety jumps Johnny," Osborne told Brownson, "we're going to go with Guy on the post."

Sure enough, the safety came up to defend Rodgers, leaving Ingles one-on-one with the corner. Ingles gave him a waggle and streaked down the field. Brownson faked a handoff to Joe Orduna and in the face of a fierce KU pass rush waited patiently for Ingles to get into his route. Then he put the ball right on the money. Ingles outraced one of the Big Eight's fastest track men into the end zone, completing a sensational 80-yard strike.

"It was as finely executed a pass as you'll see in football," Devaney said afterward. Not that Brownson saw it. He got decked on the throw.

THE JERRY AND VAN SHOW 137

Brownson turns the corner, slips a tackle and celebrates his touchdown against Kansas.

The play provided the spark that Nebraska needed to break out of its funk. After a three-and-out by the Blackshirts, Brownson dissected the KU defense with a 73-yard drive. He capped it himself, making a slick ball fake and keeping on the option for a 15-yard score. He high-stepped into the end zone and raised his left arm over his head in triumph. Then to start the second half, he led an 80-yard drive that ended with a touchdown flip to Rodgers. Brownson's short TD plunge on NU's next possession sealed Nebraska's 41-20 win.

Afterward, everyone was talking about Brownson: 10 of 15 throwing for 183 yards and two touchdowns, while also rushing 12 times for 59 yards and two scores. "Not bad for a second-string quarterback," Kansas coach Pepper Rodgers quipped. But Brownson was No. 2 no more. He had emphatically seized the job. "Big Red Van-Liner Smacks Kansas," screamed The World-Herald's banner headline the next day.

Brownson didn't let up in the weeks that followed, and neither did the Huskers. They first outgunned Oklahoma State's Cowboys 65-31. The Nebraska offense seemed to score at will against OSU, and Devaney took out Brownson late in the second quarter with a 41-7 lead. The final total was the most points Nebraska had scored in a game since 1922.

Then the Huskers went to Folsom Field in Boulder and in a game televised regionally by ABC beat a game bunch of Buffaloes 29-13. Brownson twice connected with Ingles on long touchdown plays in the first quarter. Ingles' first one bordered on the superhuman, the little receiver going high to snag the ball away from a taller defender.

But in a game played on Halloween, the Buffs put a scare into the Huskers early in the fourth quarter, narrowing NU's lead to 15-13. A failed two-point conversion — stopped by the Huskers just shy of the goal line — was all that stood in the way of a tie. From there, Kinney and Brownson took over. Kinney took the ensuing kickoff 79 yards to set up Nebraska, and Brownson eventually plunged in from the 1. After Colorado fumbled on its next possession, Brownson passed to Kinney for 22 yards before the I-back took it in from the 7 to ice the win.

Nebraska rose to 7-0-1 and No. 4 in the polls, and ran its unbeaten streak over two seasons to 15 games. The major bowl scouts in their bright-colored blazers were flocking around this NU team. What's more, for the first time, the Husker players were speaking openly in the press about a national championship. Not surprisingly, it was Jerry Murtaugh who started the bold talk.

"We're going for No. 1," he told a reporter two days after the OSU game. "We think we have a real good chance of going all the way. I think it'll be hard for anybody else to beat us."

A long kickoff return by Jeff Kinney (35) turned around a close game against Colorado in Boulder.

Brownson, playing through a first-quarter injury, threw for 173 yards and ran for 30 against Colorado.

When asked how his comments would sit with Devaney, Murtaugh didn't seem too concerned. "Well, he probably won't admit it," Murtaugh said, "but he probably feels the same way."

It was an exciting time for everyone in Lincoln, but it was an especially good time to be Van Brownson. In his three starts, Brownson as usual had shown major moxie running the ball. But he also had completed 32 of 47 passes for seven touchdowns and no interceptions. Brownson now had completed 65 percent of his passes on the season compared with Tagge's 61 percent. And Brownson's long balls had been spot-on, casting doubt on the belief that Tagge was the better thrower of the two.

Tagge could only watch on the sidelines as Brownson's star rose. He saw limited action against KU, OSU and Colorado, and threw an interception on his only pass against the Buffs. Now late in his junior year, Tagge once again was the backup. And as long as Van kept playing the way he did, Tagge knew there was no way he would get back on the field. It was tough to take.

Tagge candidly admitted in a 2014 interview that at that point, winning national championships was the furthest thing from his mind. "I was just worried about Van," he said. "I just wanted to play. My whole focus was Van."

Years later, Nebraska fans could debate the relative strengths of the era's standout quarterbacks. Ask even those who played with Tagge and Brownson and you get different answers as to which was the better thrower, the better runner, or the one you'd want playing with the game on the line.

But Jerry Tagge in the end would have one huge advantage over Van Brownson, summed up in a single word: durability. The sturdy Tagge's edge in that category ultimately would decide their four-year battle for supremacy in Lincoln. Because the injury bug would bite Brownson once again.

During the game at Colorado, Brownson ran an option to the right and was forced out along the sidelines. Folsom Field has among the narrowest sidelines of any stadium in college football, with team benches squeezed on a narrow strip of turf between the playing field and stands. Opposing players are so close to the CU student section that fans can spit on them — not a foreign concept in Boulder. On that option play, Brownson ended up whacking his problem elbow against one of the sideline benches.

It hadn't seemed a serious injury at the time. It happened in the first quarter, and Brownson played the rest of the game with it. But he could tell afterward that something wasn't right. He had visual evidence in the days that followed: His entire arm turned black and blue.

No one realized it then. But the dazzling Van Brownson had started his last game as a Nebraska Cornhusker.

> "Coach Devaney has a tough enough job just coaching and not trying to make us happy. It's going to be entirely up to him."
>
> — Tagge

They Might Be No. 1

NOT EVEN BOB DEVANEY WAS GOING to hold his tongue anymore. Standing inside the locker room in Lincoln on a bitterly cold and windy mid-November day, he responded to a reporter's question and stated his firm belief. His Cornhuskers were the best team in college football.

"I think we should be No. 1," Devaney said. "We have as much right to be No. 1 as any team in the country." And after what his team had just done to Kansas State over the previous three hours, who could argue?

On homecoming day in Lincoln, fourth-ranked Nebraska absolutely dismantled what had been considered by pollsters the No. 20 team in the country. K-State boasted one of the nation's top passers in Lynn Dickey, who wore white shoes like his idol Joe Namath and possessed a Namath-like arm and swagger. But Dickey found it pretty hard to complete passes while looking straight up into the cold blue sky. The Blackshirts hounded Dickey, knocking him to the turf and collecting an eye-popping seven interceptions.

Even Sports Illustrated, at the time the most influential voice in all of American sports, took notice of the Huskers in the wake of the 51-13 demolition. "They are unbeaten after 10 games and heading for the Orange Bowl," the writer said, "and now it is becoming apparent even outside Nebraska that they just might be the No. 1 team in the land."

The alchemy of a championship football team involves a lot of different elements, among them talent, toughness and leadership. No one yet knew whether this team had what it took. But as the 1970 college football season played out, it was becoming increasingly clear week by week that Devaney was brewing up something very special in Lincoln.

The Huskers had a great collection of talent that was fast growing and maturing right before Devaney's eyes. More than that, there was a special chemistry to this team, a unity, respect and closeness that were unlike any that the players had experienced before. "I don't remember anyone saying it at the time, but I think everyone knew there was something extraordinary going on," Jim Carstens, a reserve fullback, recalled decades later. "The chemistry between the team members, the friendships that were building, the unbelievable support of the fans and state. . . ."

Jerry Murtaugh (42) returns one of seven Nebraska interceptions of Kansas State's Lynn Dickey, as Blackshirts John Adkins (57) and Bob Terrio (45) become blockers.

Defensive end Willie Harper (81) and tackle Dave Walline (76) help make Dickey's 1970 visit to Lincoln miserable.

The offense was turning into a true juggernaut, combining Tom Osborne's game-planning mastery with a powerful line and playmakers at every skill position. While the tie with USC had been disappointing, the offense had gained a lot of confidence from it. And with each week, players' comfort with the offense's complexities was growing. The Huskers' 38-point scoring average now ranked second in the country. They were on their way to becoming the highest-scoring team in school history.

No team in the country could match Nebraska's devastatingly diverse attack. The Huskers could hit you right up the gut, outrace you around the end, burn you with play action or beat you over the top with the bomb. The run-pass balance of the attack was its strongest asset, always keeping defenses guessing.

And it didn't matter who was at the controls. When Brownson's black-and-blue arm kept him out against Iowa State, Tagge went in and played like a guy who wanted his job back. He completed 18 of 27 passes for 223 yards and two touchdowns as the Huskers put up 54 points in Ames. It was enough to earn him Big Eight player of the week honors, matching Brownson's feat against Kansas. How many teams could have two different quarterbacks win such conference honors just weeks apart? "It felt great to be playing again," Tagge told reporters afterward.

Against Kansas State, Tagge again was his reliable self, completing 13 of 19 passes for 162 yards and a touchdown — his team record 10th TD pass of the season. He also showed some Van-like ad-libbing ability on one first-half pass. Finding three defenders in his face, Tagge shrugged them off with a pump fake and then scrambled for 16 yards.

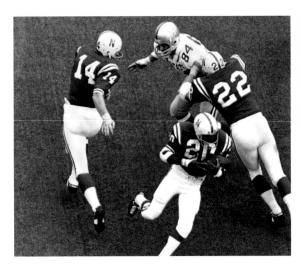

Johnny Rodgers gets the ball from Jerry Tagge on an inside reverse against Kansas State and picks up key blocks from Dan Schneiss (22), Bob Newton (74), Donnie McGhee (70), Dick Rupert (77) and Doug Dumler (54). Rodgers' 30-yard touchdown run was Nebraska's first play from scrimmage after quarterback Lynn Dickey threw an interception on the Wildcats' opening drive.

The performance had K-State coach Vince Gibson marveling at Devaney's ability to shuffle quarterbacks while keeping his team focused and united. "You don't know how tough coaching is until you've tried something like that and gotten away with it," Gibson said.

Nebraska's 1-2 punch at quarterback was mirrored at I-back. Jeff Kinney and Joe Orduna were so closely matched at the start of the season that Devaney had to flip a coin to decide which one would start. Orduna would enjoy the bigger year, winning all-conference honors, scoring 14 rushing touchdowns and becoming Devaney's leading career rusher. But both averaged 4.5 yards a carry and together amassed 1,600 yards on the ground. After having starred as a sophomore, Kinney didn't much like sharing the job. But he kept his mouth shut and had to admit it was working. With those two, Nebraska always had a fresh I-back ready to carry the load. Against KSU it was Orduna, who landed in the end zone four times.

Often underappreciated were the efforts of fullback Dan Schneiss. The offensive captain was best known for his anvil blocks, but he also was averaging nearly 5 yards a carry. And he'd emerged as a surprisingly good receiving target out of the backfield, hauling in 20 passes for the season and scoring on a 12-yarder against the Wildcats. Quipped Devaney during a booster luncheon two days later: "Dan's a pretty good football player. I think I'll tell him personally after the season is over."

The player who really set the offense apart, of course, was Johnny Rodgers. An array of counters, reverses, quick screens, long passes and punt returns got him into the end zone nearly every game. Only once during the regular season would he fail to score a touchdown. Big plays happened when he had the ball in his hands, with 32 runs, receptions or kick returns that covered 20 yards or more.

Even when he didn't touch the ball, Rodgers was a tremendous weapon as a decoy. If opposing linebackers stayed home to account for Rodgers on the scissors, things opened up for the quarterback and I-backs on the option. Defenses always had to account for Rodgers.

Guy Ingles

As the season went along, Husker players and coaches were learning a few quirks about their new star. Almost without fail, Rodgers threw up at halftime of games. He had a stomach ulcer, a condition he'd later attribute to the stresses of a childhood on the run. But despite that nervous condition, teammates also were seeing there was no spot too big for the fearless Rodgers. "Some guys back there returning punts look like they don't want the ball," Osborne recalled. "Johnny wanted the ball. He always wanted the ball." And with Rodgers returning punts, the Husker offense almost never started in a hole.

Devaney had begun the season with Rodgers and Ingles — who had done a credible job as a returner the previous two seasons — as twin returners on punts. It didn't take long for the coaches to decide Ingles' services no longer were needed back there. "You're OK, Guy," they diplomatically told him. "We just don't want you getting hurt."

Rodgers took punts back for scores against Missouri and Oklahoma State. Even when he didn't score, one or two times a game he'd get 30 or 40 yards that no one else could have. Give him a little space, and you could count on him faking the first guy right out of his scholarship. "Johnny Rodgers can break a game open better than anyone we've ever had here," Devaney said that fall.

Despite the loss of his punt-return job, Ingles was the consummate team player. In fact, he was the first player on the sideline to put his arm around the dejected Rodgers when he fumbled a kick against Missouri. And with Ingles at wide receiver and Rodgers at wingback, Nebraska possessed one of the finest pass-catching tandems in the country.

Both players had grown up in Omaha. But they might as well have come from different planets, their backgrounds as contrasting as the colors of their skin. Ingles grew up in Omaha's fashionable suburbs, the privileged son of the manager of the city's Merrill Lynch brokerage. He attended Westside High School, a wealthy, nearly all-white school where it wasn't a foreign concept for a kid to get a new Corvette on his 16th birthday.

Ingles had not been highly recruited. Coaches weren't scouring the country looking for 5-foot-8, 140-pound running backs. But he happened to have a huge game against Tech High his senior year while Husker coaches were checking out several Tech standouts — including the young John Rodgers. The subsequent scholarship from Nebraska — the only big school to make an offer — was a huge thrill for Ingles. He'd grown up going to games with his dad during Devaney's first seasons in Lincoln. Even as a Husker senior, Ingles weighed only 159 pounds. But the player fans called "Guy the Fly" was soaring toward the finish of a great career with his home-state team.

Backgrounds aside, both Rodgers and Ingles were precise route-runners with speed, hands and football instincts. Nebraska may never have had a better pair of receivers. During 1970, Rodgers would log 39 catches for 710 yards and seven touchdowns while Ingles caught 36 balls for 625 yards and eight touchdowns, finishing as the Huskers' career leader in receptions.

Doug Dumler (lower left) and Bob Newton (lower right) clear a hole for fullback Dan Schneiss to score against Kansas.

There was no way opposing teams could double-cover both of them. Throw in the emergence of tight end Jerry List, a sophomore from Michigan, and those pass-catching running backs, and Tagge and Brownson almost always could count on someone being open.

All those offensive stars were quick to point out that the success actually started up front. From the wreckage of the failed experiment with trimmed down linemen, colorful assistant coach Cletus Fischer and scholarly Carl Selmer had by 1970 built a formidable line.

Left tackle Bob Newton was the anchor. The player teammates called "Fig" possessed tremendous speed for his size, able to make blocks 20 or 30 yards downfield. He had a bad game against Missouri. That prompted a motivational side session with Devaney, who threw cold water on his hopes of playing pro ball. The next week Newton made Kansas pay and was named the Big Eight's lineman of the week. He now was putting the final touches on a dominating, consensus All-America season.

Donnie McGhee

Elsewhere on the line, Doug Dumler, a sophomore from Chicago, emerged as a pleasant surprise at center, a preseason position of worry for Devaney. Dick Rupert, like Newton a junior-college transfer from L.A., was holding down one guard spot and may have been the toughest of them all. Rounding out the unit were seniors Wally Winter and Donnie McGhee, a fast 225-pounder from Flint, Michigan, who earned All-Big Eight honors.

Fischer would ride his linemen during practice, yelling "You've got to get in there and root-hog!" It simply meant keep your head low and fight. These guys were making him proud, coming off the ball like a bunch of angry sows. Almost any back could look good behind a great, overpowering offensive line like this one.

As for Monte Kiffin's Blackshirts, there had been moments to doubt them. Oklahoma State three times had driven more than 80 yards to score. Iowa State scored four times through the air. Colorado once drove 93 yards on the Huskers, with every single yard coming on the ground. But the Blackshirts also had proved a big-play unit, intercepting a team- and conference-record 30 passes. The larcenous performance against Kansas State would prove a season highlight.

A big reason for the Blackshirts' growth was the emergence of Joe Blahak, a sophomore cornerback from Columbus, Nebraska. Called "Airhead" by teammates because of his offbeat sense of humor, Blahak's athleticism rivaled even that of Rodgers. He was one of the team's fastest runners and a sure tackler.

Ed Periard, a 5-foot-9 middle guard, wrestles down Oklahoma State running back Bobby Cole as linebackers Bob Terrio (45) and Jerry Murtaugh (42) close in.

Against K-State, Blahak would have his biggest game as a Husker, intercepting three Dickey passes to bring his season total to six. That still was short of the seven picks that would be logged by junior safety Bill Kosch. Kosch, named All-Big Eight this season, also had been Blahak's teammate at Columbus Scotus High School. It was a testament to Nebraska's homegrown talent that one small school could produce half the Huskers' starting secondary. At the other corner, Jim Anderson, Tagge's old Green Bay West teammate, had four picks and set a school record with eight pass breakups.

Jim Anderson

Bob Terrio, the California junior college player who had arrived with Newton after that epic cross-country drive a year earlier, claimed the linebacker spot next to All-Big Eight performer Murtaugh. Terrio had a great year, finishing second on the team in tackles.

Dave Morock came on strong as the new starter at monster, though Murtaugh told him it was his ugly looks rather than play that prompted Kiffin to put him at the position. Morock had four interceptions on the season and two of the best. He had a spectacular one-hander against Kansas and against Kansas State took one 43 yards for a touchdown.

Despite all the preseason questions about the defensive line, Kiffin developed a strong and quick front of Willie Harper, Dave Walline, Ed Periard, Larry Jacobson and John Adkins. Walline and Periard both made All-Big Eight. Harper, just a sophomore, Jacobson and Periard would register tackles for losses totaling nearly 300 yards. It was largely their relentless efforts that harassed Dickey into all those bad throws. "Dickey may never want to throw again," one radio announcer said after the seventh pick.

When it came to the emergence of Nebraska's offensive and defensive lines, the impact of Boyd Epley's weight program shouldn't be underestimated. Epley's novel enterprise at that point had been in place for 15 months. And it was producing some impressive results. Defensive end John Pitts in March had become the first member of the Huskers' "300-Pound Club" — able to bench press 300 pounds. He'd soon be joined by dozens of others. Newton had been an Epley disciple even before Devaney hired the pole vaulter, and he became the first Husker to press 300 pounds on an inclined bench. Dumler also make an early mark, the first to power clean 300 pounds. Epley displayed their records and others on a new tote board on the wall in the Schulte weight room. Devaney was so pleased with the results after the first year that he tripled Epley's pay.

Those gains in the weight room were beginning to clearly show up on the field. And while players were getting bigger and stronger, in keeping with Devaney's admonition, they weren't losing a step of speed. Colorado coach Eddie Crowder two weeks earlier had remarked about the "marvelous physical strength" of the Huskers, not knowing the secret behind it.

Even Nebraska papers had paid scant notice at this point to Epley and the strength program. The World-Herald in 1970 told of Epley's personal success in bodybuilding competitions, only in passing mentioning his work with the football team. The under-the-radar success gave meaning to words that would become a motto of Epley's program: Champions are made when no one is watching. As trainer George Sullivan put it years later in summing up the Huskers' steel-forged edge, "We got so far out in front of other schools in conditioning, it was kind of pathetic."

Not all the benefits of the conditioning program were physical. Much of the emotional closeness of this team had been forged in the blood and sweat of those Schulte workouts. As players went through the countless hours of lifting, sprinting and fighting over ax handles, there always was much clapping and whooping. They'd urge each other on and pick guys up when they were down or fading: "Come on! You can do it!"

The shared experience built the same kind of esprit de corps you'd expect in a Marine unit. And much like Marines, these guys went to war every Saturday not for themselves, but for the guys beside them. "You look back on it, and that's where the team was built," Steve Runty recalled. "You can't replace that kind of camaraderie."

The team's close bond fit within the larger Devaney culture of working to get better every day and pulling together toward a common goal. "When we walked on the field on Saturday, we played as one unit," Newton recalled. "It all trickled down from Bob."

As the season went on, and the wins piled up, the Huskers got into a comfortable rhythm: Learn a new game plan. Perfect it in practice. Win on Saturday. Move with confidence to the next one. The team became a threshing machine, relentlessly chewing up teams in its path like so many dry cornstalks.

Jerry Murtaugh pulls down Iowa State receiver Tom Lorenz, with monster Dave Morock (43) trailing the play. Morock broke up seven passes during the season, second on the team to Jim Anderson.

K-State's Wildcats had been warned what they were going up against, a team nothing like the one they'd taken to the wire in Manhattan the year before. Just before the kickoff, the Wildcats gathered outside the tunnel, next to a red-clad old woman sitting in a wheelchair. When one of them looked over at her, she told him matter-of-factly, "We're going to kick your ass."

The Wildcats had gone into the game with a chance to claim a share of the Big Eight title. That was a long-forgotten notion by the end. On K-State's first possession, Harper pressured Dickey into a wobbly ball that Murtaugh gobbled up. Nebraska needed just one play to get into the end zone, Rodgers working the scissors play for a ridiculously easy 30-yard score. The Huskers' onslaught was quickly on.

With the win, the Huskers claimed no worse than a share of the conference crown, with one regular-season game to go. Devaney was happy to have his sixth Big Eight title in his nine years in Lincoln. But he was thinking about bigger things afterward.

For the first time, he joined Murtaugh in the No. 1 talk. He conceded that he had been among the handful of coaches who had recently been putting Nebraska No. 1 on their ballots. In fact, he'd been voting the Huskers No. 1 all season. "I'm going to vote for us No. 1 again," he said. "At the present time, we are, in my opinion." Other players were equally unabashed.

"I think we're No. 1," Schneiss told a reporter.

"Think?" Blahak interjected.

"I know," corrected Schneiss.

Other teams in the country, however, could credibly make the same claim. Defending national champion Texas, Notre Dame, Michigan and Ohio State were unbeaten. And they all sat at the big-boy table in college football, long considered among the game's powers. The Huskers still were just upstarts.

The Sports Illustrated writer in Lincoln that day had clearly found the Huskers' performance convincing. But in an era when so few games were televised, many of the pundits voting each week never had seen Nebraska play. There still were many around the country who doubted that these once-tied Huskers were truly among college football's elite.

Among those ready to buy the Huskers, however, were the orange-jacketed representatives of the Orange Bowl. They salivated over the chance to snag the undefeated Huskers and their horde of fans. Just hours after NU beat KSU, they extended Devaney a bid for the January 1 Orange Bowl Classic in Miami.

Bob Devaney and his Huskers now had a date with destiny.

Co-captain Dan Schneiss (22) presents the game ball to Devaney after the Huskers wrapped up a 10-0-1 regular season with a 28-21 victory over Oklahoma.

Opportunity Knocks

TEAMMATES THOUGHT ED PERIARD was going to kill that bus driver. The man behind the wheel of the motor coach taking the Huskers to Miami's Orange Bowl drove through the wrong stadium gate and got stuck in a crush of spectators within a fenced-in area. It was taking an eternity for the confused driver to get to the right gate, and the bus just crawled around one end of the stadium. Periard, the Huskers' volatile little fireplug of a nose guard, finally blew his top.

Ed Periard

"WILL YOU GET THIS F****** BUS WHERE IT'S SUPPOSED TO GO!" he screamed. "NOW!"

When the bus finally parked, Periard stormed out the door. Fortunately for the poor bus driver, the Husker would unleash all that agitated energy on Louisiana State's quarterbacks this night.

Periard had good reason to be on edge going into the Orange Bowl. Not only were the Huskers about to play in one of college football's classic bowl games, they just might have a once-in-a-lifetime chance for immortality. Texas, No. 1 in the Associated Press poll of sportswriters, already had fallen in the Cotton Bowl to sixth-ranked Notre Dame. At that moment, 2,700 miles across the country in Pasadena, No. 2 Ohio State was locked in a close battle with Stanford in the Rose Bowl.

It was possible that third-ranked Nebraska would go into its game that night against LSU's Bayou Bengals as the last major unbeaten team in the country. There might be a chance to claim the school's first national championship.

When Nebraska players voted to accept the bid to the Orange Bowl, their plan all along was to play for a national title — no upsets required. As Bob Devaney met with his team the Sunday after the Kansas State win, he asked players their preference of several expected bowl invitations. Their answer: Wherever the No. 1 team is playing.

At the time, that was Notre Dame. And the Orange Bowl representatives had made it clear — both in the press and personally to Devaney — that they wanted the Irish in Miami on New Year's Day. It seemed the Orange Bowl was the place to be for the Huskers. Just to be sure, Devaney called Notre Dame coach Ara Parseghian to ask where the Irish stood on the Miami offer. Parseghian wouldn't say. By that time, though, there had been persistent reports in the press that the Irish had all but signed up for the Orange Bowl, lured by a handsome financial commitment. The Huskers took the Orange Bowl offer, dying for a chance to play the Irish.

But a week later, Notre Dame pulled a mild surprise and accepted a bid to play in the Cotton Bowl against Texas. Just days earlier, Texas had jumped Notre Dame to reclaim the No. 1 spot in the AP poll, a position the Longhorns had held most of the season. Texas, riding a phenomenal 30-game unbeaten streak, had beaten Notre Dame to win the national championship in the Cotton Bowl after the 1969 season. Notre Dame's coaches burned for a rematch, reportedly overruling players who had wanted to spend the holidays on the beach. Parseghian told his players they'd be knocked in the press if they didn't accept the challenge of playing the Longhorns in a No. 1 vs. No. 2 matchup.

Devaney talks with his team after its final practice in Miami before the Orange Bowl matchup with LSU.

The decision was a huge disappointment for Devaney and his players. The bowl picture was scrambled even more days later when Notre Dame was upset in its regular-season finale by USC — the same team Nebraska had tied in L.A. If the Huskers had known this was how it was going to play out, they would have held out for their own bid to play Texas in the Cotton Bowl rather than jumping at the Orange. To make matters worse, Ohio State vaulted over the No. 3 Huskers following a win over rival Michigan in a battle of unbeatens. The Buckeyes would be taking the nation's No. 2 ranking into the Rose Bowl.

As the rest of the bowl lineup shook out, the third-ranked Huskers drew fifth-ranked LSU, a 9-2 team that had won the Southeastern Conference championship. LSU had been just five points away from an unbeaten season of its own and weeks earlier had lost a 3-0 slugfest with Notre Dame in South Bend. The Bayou Bengals struck Devaney as much like his 1969 Huskers, a team that by the end of the season was playing as well as anybody. But even an impressive win over the Tigers wasn't going to be enough to have the Huskers leaping to the top of the polls. They would need a lot of help.

Going into New Year's Day, coach Darrell Royal's Longhorns already had the championship in the United Press International poll sewed up. The UPI board of coaches still clung to an outdated system of awarding national titles based on the regular season alone, not considering the bowls. It wouldn't be until 1974 that UPI changed its system, which over the years produced many spurious national title claims by teams that actually lost their final games. There was little question, though, that with a win over Notre Dame, Texas would lock up the AP writers' title, too.

> "If LSU beats us, they deserve to be the best team in the country."
>
> — **Devaney**

Devaney continued to believe his team was the best in the country. "We're No. 1, Texas or no Texas," he said during an Orange Bowl kickoff press conference. And he believed his team still might have a shot. Privately, he believed Notre Dame had the athletes to hang with the streaking Longhorns. He also thought Ohio State was overrated.

Of course, he had been in this same spot before, in this same stadium, five years earlier. He had seen the No. 1 and No. 2 teams lose, only to have his then-No. 3 Huskers fall to No. 4 Alabama. He was confident that if this team got an opportunity like that, they wouldn't blow it.

But as the new year dawned on January 1, 1971, Nebraska was seen by most observers as having, at best, just an outside shot. Both Texas and Ohio State would go into their bowl games as big favorites.

The Longhorns were riding that big winning streak behind a wishbone offense that had just thrashed then-No. 4 Arkansas 42-7. The big and powerful Ohio State Buckeyes had stormed unmolested through the Big Ten. Most experts now were expecting the Buckeyes to steamroll a 9-3 Stanford team that limped into the Rose Bowl with consecutive losses to Air Force and 5-5 California. Stanford was just happy to be there, making its first Rose Bowl appearance in two decades.

The chance that both Texas and Ohio State would lose was considered so remote, in fact, that The World-Herald's game-day preview story didn't mention the possibility of a Husker national title until the 32nd of 35 paragraphs. One Florida columnist suggested that the Nebraska-LSU game was "nothing more than a midwinter exercise by two plodding teams."

There are a lot of elements that go into a national championship — great athletes, hard work and team chemistry, to name a few. But almost every championship team needs some luck, too. And as the Cotton, Rose and Orange Bowls played out one by one on national television on the first day of 1971, Devaney's team would benefit from a huge dose of good fortune.

At Miami's beachfront Ivanhoe Hotel that afternoon, the Huskers were glued to their TV sets as Texas kicked off against the Irish and proceeded to fumble away its top ranking. The Longhorns put the pigskin on the ground nine times and lost five of those balls, turning the Cotton Bowl, as Sports Illustrated put it, into "an Easter egg hunt for leprechauns."

The Irish and their star quarterback, Joe Theismann, accepted the generosity. He passed for a touchdown and pranced for two more within the first 16 minutes of the game, putting the Longhorns on their heels. Theismann had changed the pronunciation of his name that season from Thees-man to Thighs-man — rhyming with Heisman — as part of his campaign for the trophy. It didn't work. But no matter how you pronounced it, the Theismann name soon became mud down in Texas. The Irish held on for a convincing 24-11 win.

The Longhorns' demise, marked at 5:01 p.m. Miami time, sent an immediate jolt of excitement through the gathered Husker coaches and players. By the time the Huskers left the Ivanhoe, the Rose Bowl also had kicked off. The Huskers were euphoric when a fumbled kickoff helped Stanford's Indians jump out to a quick 10-0 lead.

Van Brownson, left, Jerry Tagge and backup quarterback Bob Jones dip their toes in the pool at the team hotel.

No one knew it at the time, but the stumbling Buckeyes could have been exhibiting some fallout from a bowl week player revolt. The OSU players were upset with coach Woody Hayes' boot camp-like practices in Pasadena. He'd actually taped players' ankles during the plane ride out to California so they could practice immediately upon landing and cloistered his team in an old monastery. It had sucked much of the fun out of the players' bowl experience. In contrast, Devaney made sure his players enjoyed their week on the beach taking in the sunshine, waves and bikini-clad women. He even surprised his team with front-row tickets to a concert by The Temptations. Devaney didn't believe such temptations would distract his team from what it was there to do.

As the Huskers warmed up on the Orange Bowl's new artificial surface, NU sports information director Don Bryant kept Devaney and the Huskers apprised of developments out west. Ohio State shook off its slow start to take a 14-10 lead at the half. In the fourth quarter, the Buckeyes seemed poised to put Stanford away, leading 17-13 and driving inside the Stanford 20. But the much-maligned Indian defense stuffed bulldozer fullback John Brockington on fourth and one. From there, Heisman-winning Stanford quarterback Jim Plunkett passed the Buckeyes silly. By that time, three time zones away, the moon was rising over Miami. But the sun was clearly shining on these Nebraska Cornhuskers. An excited Bryant suddenly gave the word to Devaney: Stanford has taken the lead!

The Huskers retired to their locker room beneath the Orange Bowl stands. Kickoff was delayed briefly so NBC could finish its broadcast of the Rose Bowl. At 8:07, the stunning result was official: Stanford 27, No. 2 Ohio State 17. The roar from the Nebraska locker room echoed through the bowels of that old stadium.

"There it is," Devaney told his gathered team.

A national title was now there for the taking, but Devaney tried to keep his team from getting too high. His pregame message was simple: Just go out and play the kind of game I know you can play. The next 60 minutes of football would determine whether this team had what it takes to be a champion.

The Huskers went through their unique pregame rituals in the locker room. Some closed their eyes, thought about the opponents who would be lined up across from them and visualized the battle ahead. Others worked themselves into a state of simmering rage. When word came, they gathered themselves and went out into the night — a night that would change their lives forever.

Dressed in his scarlet Husker home jersey, Jerry Tagge strapped on his helmet and started for the door with the rest of his charged-up teammates. This was a colossal moment for a 20-year-old. But the Nebraska quarterback felt he was ready for it. Since taking over for the injured Van Brownson, the junior had led the Huskers to three straight wins, including a 28-21 gut-check during Nebraska's season finale against Oklahoma. The Sooners had come into that game at 6-3, a young but talented team that was just beginning to grasp the new wishbone offense that coaches had installed midseason. Many names who would become legends when the two teams got together again a year later were on the field that day in Lincoln.

In the fourth quarter, the teams were deadlocked 21-21. Everything the Huskers had worked for all year was in danger of blowing away like dandelion seeds in a breeze. That's when Tagge engineered a game-winning drive. Twice he kept it alive by hitting crucial third-down passes, including a 24-yard fingertip grab by Dan Schneiss. The play set up Tagge's game-winning plunge, keeping the Huskers' national title hopes alive.

As Tagge led the Huskers on that late-season run, he could feel things clicking for him. He had invested countless tedious hours studying Tom Osborne's offense. He'd learned all the plays Osborne wanted called in certain situations, and all the audibles off all those plays. He'd hated having to learn it. But now all the nuances of the sophisticated attack had taken up residence in his head.

"One day in practice," he'd later recall, "all of a sudden I could see the whole field." He knew what to do and when to do it. Perhaps most importantly, he knew he could do it. Something else happened over those weeks, too. As Tagge developed confidence in himself, he gradually stopped worrying about Brownson.

Devaney talks to defensive linemen Willie Harper (81), Dave Walline (76), Ed Periard (56), Larry Jacobson (75) and John Adkins (57).

Tagge knew the two quarterbacks still were competing. Indeed, Devaney deliberated right up until bowl week as to how he would utilize his quarterbacks in Miami. He had publicly hinted on his weekly television show that he might rotate Tagge and Brownson, now mostly recovered from his elbow injury.

One fan letter published by The World-Herald had argued Nebraska "would enhance its chance for a bowl victory with the dynamic Brownson at the controls," calling him the more effective runner, ball-handler and passer.

But Tagge decided worrying about whether Brownson was going to replace him wasn't going to get him — or the team — where they needed to be. "I felt at that point like the starter," he recalled later. "I just had confidence."

That was the attitude he took to the field in the Orange Bowl — the game in which he'd step up as the unquestioned leader of this team.

"Let's go get it," Tagge said.

A Night to Remember

A RECORD CROWD OF 80,699 — including some 20,000 Nebraska rooters conspicuous by their red garb and jittery looks — packed the horseshoe of Miami's Orange Bowl. The old Orange Bowl was one of the classic venues in college football, with the iconic stand of palm trees in its open east end and the big letters across the face of the upper deck: THE CITY OF MIAMI WELCOMES YOU TO THE ORANGE BOWL. But on this night, Nebraska fans had added a banner of their own across the bottom of the lower stands, also all in caps: NUMBER ONE.

Like Bob Devaney and his players, Husker fans were convinced that their team was the best in college football. And they would have continued to believe that, even if Texas and Ohio State had not fallen in the past three hours. That banner had been put up well before the final from the Rose Bowl came in. Many Husker fans also wore "Nebraska's No. 1" buttons, which had become big sellers in Lincoln in recent weeks.

The pride of Husker fans had showed hours before kickoff, when Devaney was presented the biggest telegram ever delivered by Western Union. Some 1,400 feet long — nearly the length of five football fields — it included the names of 46,200 fans who paid 15 cents each to have their names attached to a message: "Congratulations and best wishes to the finest coaching staff and players in America. You are No. 1 with us. We are very proud of you. Go Big Red!" It again spoke to the unparalleled passion of Nebraska football fans.

The Huskers struggled to contain their sky-high emotions in the locker room and tunnel as they waited through a lengthy pregame ceremony that featured high school bands, a pregame prayer and finally Anita Bryant, the TV pitchwoman for orange juice, singing the national anthem. The buzz of excitement the Huskers were feeling at kickoff was multiplied a hundred-thousandfold by their fans in the stands and those back in Nebraska mesmerized by flickering TVs. The game was being televised nationally by NBC, which boasted that it was bringing the game "live and in color." At the time, still less than half of all U.S. households had a color TV.

"Here comes Nebraska," NBC play-by-play man Jim Simpson said as the Huskers floated onto the field, riding the day's emotions. "If they can beat LSU, they can say 'We are No. 1.' They know it here in the Orange Bowl, and they are ready for this game."

The Huskers indeed were ready. Looking across the field before kickoff, LSU coach Charlie McClendon could see how supercharged the Huskers were, jumping around and waving their arms. He came into the game concerned about Nebraska's big size advantage over his team. Those big guys now looked like a herd of raging bulls, snorting and pawing the ground before a charge.

LSU kicked off, and Tagge led the offense onto the field. Across the line of scrimmage from him was one of the best defenses in all of college football. LSU had three All-Americans on that side of the ball, anchors of the nation's No. 1 run defense.

> "I haven't had to have many pep talks with my team as far as getting ready for a game."
>
> — Devaney before the Orange Bowl

An estimated 20,000 Nebraska fans made the trip to Miami, and many were ready to proclaim the Huskers No. 1 even before the game was played.

The stingy Tigers on average surrendered but 52 yards a game on the ground. They were solid against the pass, too, allowing teams to complete less than half of their throws and intercepting 25 of them.

Figuring out a way to crack that defense fell on Tom Osborne. He had scouted the Tigers hard, wearing out the film of their games. But he also had scouted himself. Looking back over the season, he saw that the Huskers had run the ball 80 percent of the time on first down. He decided to reverse that percentage against the Tigers.

Nebraska still intended to run the ball. Devaney told his team beforehand that the Huskers were not going to give up on the running game as easily as some of LSU's opponents had. But coaches figured that if the Huskers could soften up the Tigers with some effective passing, that could open up more in the run game. Even against a stout defense like LSU's, the Huskers figured they had a lot of different ways to attack.

Jerry Tagge indeed came out throwing on first down, including several long ones. Most of them misfired, as the two teams spent the game's opening minutes probing each other for weaknesses. The Huskers early on also seemed a little too wound up. Tagge overthrew some balls, and the offense was flagged four times in the first quarter alone for jumping before the snap.

Midway through the first quarter, LSU botched a handoff at midfield, and the Huskers finally got moving. Tagge hit Guy Ingles for 9 yards, beating All-American defender Tommy Casanova. Tagge kept things rolling, connecting with Jerry List for 17, running a quarterback draw for 12, and then completing another pass to List for 14 more. The drive bogged down from there. But Paul Rogers nailed a 26-yard field goal to give Nebraska a 3-0 lead.

Paul Rogers, who made eight of 13 field goal attempts for the season, gives the Huskers a first-quarter lead.

The Blackshirts had come into the game with some extra motivation. They had tired of hearing the pre-game hype about the LSU defense. In fact, Devaney had used every opportunity during practice to razz his players about it. "It kind of peeved us," big tackle Larry Jacobson would say after the game. "We were psyched."

It showed on the very first play from scrimmage after the field goal. Jacobson, a junior from South Dakota, stepped over a block, wrapped up LSU quarterback Buddy Lee behind the line and reached around with one of his long arms to strip the ball. Willie Harper came flying in to recover the fumble with an acrobatic dive — the first of several game-changing plays the 19-year-old defensive end would make this night. The turnover set up Nebraska inside the LSU 15.

Willie Harper

It took only two plays for the Huskers to overpower that vaunted LSU rush defense and get into the end zone. Joe Orduna took a pitch and behind blocks from Johnny Rodgers, Dan Schneiss and Tagge rumbled down to the 3. From there, Orduna followed a powerful block from left guard Dick Rupert, who pinned an LSU linebacker on his back in the end zone. Nebraska led 10-0 late in the first quarter against a team that surrendered an average of just 9 points a game.

The Blackshirts in the second quarter continued to play with a chip on their shoulder, chasing Lee all over the field and pushing the LSU offense backward. A Harper sack for a loss of 15. A John Adkins sack for a loss of 13. A Jacobson sack for 4. Adkins and Harper combining to blow up a reverse for a loss of 14. And then an Ed Periard sack for a loss of 14 more. LSU's first 24 plays from scrimmage netted -1 yard.

Nebraska's Willie Harper (81) is going to win the race to the ball after teammate Larry Jacobson forced a fumble by LSU quarterback Buddy Lee.

Nebraska I-back Joe Orduna found an opening in LSU's heralded defense to score late in the first quarter.

This game would be a coming-out party for Harper, a self-described ghetto kid out of Toledo, Ohio.

The defensive end essentially had followed his high school coach, Thunder Thornton, to Lincoln when Thornton was hired as a Nebraska assistant a year earlier. Harper had gotten an opportunity this year as a sophomore because of injuries to other players. But Devaney later would say he could tell the minute Harper stepped on the field in Lincoln that the Huskers had a potential All-American on their hands.

An awe-inspiring 6-foot-3, 205-pound body made him look like some kind of Greek god. He wasn't afraid to show it off, either. He'd wear fashionable see-through lace shirts over his tight bell bottom jeans. Such youthful vanity had cost him late in the season when he decided not to wear hip pads against Kansas State, wanting to look more trim with his mom and sister in the stands. "I felt better without them," he'd later say, "until I got hit."

The bangs and bruises forced him to miss the Oklahoma game. But Harper was wearing all his pads for the Orange Bowl, and he had come to play some football. Before the game was over, he would rack up two fumble recoveries, a partially blocked punt and four tackles behind the line for nearly 50 yards in losses.

> "You have to have a middle guard who is too much for the center to handle to make our defense work."
>
> —Assistant coach Warren Powers

It also was hard to keep your eyes off Periard — though the senior didn't so much awe as amaze. At 5-9, 201 pounds, he hardly looked like a football player and certainly not a middle guard.

The undersized native of Birch Run, Michigan, and his parents had come to Lincoln years earlier and begged Devaney just for the chance to walk on. He still almost didn't make it when he failed his physical because of an old knee injury. Periard marched into Devaney's office. "Look, I didn't come to Nebraska for a knee operation," he declared. "I came to play football." Devaney figured any player with that attitude deserved a chance.

Periard was dwarfed by all the linemen on both sides of the ball, especially the 6-6 Jacobson, who lined up next to him. But over the course of this season the feisty Periard had emerged as one of the biggest surprises on the team, becoming a consensus All-Big Eight performer. In Monte Kiffin's 50 defense, the middle guard lined up with his nose right up against the center. Periard was so quick that centers found it tough to find him after they'd snapped the ball. They'd often end up chasing him into the backfield.

For Periard, any lack of size was more than offset by his passion to play. You could not get him off the field. When he went down during a game earlier that season, he refused to let Jerry Murtaugh call trainers over. The player teammates called "Fast Eddie" also was one of the Blackshirts' emotional leaders, screaming, slapping guys and jumping around. "It doesn't matter how tall you are or how much you can bench press, it's how big is your heart," Kiffin later recalled of Periard. "For Ed, it was all heart."

Maybe it was pent-up frustration from that bus ride to the game. But on this night, Periard would play the game of his life. Like a rabid terrier, Periard chased down LSU quarterbacks for three sacks and 30 yards in losses. Even when he didn't get the sack, "that little short guy" — as LSU's Lee referred to him later — was frequently in the backfield causing disruptions. "This Periard is really something," NBC color man Al DeRogatis marveled at one point.

Nebraska's Willie Harper drags down LSU quarterback Buddy Lee, with Bill Janssen (55) ready to lend a hand.

Despite the great field position the Blackshirts constantly were handing the offense, Nebraska's attack stalled during the second quarter, squandering opportunity after opportunity. Rodgers fumbled a punt. He and Ingles both dropped passes. Tagge missed a couple of more throws. More penalties. In their first appearance on the biggest of national stages, the Huskers were looking a little wide-eyed.

Devaney decided to give Van Brownson a couple of series to throw a new look at the Tigers. Instead he threw into coverage for an interception. The LSU defense was living up to its savage billing, showing that it had been no fluke when it held Notre Dame to just 3 points. But Nebraska's shaky play certainly was giving the Tigers a big assist.

Then LSU finally got its own offense out of reverse late in the half. Lee started to sprint out to avoid the ferocious Husker pass rush. He found receiver Andy Hamilton three times to drive the Tigers from the LSU 24 all the way to the Nebraska 10. Harper made yet another huge play, flying around left tackle to bury the quarterback for a 10-yard loss. It was the sixth sack of the first half for the Huskers, who for the game would record 14 tackles behind the line for 115 yards in losses. Pushed back again by the sack, LSU kicked a field goal.

The Huskers went into halftime with a 10-3 lead but couldn't help feeling frustrated, particularly on offense. It seemed on just about every play that something was going wrong. "It should be 21-0," Tagge thought. "This game should be over."

The Tigers got the ball to start the second half and once again moved on the Blackshirts. They used two long runs and a pass interference call to drive 63 yards to the Nebraska 7. But the Blackshirts again stiffened, keyed by a Dave Walline tackle for loss. LSU settled for another field goal to make it 10-6.

The Huskers needed to answer. Tagge decided to run the ball right at the Tigers to try to get some rhythm going on offense. On the Huskers' first drive, he called the same counter dive on three of the first four plays. The Huskers quickly reached midfield.

But that drive, too, would self-destruct. Orduna slipped in the backfield on a handoff, forcing Tagge to eat the ball. Center Doug Dumler failed to snap the ball, and the whole offense was called for motion. Then Tagge threw an interception after he thought the Tigers had jumped offside, mistakenly thinking he had a free play.

The frustrations only continued to build on the next two Husker possessions. Someone lined up offside before the ball was snapped. Ingles just missed snagging a long pass in traffic. Even the dependable Jeff Kinney dropped a pass. It seemed that everyone was taking a turn flubbing up.

As in the tie with USC, the mistakes finally caught up to Nebraska. Late in the third quarter, LSU took over on its 25 and again started to hurt the Huskers with the pass. Hamilton found a hole in the Husker zone for a big third-down catch. Then the ball was moved inside the Nebraska 40 on a questionable late-hit call on a Husker who already was airborne before the ball carrier went down.

Then on third down from the NU 31, LSU slot back Al Coffee ran a hook and go on Husker cornerback Jim Anderson, faking a short route and then running for the end zone. Tagge's old Green Bay teammate had been playing a solid game. But on this play, he suddenly slipped on the turf when Coffee made his cut. As Anderson frantically scrambled to his feet, the next several seconds played out in slow motion like something out of a bad dream. Coffee broke wide open in the end zone. The Husker help in the secondary came too late. Coffee gobbled up Lee's pass. Touchdown. LSU led 12-10. As the third quarter ended, there was jubilation on the Tiger sideline.

Nebraska was staggering, having surrendered 12 straight points. Over the last two quarters, they'd done almost nothing on offense.

Devaney paced the sideline, concerned but calm. He knew his team had been in tighter spots during its current run, including that 1969 win over Kansas that started it all. If the Huskers could just get out of their own way. He talked to Tagge. We need to have something, now. Implicit in that statement was that if Tagge couldn't get the offense going, the coach would have to give Brownson another shot.

As a TV timeout at the quarter break wound down, Tagge stood with his hands on his hips looking at the ground, quietly thinking about the upcoming possession. He knew from experience that he could rally his team, as he had done in the previous game against Oklahoma. As Schneiss had said of his steady teammate after the winning drive that day, "He makes the right play at the right time." It again was time for Tagge.

Near the quarterback, Ingles also stood with hands on hips, a look of angry determination across his face. There's a saying in football that defense wins championships. But as Ingles would say decades later, that's just bunk. What wins championships, he'd say, is the ability of the offense to score points when the game is on the line. If the Huskers indeed were a championship team, this was the time to prove it.

> "LSU took the momentum away from us, and we helped them with some mistakes."
>
> — Devaney

Ingles, Tagge and the rest of the offense trotted onto the field. And against one of the nation's stingiest defenses, the coming-of-age Huskers proceeded to deliver a gritty, beautiful 14-play drive to glory.

Tagge started by handing to Orduna, who ripped off 7 yards right up the middle. The Huskers then lost 5 yards on yet another motion penalty, List firing off the ball well before the snap. While List looked like he wanted to climb into a hole, Orduna calmly tapped him on the bottom to assure him everything was OK. Indeed, Tagge made sure that this time the mistake would not stop the Huskers.

On second down, he rolled out looking to pass, saw no one open and coolly scrambled for 14 big yards. This was a far quicker Tagge than the sluggish freshman who had shown up in Lincoln two years earlier. Someone later this night would remark that Tagge had run faster than they'd ever seen him. "I was just scared to death," he replied. It didn't show.

Orduna followed with a 2-yard run and clearly fumbled at the end of the play, but the Huskers benefited from a quick whistle. More good fortune for the Huskers on a night of destiny. Tagge connected on a short pass to Schneiss, the first of three straight passes Tagge would complete on the march. Then, calling for an outside run for the first time on the drive, Tagge pitched to Orduna. The big back raced around left end for 7 yards and another first down to keep the Huskers rolling.

LSU had managed to hold Rodgers mostly in check to this point, blanketing him in coverage with two or three defenders. But Tagge on the next play found him on a first-down pass that was good for 9. Behind a massive line surge, Tagge sneaked for the third first down of the drive.

None of it was coming easily. The Tiger defense remained grudging, not conceding an inch. Longtime Orange Bowl observers afterward would call this game one of the most bitter, physical battles they'd ever seen in Miami. But this drive was perhaps where Nebraska's advantage in the weight room began to reveal itself. LSU's McClendon would say after the game that his team endured "an awful lot of punishment" on the final Husker march. "Call any play you want," one Husker lineman had told Tagge at the start of the drive. "We'll make it work."

From the LSU 25, Kinney — alternating with Orduna to keep both fresh — picked up just a yard on a smash up the middle. A Tagge scramble netted just two more, leaving the Huskers facing third and long.

At that point, the Huskers were within Rogers' field goal range. But Nebraska wasn't going to be conservative now. Osborne made the call from his press box perch, and Kinney brought in the play from the NU sideline: 71 Wingback Pass.

Tagge took the snap and dropped back on what would prove the most crucial play of the drive. From the left slot, Kinney jammed the linebacker in front of him as if blocking on a running play. By then Rodgers and Ingles were well into their deep routes, with the LSU safeties dropping back into their zone, while List ran a crossing route from left to right, clearing out the linebackers.

Kinney suddenly came off his block and sprinted left to right across the wide-open middle of the field. It was an easy throw for Tagge, who hit him in stride. The I-back suddenly was in the clear, racing toward the end zone. His breathless 17-yard sprint was cut down just inside the LSU 5. Nebraska was now set up first and goal.

Tagge called Kinney's number again on first down, and he pounded off left guard for 3 tough yards. This was the kind of determined running that was becoming his trademark. The gain was among 39 rushing yards on the drive, not far below what the LSU defense averaged for an entire game.

For the night, Nebraska's 132 rushing yards would be the most the Tigers had surrendered in two years. The Huskers also were poised to equal the number of rushing touchdowns the Tigers had given up all year. As John Sage, LSU's All-America tackle, would say after the game, "Nobody ran on us the way they did."

Tight end Jerry List (85) led Nebraska with 63 yards in receptions.

With Nebraska at the Tiger 2, LSU called timeout to get bigger bodies onto the field. Tagge went to the sidelines to talk with Devaney and coach Carl Selmer, who was connected by headphones to Osborne up above. They decided Tagge should just keep it on a sneak.

The quarterback sneak obviously is a simple play — a man-against-man scrum over a small patch of earth. It isn't just about physical strength. It's a battle of wills. As Paul Dietzel, McClendon's predecessor at LSU, once said, "You can learn more character on the 2-yard line than anywhere else in life."

Eight LSU linemen crouched shoulder to shoulder over the ball. They had made many such stands during this season. Even the one time they did surrender a touchdown at the goal line, it took Tulane four plays to get it in.

The Husker line formed a V-shaped human wedge. And on the snap, they hammered right into the Tigers. Tagge tucked the ball under his arm and ducked behind center Dumler and guard Donnie McGhee. The quarterback surged forward toward pay dirt ... and was stopped short. Tackle Bobby Joe King met him over the top and shoved him back at the 1.

Now facing third down, Tagge again called his own number in the huddle. But this time he would employ a tactic he had rehearsed in his mind before. After taking the snap, Tagge delayed just for a moment as the lines collided with each other. He spotted a gap, took a quick step to the right, tucked the ball under his right arm and again pushed his sturdy body ahead behind Dumler and McGhee.

Tagge's momentum was stopped right as the ball appeared to reach the end zone. But to leave no doubt, he twisted and — with two strong hands — extended the ball far over the goal line.

In Nebraska, the image of Tagge stretching the ball over the line would become part of the state's heritage. Even later generations would come to know the name Jerry Tagge and the picture of his goal-line reach. Decades later as athletic director, Devaney would have the Tagge photograph hanging over his desk. He never would forget what that moment meant to him, his program and his adopted state. As he'd say of his team's nerveless 67-yard drive: "When we had to have it, we did."

Rogers kicked the point after the touchdown, and Nebraska now was up 17-12. But before the Tagge touchdown could be frozen in time as the game-clincher, nearly nine minutes of football still had to be played.

The rest of the game would play out in a topsy-turvy, emotional fashion that would have many Nebraska fans at home reaching for a Salem, one of the numerous cigarette brands whose ads were featured in the NBC broadcast. These were among the very last tobacco ads to appear on American television. Congress' 1970 ban on them took effect about two hours after the game concluded.

The back-and-forth craziness that had Husker fans alternately exalting and despairing started minutes after the Tagge score. The Huskers were driving for what would have been a clinching score when Orduna was hit and fumbled at the LSU 13. Husker fans gasped in the cool 55-degree Miami air as LSU pounced on the loose ball.

The Blackshirts subsequently had LSU backed up at third and 30, but they somehow managed to give up a 31-yard pass to keep the drive alive. It took Harper to bail them back out. Tiger quarterback Bert Jones dropped back to pass and was wrapped up by Harper. The Husker defensive end suddenly emerged with the ball, having ripped it right out of Jones' hands. With less than two minutes on the clock, a Husker win again seemed all but assured.

170   A NIGHT TO REMEMBER

Tagge reaches across the goal line to score the winning points against LSU.

But as Tagge was going for a first down that could have allowed the Huskers to run out the clock, he had the ball poked out of his arm from behind. To the agony of Husker fans everywhere, LSU again recovered.

With 48 seconds left, Jones and LSU had one more chance. The Tigers once again would be foiled by a pilfering Blackshirt. This time, it was one of those junior college players Osborne had pulled out of California two years earlier — just one more among the many building blocks it took to construct a championship team.

After the cross-country odyssey driving in that VW with Bob Newton, Bob Terrio didn't see the field at all in 1969, buried on the depth chart at fullback and taking a redshirt. During spring ball in 1970, Kiffin, looking for more speed at linebacker, suggested that the Huskers give Terrio a tryout. After just one scrimmage, coach John Melton tossed the junior a black practice jersey.

Throughout the 1970 season, Terrio had played side-by-side with Murtaugh. Possessing some of the best lateral speed on the team, he was a sure tackler who also had proved effective in pass coverage. On this play, he would surprise even himself by just how far he would go to get to the football. Jones dropped back, and under extreme pressure from Adkins and Harper, heaved the ball downfield in the direction of the dangerous Hamilton. As the ball flew through the air, a Husker defender leaped in desperation to try to knock it down, coming up short.

Terrio also was flying, coming from the opposite side of the field after dropping deep into coverage. The Husker arrived just as the ball did, his eyes by that point as big as the Miami moon. Terrio leaped in front of Hamilton, clutched the ball to his chest and fell to the turf.

Terrio sprung up and held the ball aloft in triumph as officials signaled the interception. Monster Dave Morock threw his arms around him, and the two sprinted toward a giddy Nebraska sideline. The first player to greet Terrio was a beaming Newton, who gave his driving buddy a celebratory shot in the chest. The play capped a night of big plays for the Blackshirts, especially sweet given all the doubts they had faced at the start of the season.

There was no stopping the Huskers now. Killing off the clock, Tagge dropped to the turf untouched. As Husker fans gleefully counted down the game's final 10 seconds, Ingles punched the air and stomped his foot. Rodgers ecstatically pulled off his helmet. And Tagge and Kinney both ran from the field holding their arms aloft, index fingers extended into the air.

The Huskers had believed all season that they were the best team, even when nobody else did. Now they had proved it. "We made it, we made it!" screamed Tagge. "They know who's No. 1 now."

On the sideline, Devaney enthusiastically shook Mike Corgan's hand and was lifted onto the shoulders of two Huskers for a ride to midfield. Then the Huskers danced and frolicked their way to the locker room as their fans' chants of "We're No. 1!" rained down from above.

The Nebraska locker room was a wild and jubilant scene, players and coaches hugging and hooting. Rodgers and Ingles, two native Nebraskans who knew just how much this meant to the state, had their arms around each other. Ingles felt so happy he could cry. Rodgers climbed atop a bench. "We're No. 1 in the nation," he proclaimed, "and No. 1 in the world, too."

Devaney was elated, the happiest anyone had ever seen him. He was so proud of this team. His players always had shown so much spirit and resolve, not needing a lot of motivation. And tonight, against all the adversity, and with the outcome hanging in the balance, they had shown the heart of a champion. As the last major unbeaten team standing, these Huskers had earned the right to be No. 1. "We weren't a great team that night," Devaney would recall of this team's last game. "But we got the job done."

Three Huskers grabbed their coach and hauled him, red blazer and all, off to the showers. Devaney emerged wearing a gray Husker sweatshirt and a borrowed pair of pants that seemed a couple of sizes too small. He did look a bit like the poorly dressed Willy Loman Sports Illustrated once had likened him to. But Devaney would have the last laugh on this night. It was in that wet and rumpled fashion that Devaney began the post-game meeting with reporters. They were now asking the obvious question: Is Nebraska the best?

"Hell, yes, we're No. 1," Devaney blurted, famously following with, "I don't see how even the pope himself could vote for Notre Dame."

Devaney was addressing head-on the debate that would be playing out over the next four days, until the final vote by the Associated Press football writers was released. In fact, Notre Dame coach Ara Parseghian already was arguing that his Irish had taken on the greater challenge by beating the No. 1 team head-to-head and now should be voted No. 1.

Devaney told reporters that night that if the Huskers weren't voted No. 1, the writers ought to just stop doing their poll. Not only was Nebraska the last unbeaten team, it had gone to Los Angeles and tied the same USC team that beat Notre Dame 38-28. LSU was another common opponent. Nebraska beat the Tigers by 5 points on a neutral field; the Irish beat them by 3 points at home. Devaney was confident that the plain facts would prevail. But all the Huskers and their fans could do now was wait.

Devaney peeled off his wet clothing as he talked with reporters after the game.

As Nebraska wrapped up business in Miami — their return delayed for two days by the biggest blizzard in a generation back home — the debate would continue to play out in the papers. One Florida columnist the day after the bowls proclaimed that "sentiment may be flowing strongly for the Irish." A Miami Herald columnist disagreed. "If Nebraska isn't No. 1," Ed Pope wrote, "there isn't any justice."

On Sunday, two days after the Friday bowl games, Parseghian campaigned for the top ranking in an Associated Press interview. "The automatic assumption that they should be No. 1 disturbs me," the Notre Dame coach said. "Our team should get a great deal of credit for accepting the challenge of taking on the top-ranked team."

When Devaney was told of Parseghian's words, he fired back, "He's full of B.S. to make statements like that."

In the end, the pollsters agreed with Devaney. Nebraska received a whopping 39 first-place votes to eight for Notre Dame in the final AP poll, released on Tuesday, January 5. The Cornhuskers were the 1970 Associated Press national champions, the first national title in school history. "Now It's Official — We ARE No. 1!" The World-Herald proclaimed on the front page of its late edition that day.

Devaney told reporters that the title probably was the biggest thing ever to happen to the university. It also was one of the biggest things ever for the entire state. Sports Illustrated termed the title "the greatest thing to happen to Nebraska since the Union Pacific started laying track out of Omaha."

From Omaha to tiny Henry on the Wyoming state line, the championship unleashed pure joy and pride. For a state with an inferiority complex, especially when compared with the flourishing coasts, this Big Red title was something everyone could rally around.

Old coach Bill Jennings had been wrong. Nebraska could be the best at something, and it should not be afraid to aspire for more.

So many people across the country thought of Nebraska as a flat and dismal outpost populated by overweight farmers and rubes and home to notorious mass murderer Charles Starkweather. Even if many still believed such things, they also would now know that Nebraska had a bunch of solid, hardworking boys who played some awfully good football.

This championship also would mark the starting point of a notable shift in the college football landscape. While the Huskers under Devaney often had resided in college football's upper echelon, this badge gave NU the status of a true national power. From this point on, the name Nebraska would join the likes of Texas, Notre Dame, Alabama and Southern Cal when people talked of college football's elite.

The president of the United States himself would make Nebraska's championship status official. Richard Nixon was a huge college football fan and, in recent years, had taken to annually recognizing the national champion with a presidential proclamation.

In Nebraska's case, Nixon was urged to abstain. In a January 6 memo drafted by White House aide Pat Buchanan — later a conservative talk-show host and Republican presidential candidate — Nixon was strongly discouraged from picking any champion. The memo, unearthed from Nixon presidential archives years later, made several arguments. It might upset Catholics and Notre Dame's fans. It would be an affront to Texans. Ohio State coach Woody Hayes was a good Nixon man. It would provide the president little political benefit, given that conservative Nebraska already was among his strongest states.

Rejecting the advice, Nixon flew aboard Air Force One into Lincoln on January 14, 1971. And standing with Devaney, Murtaugh and Schneiss before an overflow crowd of 8,500 students and fans at the NU Coliseum, Nixon awarded the team a plaque proclaiming the Cornhuskers the "Number One team in the nation." Noting Devaney's obvious popularity among the crowd, Nixon told the coach, "You ought to run for something in this state."

Devaney hung the plaque Nixon gave him that day on the wall of his office, considering it the greatest honor he had ever received. But he never forgot just how fine the line was between success and failure in college football. While the president was suggesting that he could run for governor, just two years earlier many folks in Lincoln had been calling for his head.

As if to underscore that point, just below the prized presidential plaque, Devaney hung a framed copy of his favorite cartoon. The drawing featured two bums sharing their woeful life stories, one saying to the other, "Then we lost our sixth game to Keen State … "

Indeed, it's amazing to look back now to see the dramatic turnaround Devaney engineered in those two short years: From 6-4 and a losing conference record to Big Eight champions, national champions and an unbeaten streak that had now stretched over two years to 19 games.

But Bob Devaney wasn't done yet. It wouldn't be long before people would start talking about his next Husker team as perhaps the greatest ever to set foot on a college football field.

President Nixon presents the national championship plaque to Devaney, Schneiss and Murtaugh.

Standing by His Man

MONTHS AFTER THAT GLORIOUS NIGHT in Miami, the Cornhusker State remained a state of euphoria. Nebraskans still beamed at the very thought of the Huskers' 1970 national championship. And they were going out and buying anything they could find that proclaimed Nebraska the No. 1 team in the land. Nebraska retailers always counted on making a killing selling anything red. But now they were setting aside whole new departments to accommodate even more clothing and memorabilia, many with a No. 1 theme. The Go Big Red business was booming.

J.L. Brandeis & Sons reported selling $17,000 worth of "Nebraska No. 1" mugs in just the first three months after the Orange Bowl. Brandeis also placed an order for 1,000 music boxes that would play the school's fight song. Other new items offered by various retailers included T-shirts saying "Nebraska #1," Husker whiskey decanters shaped like a 1, helmet-shaped lamps with the new N logo, and clocks, posters and pennants featuring the numeral 1. There even was a toy action figure featuring Jerry Tagge's No. 14 jersey. Other businesses also attempted to tap into Big Red fever, with Goodrich Dairy in Omaha marketing a Go Big Red milk.

But amid all the giddiness, the Husker nation soon would be hit with a huge jolt of reality. It landed hardest on Bob Devaney. In late May 1971, he was attending Big Eight athletic director meetings in Stillwater, Oklahoma, when he was called out of the room to take an urgent phone call. Soon, both he and sports information director Don Bryant were on the line with their secretaries back in Lincoln. After hanging up, they stared at each other in utter disbelief.

Johnny Rodgers, the game-breaking sensation on the national champion Huskers — and a player who would figure to play prominently in Nebraska's drive for a repeat title — had been arrested in Lincoln for armed robbery.

Devaney would recall that at that moment, he had just one thought in his head: It's over. Johnny Rodgers has played his last down of football for the University of Nebraska. "There was no way he was going to play football again," Devaney would write in a 1982 memoir. "I pictured him behind bars, not in the end zone."

The crime for which Rodgers now stood accused actually had taken place a full year earlier, months before Rodgers had exploded onto the college football scene. Though Rodgers' arrest would cause a media sensation in Nebraska, many of the details of that night wouldn't come to light for another four decades, when Rodgers sought a pardon from the state for his crime.

Johnny Rodgers

Rodgers takes a breather after a long punt return in 1970 with Devaney, assistant Mike Corgan and Guy Ingles.

Rodgers and childhood friend James Glass, a fellow freshman at the university, decided to celebrate the last day of school, May 19, 1970, with vodka and orange juice. As the evening went along, the two Omahans were joined by two students from Ord, Nebraska, who lived across the hall of their dormitory. They introduced Rodgers to another student from back home, 19-year-old Randy McCall.

Eventually the revelers' alcohol supply ran dry. McCall wanted to keep the night going. Glass had money. And Rodgers had a car. So they piled into Rodgers' Ford Mustang and headed out into the warm spring night looking for some beer.

They stopped at a package store where the clerk also had to tend bar, and Glass would recall commenting on how easy it would be to grab the money out of the register. That seemed to plant a seed. Glass also would remember McCall, who was white, saying: "You black guys are always talking about what you can do. I double-dog dare you."

Rodgers and McCall later would say they didn't recall the details of that conversation. But Rodgers has said the group was looking to do something daring that night. "It wasn't about money," Rodgers would say in an interview years later. "It was about the thrill of being wild and daring — part of my makeup."

Rodgers would be quoted saying in a 1985 book that he was the one who masterminded what came next, convincing the others it was a perfect plan. Rodgers drove south from downtown to the Derby gas station at Ninth and South Streets, parking just outside the view of the station attendant. In the 3 a.m. darkness of May 20, McCall walked into the gas station first and asked 64-year-old attendant Glen Griggs for a pack of cigarettes. Then Rodgers joined him at the counter.

According to Griggs' account to police, the black man at the counter held a small-caliber handgun and demanded cash. Griggs handed over a leather pouch containing $91.50. He was told by the robbers that an armed accomplice outside would be watching to make sure he didn't call the police. The two students high-tailed it for the door. The adrenaline-charged McCall later recalled that he even outran Rodgers — something few on a football field could claim. Glass, who later said he watched from across the street and never participated, also got back into Rodgers' car, and they sped off.

Rodgers and his accomplices thought they had gotten away with the robbery. For several days, they nervously watched news reports. Police seemed to have no suspects or leads. After a while, it seemed to blow over. A clean getaway.

But then on May 19, almost a year to the date of the crime, Rodgers got a surprise visit from Lincoln police. They arrested him for armed robbery and hauled him off to jail. McCall and Glass also were tracked down and arrested.

How police cracked the case still remains something of a mystery. Prosecutors at the time would say only that an informant had told them of Rodgers' involvement. Rodgers later would say he suspected the informant was one of his accomplices. And indeed it does appear one of them fessed up. Lancaster County Attorney Paul Douglas would say in an interview decades later that the case was solved only when one of the young men, under pressure from his girlfriend, came forward.

Tom Osborne went to the city jail to see Rodgers. At first Rodgers denied it, and Osborne believed him. It did seem out of character. Then Rodgers admitted his involvement, saying it had been a prank. The morning after the arrest, Rodgers appeared in court and was arraigned on a felony charge of larceny from a person, a lesser charge than armed robbery. As coaches Osborne, Thunder Thornton and John Melton looked on, Rodgers pleaded guilty. Osborne then posted the $2,000 bail to secure his release until sentencing.

The arrest was splashed across the front page of Nebraska newspapers from border to border. Unlike the fits of Husker mischief that had been handled privately by Devaney and the authorities, there was no keeping a lid on a robbery.

Rodgers' future was clearly in limbo. He faced the threat of time behind bars, with the conviction carrying a sentence of up to seven years in prison. Some thought Devaney should immediately kick Rodgers off the team. Across the state, Nebraskans were asking the question: "What's going to happen to Johnny Rodgers?"

Devaney sent word from Stillwater that he would wait until he got back and talked to Rodgers before he would comment in detail on the incident.

Osborne spoke for the other coaches, telling a reporter that they all "hope John has a fine future." He described Rodgers as "basically a very decent person."

Rodgers was repentant and dismayed when he spoke to a World-Herald reporter the next day in the lobby of his dormitory. His voice quavered with emotion. He rolled two books in his hands. He was nervous, his smiles forced.

But he also at times appeared to be relieved of a burden. "Why did I do it? I can't tell you," he said. "I don't know myself." The 19-year-old did say it wasn't about money. He even thought that night about returning the cash, he said, but he decided he couldn't go back to the station. He instead tried to just forget it happened.

Rodgers sullenly told the reporter that he had let Devaney and Osborne down. "I feel rotten," he said. "Very rotten." He would not ask Devaney for mercy but made it clear he still wanted to play for the Cornhuskers. "I hope I get another chance," he said. "But I will take what comes. It's my fault. My fault."

World-Herald sports columnist Wally Provost defended Rodgers' character, noting he knew him to be bright and personable, not defiant or anti-social. However, Provost opined that there was no way Rodgers should see the field during the 1971 Cornhusker season:

"Even if he receives probation, and the university agrees to let him remain in school, it is almost inconceivable that he would be permitted to play next season. Nebraska would be showered with scorn and contempt by outsiders. It would be accused of the rankest expediency. It is not unlikely that some of the school's own boosters would turn against the football program. I cannot see Johnny Rodgers in the 1971 Cornhusker future. I can see him adjusting to whatever punishment is dealt and, eventually, regaining the admiration and respect with which he was regarded until the regrettable turn of events."

Provost no doubt spoke for many in Nebraska. But the opinion piece drew strong rebukes from some Husker fans, too. "Get off his back," one woman wrote to the paper. Another Rodgers defender wrote that if people were going to be so conscience-smitten and force Devaney to kick Rodgers off the team, then it followed that Nebraska also should forfeit all 1970 victories and "give back the No. 1 trophy." A small-town Nebraska editor wrote that Big Red fans were "torn between their sense of duty and responsibility to law and order and their desire to see the Cornhuskers continue as the No. 1 gridiron power of the country."

At that moment, Rodgers had three big hurdles: his criminal case, a university discipline hearing to determine whether he remained a student in good standing, and then Devaney. Rodgers would have to clear all three if he was going to return to the football field.

Rodgers got over one bar with relative ease. Even before his case had gone through the courts, a university tribunal made up of two faculty members and seven students quickly decided that, as long as no prison sentence was imposed, Rodgers could remain a student.

No details of the deliberations were revealed. But officials said such tribunals considered two criteria when a student was convicted of a crime: whether it would raise problems with the rest of the university community for the student to remain in school, and what was best for the student. The tribunal obviously decided in Rodgers' favor on both counts.

Then on June 25, Rodgers was placed on two years' probation by a district judge. The judge said such a sentence was consistent and appropriate for someone with no previous criminal record. The only troubling thing the court could find in Rodgers' past was what the judge termed a "lousy" driving record, one that spoke to his immaturity. And the judge praised Rodgers for his past work with the Boys Club in Omaha. He said the most unfortunate aspect of the whole incident was how Rodgers had let down those young boys in north Omaha.

Rodgers received an award in December 1971 from community leader Rodney Wead for "inspiration to ghetto youth."

So Rodgers would face no jail time as long as he complied with probation, and he could enroll as a student come fall. Now it was up to Devaney to decide whether he would remain a Cornhusker.

Devaney in his memoir would describe it as one of the toughest decisions he ever faced as a coach. He agonized over it, staying awake at night. "I knew there was no right answer," he would write. "If we kept him on the team, people would think we'd do anything just to win. If we kicked him off, we'd be kicking his life away. Most people would think justice had prevailed. But what would that do to the only person who really mattered?"

The issue came up in every meeting of the coaches. Devaney at first didn't see how they could allow Rodgers back on the team. But in one of those meetings, Devaney would recall it was Osborne who came up with a strong rationale for keeping Rodgers. "If the courts decide to put Johnny on probation," Devaney recalled Osborne saying, "why shouldn't we do the same thing?"

Indeed, Devaney came to think that revoking Rodgers' scholarship now would punish him more than even the courts had. Taking away football and his college education would be the most severe of punishments — one he didn't believe was appropriate for a kid who never had been arrested before.

Devaney knew he would face personal criticism, but he didn't care. He'd like to know how damn well his critics would have turned out if they had grown up in poverty and without a father.

"I'm glad that the law saw fit to give him another chance for a mistake he made as a freshman."

— Devaney, contemplating his decision whether Johnny Rodgers would remain on the team

When Devaney returned from coaching an all-star football game on July 6, he announced his decision. He would impose the same sentence as the courts, putting Rodgers on athletic department probation for the next two years. During that time, he would be able to play. To deprive him of that opportunity, Devaney said, would work against the aims of Rodgers' rehabilitation.

Rodgers was ecstatic, saying he wanted to play football more than anything in life. "There is not even a slim chance I'll ever get into any more trouble of any kind," he declared.

Much division remained among Nebraska fans after Devaney's decision. One said it "brings the university awfully close to mercenary or a paid type of football." Others thought Devaney was taking a tough, principled stand on behalf of a young man's future.

Still, the reaction overall in Nebraska was somewhat tame. As the coach who had just delivered the state a national championship, Devaney had lots of influence with the public. As further evidence of that, during this off-season he would convince the Nebraska Legislature to increase the state's cigarette tax to pay for a new campus basketball arena — a proposition lawmakers had been cool toward previously. The senators even allowed Devaney to sit in the chamber as they debated the bill, something they normally wouldn't allow because of perceptions of undue influence.

Devaney, in most people's eyes, could do no wrong at that point. Regardless of how Nebraskans personally felt, most trusted him to know what he was doing. "If Devaney's encouragement and display of faith in the young man can help him make the right turn, more power to them both," The World-Herald concluded in an editorial.

More than four decades later, the question is as relevant as it was in 1971: Did Rodgers catch a break — one that no one else would have gotten — simply because he was the biggest star on the Nebraska football team? Looking back, there seems almost no question that on some level he did. Just how big a break is debatable.

Prosecutors charged Rodgers with theft from a person, even though it appears that he could have been charged with armed robbery. Griggs said one of the robbers had a handgun, a statement he never backed away from during repeated interviews with Lincoln police. The presence of a gun usually ratchets up the severity of any crime — and the punishment.

Paul Douglas

County Atttorney Douglas would defend the decision to go with the lesser theft charge in a World-Herald interview in mid-July 1971. He said he considered filing armed robbery charges against Rodgers but settled for felony theft after Rodgers' attorney said the Husker immediately would plead guilty to the lesser charge. It's not unusual for prosecutors to accept such a deal to get a quick disposition of a case, no matter the defendant. Douglas said during the interview that other factors would have made it difficult to get an armed robbery conviction, including the fact that the crime had occurred a year earlier.

In 2013, when Rodgers sought a state pardon on his felony conviction, he'd insist there was no gun involved whatsoever. He pointed to the theft charge he pleaded to as evidence of that. Rodgers' claim obviously went against the account of the victim, who would have had no motive to make up such a detail. And Rodgers wasn't exactly backed up by his accomplices, either.

Glass told The World-Herald in 2013 that he clearly remembered that Rodgers used a gun that night. He said he watched Rodgers reach into the glove compartment of his Mustang and pull out a handgun, though he said he thought it was a starter's pistol that shot blanks. McCall neither confirmed nor denied the presence of a gun, saying he was too scared at the time to notice.

While Rodgers and his supporters would say the crime was out of character, Rodgers would over the years tell of other reckless incidents around that time that involved guns, violence and trouble. That included a time he was shot.

One night, Husker teammate John Pitts was beaten in the face with the butt of a shotgun during a confrontation with a group of Lincoln men. There long had been conflict in Lincoln between black NU athletes and the young men in the city's small black community, concentrated about a mile east of campus in an area known locally as T-Town. Rodgers recruited a group of teammates and friends from Omaha to seek out Pitts' attackers.

Later, Rodgers parked his car and was walking back to his dorm when the local hoods confronted him. As Rodgers fled down 17th Street, one of them fired several shots at him. Rodgers ducked into the doorway of another dorm for cover. He soon discovered that one of the shots had grazed his knee. Luckily, while the bullet left a scar, it did no real damage. "If they shoot me an inch deeper," he'd say years later, "I never would have won the Heisman." Another time, Rodgers ended up in a ruckus and was hit over the head with a table.

In spite of Rodgers' gun denials, Lincoln police more than four decades later weren't backing off their original contention that a gun was used in the robbery. At the request of The World-Herald in 2013, a Lincoln police spokeswoman looked into the department's microfilm library for original investigatory reports in Rodgers' case.

She declined to release all the documents, but she noted repeated interviews in which the station attendant said there was a gun. Through other interviews and investigation, not only did Lincoln detectives conclude that a gun was used, the spokeswoman said, but they concluded it was a .22-calber handgun that belonged to Johnny Rodgers.

The close relationship between Devaney and Douglas, the prosecutor, also has to be considered as a factor that worked in Rodgers' favor. Both Rodgers and Devaney's son years later would acknowledge that Devaney and Douglas were good friends. There's not necessarily anything insidious about that. Because Douglas knew Devaney, it's conceivable he simply had faith in his friend to make sure Rodgers stayed in line. But there's also some evidence that the friendship allowed Devaney to get directly involved in the disposition of the case.

After his arrest, Glass continued to insist that he had played no part in the robbery. For several days, he refused to accept the plea deal that Rodgers and McCall had taken. In a 2013 interview with The World-Herald, Glass recalled that on his third day of confinement, a jailer led him into a visiting room. On the other side of the glass were the prosecutor and Bob Devaney.

The prosecutor told Glass that if he pleaded guilty to the theft charge, he would get two years of probation, the same sentence recommended for Rodgers and McCall. Glass again balked. Not only did he not take part in the crime, he said, but he had tried to talk Rodgers out of it.

That, Glass said, gave Devaney an opening. "Don't rock the boat for Johnny," he recalled Devaney saying. "Johnny's on the verge of doing great things." Glass eventually would accept the plea deal, though he said it was not influenced by anything Devaney had said.

Even if law enforcement authorities handled Rodgers' case without taking into consideration his football future, there remain questions whether the university and Devaney did.

It's not hard to imagine that Rodgers could have caught a break from the university panel. Could faculty and students be completely impartial in dealing with a football player who had helped bring great esteem and acclaim to the university? It certainly would benefit NU if he were allowed to continue to represent the school on the field.

As for Devaney, it's hard to view the coach's decision as a completely selfless act. He wanted to win as much as anybody and knew that Rodgers was a difference-maker for his team. Devaney nearly said as much in his own memoir. "I'm not going to deny that as a coach," he wrote, "it wasn't a pleasant thought to picture a football team without John when you've already seen what he can do." Even the straightest of coaches, he wrote, would roll with any criticism if he felt such a decision would help the player and keep the team "in the winning column."

> "We didn't have a perfect case for an armed robbery conviction by a long shot."
>
> — Lancaster County Attorney Paul Douglas

It's also notable that Devaney in the end would not suspend Rodgers for his crime, not even for a single game. On that count, Rodgers almost certainly caught a break.

Just two years earlier, a starting defensive lineman had pleaded guilty to a misdemeanor charge of obtaining money under false pretenses and was forced by Devaney to sit out a game. Osborne years later said he argued for suspending Rodgers for several games. Devaney never agreed. "It won't do him any good not to play," Osborne recalled Devaney saying. Osborne believed the head coach was rationalizing a little bit — something Devaney even admitted might be true.

As imposed by Devaney, Rodgers' main punishment was to report to Schulte Field House at 6 a.m. every day to run laps with Osborne. Devaney later explained that the punishment combined two things Rodgers hated: getting up early and running.

Devaney said he also trusted that Osborne, as Rodgers' position coach, would keep him in line. And indeed, coach and pupil would form an even stronger bond during those early morning running sessions. "We talked and we ran, and we ran and we talked," Rodgers would recall. With Osborne riding herd that fall, Devaney later said, Rodgers racked up a 4.0 GPA in the classroom.

Those who knew Devaney best later would say that you can't overlook his own hardscrabble upbringing when considering how he handled Rodgers' case. If it weren't for second chances, Devaney didn't know where he would have ended up, either. "Bob was an outlaw," Melton said, "and I think he always had a warm spot in his heart for a kid who was an outlaw."

Said Osborne: "One thing you have to understand about Bob is he understood people having trouble and how that can happen, and how even if you did get in trouble, you need to have another chance. Johnny should thank his lucky stars it happened when it did. Because if it happens today, he's gone."

When all was said and done, after Rodgers had played his last down as a Husker, it should be noted that the coach's faith in Rodgers' character largely was validated. Under Osborne's personal guidance, the Husker star avoided any serious brushes with the law during his remaining two years in Lincoln.

A year later, Rodgers was a passenger in a car that police apparently had been tipped was carrying marijuana. Rodgers said the officer who arrested him referred to him by his first name before even checking his ID. But an extensive search of the car revealed no pot stash, and Rodgers later was cleared of any wrongdoing. He faced unjustified publicity because of the incident.

The only real mark against Rodgers was that he continued to be a lousy driver, eventually convicted of driving on a suspended license and even serving a few days in jail in 1973. Rodgers chose to serve the jail time to spare Devaney criticism after he originally was set to do work-release time as a helper in the Husker weight room.

Years after his coaching days were done, Devaney would say he had no regrets about his decision to keep Rodgers in a Husker uniform.

And Rodgers always would appreciate the faith Devaney put in him during those difficult days in the summer of 1971. "When I got in trouble, he stood by me the whole time," he'd say years later.

As a reward for that faith, Rodgers would deliver two of the finest seasons that the college football world has ever seen. As Devaney himself would put it one day in summing up Rodgers' career in Lincoln: "John had a knack for being in the wrong place at the wrong time — except when he had a football in his hands."

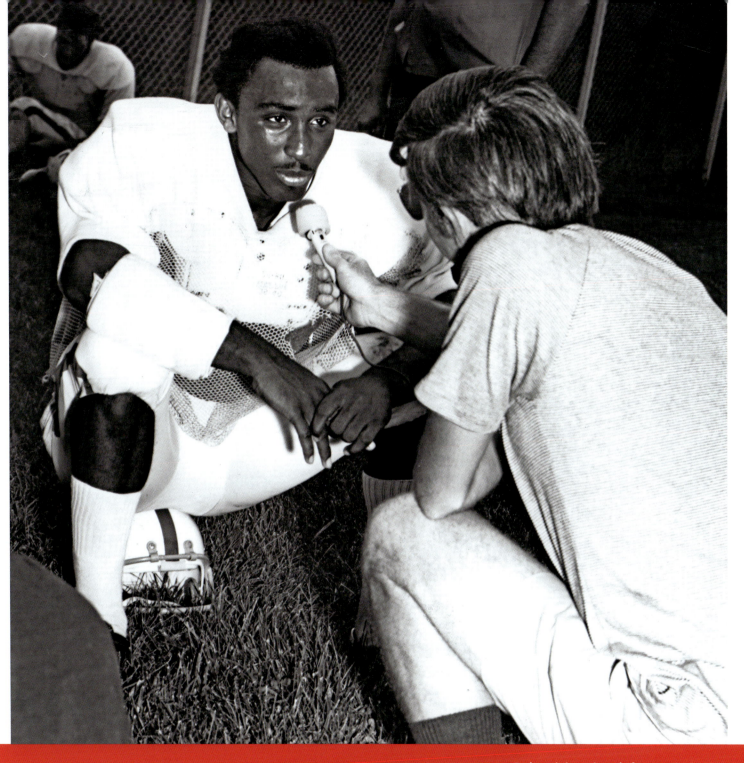

Rodgers is interviewed after practice in 1971.

Great Expectations

A MEMBER OF NEBRASKA'S MASSIVE OFFENSIVE LINE would recall that it happened during the first quarter of the Huskers' sultry 1971 season opener against Oregon. They were down at the goal line getting ready to punch it in. And then one of them noticed her. Check out the leggy blonde, he said, pointing to the young woman in the short skirt. She was standing a few rows up, just behind the end zone, on the bright, hot September afternoon. The group took a moment to discuss the young woman's attributes until Jerry Tagge huddled the offense up and called the next play.

To be ogling a woman in the middle of the game, you might think these guys were cocky. Or, at the very least, easily distracted. But it was neither, when you got right down to it. It was just that these Huskers simply were that good. There was a relaxed confidence about this group. And once they had their orders, they quickly got down to business. On the next play, the Huskers pounded the ball into the end zone.

That score was one of five short TD plunges by I-back Jeff Kinney and his backups during the Huskers' 34-7 victory in Lincoln. The Blackshirts were physically dominating that day, too.

Oregon boasted the potent tandem of quarterback Dan Fouts and running back Bobby Moore, both future NFL Hall-of-Famers. But Fouts was harassed into three interceptions. Moore, later known as Ahmad Rashad, was held to 53 yards by a Blackshirt unit he summed up afterward with a single word: "Dynamite." Indeed, this entire Nebraska team simply was that good.

> **"It's as good as I've faced."**
> — Oregon quarterback Dan Fouts, when asked about Nebraska's defense

"You can't win them all unless you win the first one," Bob Devaney said after the game. And winning them all was certainly the goal of his 1971 Cornhuskers. This team, Devaney's 10th in Lincoln, was driven to win a second consecutive national championship. They wanted to become just the sixth team in the four decades since the Associated Press initiated its college football poll to finish No. 1 in back-to-back years. They wanted to be great. And so did Devaney. "Frankly, we don't want to admit that anybody is as good," he'd said earlier that spring.

There also was little reason to think they couldn't again win it all. The team that took the field against Oregon that day was uber-talented. Six Huskers would be named to various All-America teams by the end of the year, three on each side of the ball. Before then, only 21 Huskers had been so honored in the school's 81-year football history.

In addition to those six standouts, eight other starters returned from the 1970 championship team. And behind them, the Huskers were stacked two or three deep at every position.

Nebraska's Willie Harper, left, and Larry Jacobson put the squeeze on Oregon quarterback Dan Fouts, who threw three interceptions in the game.

THE KEY OFFENSIVE PLAYERS — Kinney, Tagge and Johnny Rodgers — were back. There were big losses on defense, including Jerry Murtaugh and Ed Periard. But coaches by spring thought they might have someone ready to step into Periard's shoes, a fast-rising junior named Rich Glover. Devaney and his players weren't the only believers. The Huskers started the season as overwhelming favorites nationally to again win it all.

Given the expectations, Devaney had been worried about fat-headedness setting in. In January at the team's post-season banquet, just days after Richard Nixon had recognized their champion status, Devaney had reminded the underclassmen that "back-to-earth day starts tomorrow." Before the fall, Devaney gathered his team, telling of a prank he and his buddies used to pull as kids back in Michigan. They'd put some dog poo in a newspaper, leave it on a neighbor's porch, set it on fire and ring the doorbell. When the victim came out to stomp out the fire, he'd get the poo all over his shoe. The moral of the story, Devaney told them: Watch out for the crap in the newspapers.

But Devaney soon learned that this wasn't a team he had to prod to get to work. Winning that national championship in 1970 had only motivated them all the more. They were a proud team, and they relished the challenge ahead of them. To get where they wanted to go this year, it wouldn't take any luck. It was all out there right in front of them. "We knew we'd been in the right place at the right time to win our first national championship," Rodgers would recall in a 2014 interview. "In 1971, we wanted to dominate."

Middle guard Rich Glover (79) and cornerback Joe Blahak (27) led the Huskers with five unassisted and two assisted tackles each against Utah State.

And from the first minute of the opener against Oregon, they did. They subsequently dispatched Minnesota, Texas A&M and Utah State by nearly identical 35-7, 34-7 and 42-6 scores. It was as easy as spitting out watermelon seeds. Week after week, teams would come in gunning for the No. 1 Huskers, and by halftime they'd be looking for a soft spot to land.

Jim Carstens

All the while, the Huskers never became complacent. They just got better. There was no game they wanted to win more than the next one. And they never played down to the level of their opponent. It might seem boring to look back and see a team beating everyone by four or five touchdowns every week. But they were having a blast. This truly was a Big Red machine, one that in the Huskers' minds was unstoppable. As Joe Blahak would put it years later, "It never entered our minds that we could lose."

Blahak and other players would say it wasn't just the talent that made this team such a force. They would speak of the special chemistry of the 1971 Huskers. Every day they took the field, they played hard, picked each other up and fed off each other's energy. Success on one side of the ball would breed success on the other. And despite the team's star power, there really were no prima donnas. First and foremost, the Huskers were a team.

That was something Devaney continued to reinforce with his players. Jim Carstens, a fullback from Chicago, had been down during the spring of 1971 after being passed on the depth chart by Bill Olds. He went into Devaney's office intent on quitting. "Now Jim, I can't think of anyone that's more valuable to my program than you," Devaney told him.

Carstens doubted the truth of those words. Last time he'd checked, Rodgers, Tagge and Kinney still were part of this team. After the meeting, Carstens turned around and went back to the locker room. But rather than cleaning out his locker, he put on his pads. Devaney made him understand that even as a reserve, he did have value. He had a role on this team. Everyone had his role.

There wasn't a player on the roster who didn't come to Lincoln with dreams of becoming a starter and a star. With this collection of talent, it couldn't happen for everyone.

Junior defensive tackle Monte Johnson rarely saw the field in 1971 and never would start a game for the Huskers in his career. Yet he went on to become a second-round draft pick and play in the NFL for eight years.

John Dutton, a future first-rounder and 14-year pro, couldn't crack the 1971 team's starting lineup, either. But with such depth of talent, each Husker starter always knew there was a capable, driven player working hard every day to take his job. That made everybody work that much harder.

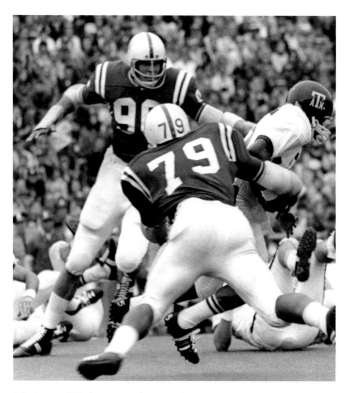

John Dutton (90) closes in as Glover gets his grips on Texas A&M running back Hugh McElroy. Dutton, a backup tackle in 1971, was an All-American in 1973.

It wasn't just the highly recruited players who were contributing to that work ethic. Junior Mike Beran of Ord, Nebraska, had come to Lincoln in 1968 as a 5-11, 186-pound walk-on. But through maniacal work under Boyd Epley in the weight room, he had transformed himself into a 225-pound backup on the offensive line. Not only did he amaze his teammates, but he would serve as the model for a new kind of Husker for generations to come: the passionate, home-grown country kid who through sheer desire and dedication in the weight room became an offensive-line mainstay on a championship team. Every player on this team, no matter where he came from, was a link in the same chain.

This team was a brotherhood. They truly loved each other. During the 1971 spring game, Carstens tripped and landed on the ball, getting the wind knocked out of him. After the game, his dad told him of the moment in the game that had given him his biggest thrill: When all the players on both benches spilled out onto the field to make sure Carstens was OK. His dad now understood why his son loved it at Nebraska so much.

> "I just automatically come in the dressing room and grab a towel. It's something I've been doing for a long time."
>
> — Johnny Rodgers,
> explaining that he gets sick at halftime of every game

They were a loose group, too. Months earlier, a friendly rivalry between Carstens and Bob Jones, a scout team quarterback and fellow Chicagoan, turned into a challenge for a boxing match. It was all worked out, with a ring set up in Schulte Field House. Coaches tried to nix it, but the one who stood up for it was Devaney. He loved a good fight. We're going to box, he said.

The two-rounder went on, and it turned into a great bonding experience. Practically the whole team was in attendance, many placing wagers. Doug "Chi-Chi" Jamail, a second-team center but a first-team character, rented a tuxedo and served as the ring announcer. Throughout the 1971 season, Jamail — a player from Houston with almost no profile outside the program — often would show up at practice on Thursdays wearing bright red boxing shorts, jumping around like a prizefighter and firing guys up. Again, everyone had his role. From this eclectic mix of talent and personalities, Devaney had molded a determined, poised and harmonious team.

Another player who was critical to the internal makeup of the Huskers was the one who outside the program now faced a self-inflicted public stigma: Rodgers. In spite of his new rap sheet, teammates would recall that he in many ways was the team's spiritual leader, someone they looked up to on and off the field.

Rodgers was an unmistakable presence in the locker room. He'd wear sunglasses and some of the most outrageous outfits. And when he was around, the soulful strains of the Temptations were sure to be playing. It was fullback Dan Schneiss who the previous year had given him the nickname Johnny R. Superstar. It stuck. He was the soul of this team.

On the field in 1971, Rodgers would take his game-changing abilities to a new level. Against Minnesota he hauled in a school-record three touchdown passes, covering 28, 20 and 37 yards. It led to a postgame question whether there was anyone who could cover Rodgers. "Nobody's done it yet, have they?" replied Tagge.

Against Kansas State, Rodgers broke NU records for touchdown receptions in a season (10) and career receptions.

The next week, Rodgers burned Texas A&M with a 98-yard kickoff return, breaking open what had been a fairly tight game. It was the first of five kicks Rodgers would take back for scores on the season. He'd set another school record with a 92-yard punt return against Oklahoma State. During another weaving return later against Colorado, teammates would later swear that Rodgers broke almost two dozen tackles, everyone getting at least a couple of shots at him. Every time Rodgers got his hands on the ball, he wanted to score. As Tom Osborne would say years later, "Of all the players I was around, Johnny could make more of a difference in a game, in more different ways, than anybody."

In fact, Rodgers arguably would have a better season in 1971 than he did in 1972, when he'd win the Heisman Trophy. He'd have five kick return TDs compared to two; he'd average 7.2 yards per rush compared to 4.8; and his punt and kick return averages would be higher. But his status as an underclassman — and a recently convicted felon — left him with no chance at the award.

> "We'd like to have a Heisman Trophy winner some day, but I'd hell of a lot rather have a football team play like last year."
>
> — **Devaney responding to a question about Tagge being a 1971 Heisman candidate**

Not only did Rodgers' playmaking make a big dent on the scoreboard, but Husker players years later would say it sparked the whole team. Even the Blackshirts were inspired to strive to bring their own play up to Rodgers' lofty level. "Everyone followed after him," linebacker Bob Terrio would recall.

Rodgers brought other intangibles to the Huskers, too. Teammates marveled at his guts. Pound for pound, he was the toughest player on the field. He would catch the ball over the middle completely exposed to the head-hunting defensive backs, bouncing around like a pinball. He'd always get right back on his feet, but you sensed that inside his helmet he was biting his lip.

Rodgers would get so banged up on Saturdays that he almost never practiced on Mondays and often was held out on Tuesdays, too. He'd instead spend that time in George Sullivan's training room taking ice baths.

When he was out on the field or in the weight room, Rodgers was no loafer. Epley would recall Rodgers as having amazingly strong legs, able to squat lift nearly 500 pounds. And when a star like Rodgers worked hard to get better, everyone paid attention. One teammate would recall going to Omaha with Rodgers to hear him speak at a school. His message: Whenever you think you have gone as far as you can, take another step. "When your best player has an attitude like that," Jim Branch would recall, "how can you lose?"

As good as Rodgers was proving to be in 1971, he still arguably wasn't the most important player on the Husker offense. That was Tagge. And by the fall of 1971, there would be no more spinning of the quarterback carousel at Nebraska. Going into his final Husker season, the senior from Green Bay clearly had taken over.

In the previous two years, Devaney had changed starting quarterbacks an eye-popping seven times. It was simply amazing that Nebraska could put together a 20-2-1 run over two seasons with Tagge starting 14 games and Van Brownson nine. Often, one had come on in relief and bailed the Huskers out, saving a game that otherwise might have been lost.

For three years, even when Tagge had been in Brownson's shadow, he had hung in there, just getting better and better. Devaney later would say he'd never seen a quarterback work harder over his career. As recently as the previous October, Tagge had been Brownson's backup. And he certainly had not played a great game in the Orange Bowl. But he had led the Huskers with confidence that night, especially when it mattered most.

In the wake of the bowl win, Tagge continued to assert himself. And his game just took off. By the start of the 1971 season, teammates recognized his clear ascendancy, voting him the team's offensive captain. The coaches never did tell Tagge he was the starter. But they didn't have to. He knew he was. Said Tagge years later: "I just felt this was my team."

So strong was Tagge's command of the offense now, he wouldn't just go into the huddle and call a play. He'd remind center Doug Dumler to make a good snap before trying to get into his block. He'd tell Kinney he'd be his primary receiver if he got into trouble. He'd take into account the position of the sun when he called a pass play, making sure the receiver wouldn't be blinded. That's how detail-oriented he was. And he was calling plays with confidence. After two years of being immersed in the Osborne offense, he knew it by rote. He'd even get a little upset when Osborne sent in plays from the sidelines, feeling it messed with the play-calling sequence he had set in his head.

Tagge follows Husker guard Bruce Weber (61), looking to block for I-back Gary Dixon (22), during the 41-13 victory over Oklahoma State in Stillwater.

And Tagge made it clear to teammates: When they were on the field, this was his huddle. During the Huskers' first drive against Oregon, the hay fever-suffering Kinney had asked Tagge to call someone else's number after he carried it three straight times. He needed a break. "Get in the huddle and play football," Tagge told him. And then he called Kinney's number again, the I-back gaining 22 yards. Tagge's message was clear: I call the plays. "Jerry was a general," Rodgers said years later.

GREAT EXPECTATIONS 193

There still was nothing flashy about him. But with the consistent Tagge, you could count on a lot of things. He'd be meticulous in his film study and be prepared every Saturday. He was going to get you into the right play. And then he'd execute it. If the play was a pass, he'd find the right receiver and put the ball in a place only the receiver could catch it.

The quarterback statistic "passing efficiency" had not yet been invented. But had it been, Tagge's numbers would have led all college quarterbacks in 1971. During the entire season, he'd put the ball up 258 times and throw only four interceptions. Auburn quarterback Pat Sullivan would throw 13 picks while winning the Heisman that year. Tagge just wasn't going to make a lot of mistakes. From Devaney's perspective, you couldn't ask for more from a quarterback.

And what of Brownson? While Tagge's star was rising, Brownson once again would be bitten by the injury bug. Midway through 1971 spring practice, Brownson was having what Devaney later described as "a hell of a spring," playing with his usual athleticism and flair. But then he went down on the turf and dislocated his nonthrowing shoulder, requiring surgery. It was the third time a serious injury had sidelined him in Lincoln.

As he'd found before, it's hard to sharpen your skills when you're standing on the sidelines in a sling. After all the injuries had healed, Brownson still couldn't throw the ball the way he used to. Instead of that great catchable ball he was known for, the nose just dropped. Brownson's desire remained strong, but his confidence was shot. "If I could just throw it the way I did in high school," he thought.

> "I still say, with Jerry or Van Brownson playing, we'd be the same as we are."
>
> — Devaney

Brownson had some good moments in fall camp with the second team. And Devaney said publicly right up until the opener that he was in the mix. But in reality, he had almost no shot at being the starter. As Osborne summed it up decades later, "Jerry kept getting better, and Van didn't."

It's also quite possible that Brownson's fun-loving ways had caught up to him. Devaney was aware by then of Van's extracurriculars. Days after the 1970 Oklahoma game, Brownson and some other players went to Omaha to see a hypnotist, Dr. Jay B. Zee, perform at Omaha's Suite 4 Lounge. Van ended up on stage and did a few crazy things, including pretending he was Wyatt Earp and yelling some profanities. He was more under the influence of alcohol than hypnosis, he'd later say.

His stage act made the paper in Omaha, complete with a photograph. It prompted Devaney to call him in. "You can't go around making a spectacle of yourself," Devaney said. He told Brownson to cool it.

But as Brownson stepped from the spotlight into the shadows during his senior year, things only careened further out of control. He was at times living out of his car, at other times crashing on teammates' couches. His scholarship check would have included enough money to pay for housing, but he decided that there were "more worthwhile things than paying rent."

Like having a good time. "Van was wilder than everybody," Rodgers would recall. "He wouldn't miss practice, but you knew he'd been out late at night." Brownson also was lax about getting up and going to class. Devaney was asked repeatedly to address rumors about Brownson's academic eligibility. It wasn't the kind of stuff that was going to give coaches a lot of faith in him.

Years later, Brownson didn't discount the possibility that his drinking and partying were damaging his performance on the field. "The drinking does many things to you, and may have changed my body," he said. "It could have had an effect on my mental approach. I'd never argue any of those points."

Brownson continued to work in practice. But as the 1971 season went along, he would be struck by a sudden realization that sapped his spirit. Devaney's rule was to stick with his starting quarterback unless the offense was faltering. Only then would he put in the backup.

Now Brownson could see: This offense is so good, it's never going to stumble. I won't get another chance to prove myself. There's no way I'll get the chance to win back the starting job. It was clear that he was now just there in case Tagge got hurt — a human insurance policy. He knew he had in all likelihood taken his last meaningful snap as a Husker. "It just felt futile," he'd recall. His desire waned.

Jeff Kinney finds plenty of room to run against Missouri, thanks to blocks from guard Dick Rupert and fullback Bill Olds. Kinney scored two touchdowns in the 36-0 rout.

When healthy, Brownson remained a talented and capable quarterback. Devaney would publicly say by the end of the year that the Huskers would in all likelihood have won as many games with Brownson starting. The coach also would admit that his policy of sticking with his starter didn't give Brownson much of an opportunity during his senior year.

But he would have done the same if the two quarterbacks' situations had been reversed. And he wasn't going to monkey around with an alternating quarterback system. He'd rather take the criticism for not playing one enough than risk spoiling the continuity of the offense.

Brownson well understood why he wasn't starting. And he never complained. Teammates would recall that there also was never any jealousy on Brownson's part as he watched Tagge lead the team week in and week out. Brownson's dad back in Shenandoah would get more frustrated than he would, saying, "If only you'd been in there …" In reality, it simply didn't matter. The Huskers won anyway.

BROWNSON WASN'T BITTER, he'd later say. He had a lot of great memories. One was that great touchdown pass he threw to Guy Ingles against KU in 1970, the one Devaney had said was as fine as he'd ever seen. When the season highlight video for the Huskers' national championship season came out in early 1971, it featured the play. As Brownson's finest moment in his finest game flashed on the screen, the narrator said, "Now, here it is, Jerry Tagge's perfect 80-yard touchdown strike. "

Van Brownson was struck by the irony.

The 1971 season became an awfully disappointing way to end a career that had started out with so much promise and hope. While there wasn't much glory in it, he still would see a lot of playing time that fall. With the way the Huskers were thrashing teams, Brownson and the other reserves often would be in by early in the third quarter.

To Brownson's credit, he wouldn't use that playing time to try to force big plays or hog the ball in an effort to impress the coaches. He would attempt only 40 passes all year, completing 16 for just 133 yards.

He was more likely to try to get the ball to his buddies on the second and third teams who had worked hard in practice, giving them the thrill of scoring in a Husker game. Against Utah State, he'd deliver Nebraska native Frosty Anderson his first Husker touchdown with a nifty pass. Teammates always would respect the way Brownson handled a difficult situation. "He held his head high," reserve QB Steve Runty would recall. "He remained a team player."

Tagge had sympathy for Brownson. He knew exactly how he felt — not that they ever talked about it. The teammates never would share a conversation about what it was like to stand in the same pair of cleats — and try to share a single football — during four of the most memorable and formative years of their lives.

Tagge was his dependable, steady self as he led the Huskers through the early 1971 slate. He posted typical numbers against Minnesota: 14 of 21 for 218 yards and those three touchdowns to Rodgers, one on an audible he called at the line. Two weeks later against Utah State, he threw for two more scores, becoming the Huskers' all-time career leader in both touchdown passes and passing yardage.

The following week the Huskers traveled to Missouri, the site of Nebraska's last loss two years earlier. In the previous two years, the Tigers had given Tagge and the Huskers fits. This time, it was no contest. Tagge broke his own Nebraska record with 319 yards running and passing as the Huskers blasted the Tigers 36-0. Osborne told him he always had possessed that kind of ability. "Jerry, you could have done that the last two years," Osborne said. Tagge had just lacked the confidence. He had it now.

Tagge was growing comfortable as the quarterback of the nation's No. 1 team. Before the season started, Devaney told him how he needed to deal with questions from the reporters. "They're going to try to get you to say something you don't want to say, and you'll know it because the hair will stick up on the back of your neck," Devaney said. "When they do that, you just tell them, 'That's not really important, but I'll tell you what is,' and then compliment the other team."

That's just what Tagge did — week after week complimenting the other guys, going out and whipping them, then moving on to the next one. But with the Big Eight season now in full tilt, Tagge and his teammates knew a major challenge was looming out there. Another Big Red on the Great Plains was suddenly inspiring its own No. 1 talk: the newly resurgent Oklahoma Sooners.

Tagge tosses to Jeff Kinney as fullback Bill Olds heads upfield to block in the 37-0 win over Iowa State.

Storm Brewing on the Plains

THE PLANNING ACTUALLY HAD BEGUN IN OCTOBER, unknown even to the Husker players. Each night, Monte Kiffin, Warren Powers and John Melton would finish their preparations for that week's Big Eight game. And then they'd grab some grub, alter their focus and keep the lights in the Husker coaching offices burning late into the night. They'd watch film. They'd brainstorm. They'd doodle formations on the chalkboard. All in an effort to answer what assuredly had become the season's most burning question: How are we going to stop the Oklahoma wishbone T?

Bob Devaney and his coaches always preached the same messages to their players: Don't look ahead. Respect every opponent the same. And while in 1971 they would keep the players on that message, when it came to Oklahoma, the coaches didn't feel they had that luxury.

OU's wishbone offense was setting the prairie afire this season as the most prolific offense ever seen in college football. And with the game still weeks away, set for Thanksgiving Day in Norman, it would have been absolute folly to think the Husker staff could just pick up a piece of chalk the week before the game and figure out a way to stop the Sooners. During this college football season, no other team had.

It's become part of the legend of the 1971 Nebraska-Oklahoma game that the heavyweights were on a No. 1 vs. No. 2 collision course from the season's first kickoff. That's not true in a literal sense. The Sooners certainly were highly regarded nationally, coming in at No. 9 in the preseason Associated Press poll. But that put them behind three schools on Oklahoma's schedule: preseason No. 1 Nebraska, No. 3 Texas and No. 5 Southern Cal. Sports Illustrated ranked Oklahoma No. 17, behind the likes of Georgia Tech, Texas Tech and Houston.

Big Eight coaches knew better. During Big Eight media days in Kansas City, K-State Coach Vince Gibson had predicted that the whole conference would be seeing a lot of red in 1971, a reference to both Nebraska and Oklahoma. The Big Eight schools had gotten an initial peek at the new Oklahoma wishbone the year before. What they'd seen scared the hell out of them.

At the start of the 1970 season, the seat in Norman was getting a little hot under coach Chuck Fairbanks. The Sooners were coming off a pair of four-loss seasons. And things didn't cool off any when OU in its third game lost at home to Oregon State.

Devaney didn't appear to be coaching an undefeated team against a Big Eight also-ran when he argued a call in a 55-0 rout of Kansas.

Nebraska coach Bob Devaney and Oklahoma Coach Chuck Fairbanks meet after the Huskers beat the Sooners 28-21 in Lincoln in 1970.

Jack Mildren

Joe Wylie

Greg Pruitt

Fairbanks could see that the Okies' recent switch to a multiple pass-run offense was floundering like a prairie schooner in the mud. In desperation, he gambled. Weeks into the season, he and offensive coordinator Barry Switzer scrapped everything they were doing. They instead copied Texas coach Darrell Royal's wishbone T, the vaunted offense that had the Longhorns in the midst of their historic 30-game win streak. After just a week's preparation, the new Sooner attack made its surprising debut at the State Fairgrounds in Dallas against none other than Texas. It wasn't the most auspicious start, the Sooners losing 41-9.

But the next week, OU went to Boulder and drilled a ranked Colorado team. And as the Big Eight season went on, the Sooners would suffer only a last-minute loss to K-State. They came to Lincoln in November with a chance to force Devaney and Nebraska to share their Big Eight title. The Sooners gave those Huskers and their dreams of No. 1 rankings all they could handle. Trailing 28-21, quarterback Jack Mildren on the last play threw a Hail Mary pass that got tipped into the air, hanging above the end zone for the taking. Jim Anderson had to leap up to snag it and save the day for Nebraska.

In that game, the Sooners felt they had come into their own. And going into 1971, nine of the 11 offensive starters were back, including Mildren and halfback Joe Wylie. They also had a budding star in junior halfback Greg Pruitt, who came on at the end of 1970. Through tireless repetition, the hungry Sooners worked to hone their new attack.

In the triple-option wishbone, three running backs are set behind the quarterback — a fullback directly behind and two halfbacks behind the fullback, flanked to either side. The ball carriers' formation looks kind of like a turkey wishbone, hence the name. Running the wishbone involves a series of critical reads by the quarterback. Depending on how the defense is lined up or reacts on the snap, the quarterback might give it to the fullback up the middle. If not, the quarterback takes it on the option to the left or right.

The quarterback then has to decide whether to pitch the ball to the trailing halfback or keep it. The quarterback tries to isolate the defender on the outside and force him to commit. If the defender goes for the halfback, the quarterback keeps it. If he goes for the quarterback, he pitches. On the pitch play, the other halfback serves as the lead blocker. It's those pitch plays, out on the edge of the defense, where the attack does its real damage. Spring a halfback out there, and there's lots of room to run.

It's a high-risk, precision offense. A rushed or late pitch can lead to a ball on the turf. To get the timing and steps right, Switzer and Fairbanks had their backs practice on a well-worn piece of AstroTurf that had white lines drawn on it indicating the path each back was to take on the play. Every step they took was drilled into their heads, keeping Mildren and the three running backs in sync.

With Mildren, Oklahoma had a player most adept at running the wishbone. He was particularly good when it came to forcing the outside defender to make a decision. The poor sap couldn't afford to hesitate even a moment. All the athletic Mildren or his halfback needed was a half step, and he'd be gone.

Mildren was tough, too. Whether he keeps or pitches, a wishbone quarterback can expect to be blasted about every play. Mildren would bounce up every time.

But it was the phenomenal speed of the Oklahoma backfield that set the Sooner wishbone apart from all other teams running it. Pruitt was nothing short of a stallion, strong and fast as the famed Oklahoma wind. During the 1971 season, the 5-foot-9 Houston native could be seen around campus wearing an OU T-shirt that said "Hello" on the front and "Goodbye" on the back. That's the way he appeared to opponents on Saturdays, too.

Wylie, the halfback on the other side of the bone, also possessed sprinter's speed. And even the backups to Pruitt and Wylie could go under 10 seconds in the 100-yard dash. The Sooners' halfbacks had the makings of an Olympic sprint relay team.

Everyone would get to see just how good the OU wishbone was once the Sooners started into

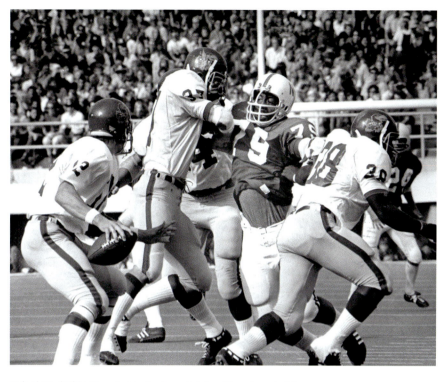

Rich Glover (79) had four tackles for losses totaling 38 yards against Kansas.

that meat-grinder of a 1971 schedule. It became a case of the meat churning the grinder into so many metal shavings.

The Sooners toppled USC 33-20, making the Los Angeles city slickers look like a bunch of rubes. The Sooners gained 516 yards that day, every single one on the ground. In fact, the Sooners threw only one pass, a fourth-quarter incompletion. "We threw that one to loosen them up," Fairbanks quipped.

Then OU the next week went back to Dallas and walloped the No. 3 Longhorns 48-27. The wishbone T monster that Royal had created had turned into Frankenstein and mauled him. Sooner fans tore down the goalposts and chanted, "We're No. 1." Mildren agreed, afterward saying the Sooners should top the polls. The win did earn the eighth-ranked Sooners a major promotion — all the way to No. 2, just behind Nebraska.

From that point on, the Huskers couldn't help doing some Big Eight scoreboard watching each week. The same day the Blackshirts posted their second straight Big Eight shutout in a 55-0 pummeling of Kansas, the Sooners blasted sixth-ranked Colorado 45-17.

Then the Sooners went to Manhattan and showed they had pretty much achieved wishbone perfection. Oklahoma drove down the field for touchdowns on its first 10 possessions. Then after a lost fumble, the Sooners went down and scored again, the final points in their 75-28 victory. The Sooners ran up a jaw-dropping 711 yards on the ground that day, smashing the NCAA record by 66 yards. Pruitt gained 298 yards on just 19 carries, breaking the single-game Big Eight record set by Gale Sayers in 1962. Some pundits began saying the Sooner wishbone was impossible to defend.

Kiffin surely took notice. And by then, the fan bases of the two schools, along with the media, were openly talking about the NU-OU showdown scheduled for November 25 in Norman. The story line already was developing: Oklahoma's explosive wishbone vs. Nebraska's impenetrable defense. The Huskers weekly faced the questions. Can you beat Oklahoma? How are you going to stop Oklahoma?

The Sooners never let up. By the end of the season, their 45 points per game would set an NCAA record, as would their 6.8 yards per carry, 470 rushing yards per game and 557 total yards per game. Pruitt was averaging an amazing 9 yards a carry. Sooner Steve Owens had averaged about half that when he won the Heisman two years earlier. "You'd have to play defense now," Pruitt told Owens, who was starring for the NFL's Detroit Lions. By just the Sooners' sixth game, Pruitt already had eclipsed 1,000 yards on the season.

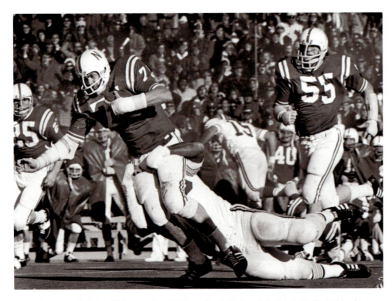
Iowa State was held to 106 yards in a 37-0 shutout, Nebraska's third Big Eight blanking.

The Blackshirts, however, also were terrorizing the Big Eight. Up front, Larry Jacobson, Rich Glover and Willie Harper were just devouring teams. Against KU, the Huskers recovered five fumbles, intercepted three passes and totaled 100 yards of tackles for loss. Iowa State was held to 106 yards in a 37-0 shutout, Nebraska's third Big Eight blanking. After the pain the Blackshirts inflicted on his Top 20 team, Cyclone coach Johnny Majors said he thought only the Minnesota Vikings had a better defense.

For the season, the Huskers would set an NCAA record by allowing just 2.06 yards per rushing attempt. The Huskers came into the Oklahoma game surrendering just 6 points a contest, a figure that ranked second in the country. In the Huskers' first 10 games, opponents would score only five touchdowns while the Blackshirts still were on the field.

Of course, the Husker offense was no slouch, either. The balanced run-pass attack wasn't putting up the kinds of numbers the Sooners were. But Tagge's unit was methodical and efficient, averaging 39 points a game and avoiding the back-breaking mistakes that cost games.

Week by week, both the Sooners and Huskers flattened their opposition. The Huskers never were threatened, beating every opponent by at least 24 points. Still, by November, the impressive Sooners were receiving 21 first-place votes in the Associated Press poll, just 10 fewer than the Huskers.

Back then, ESPN wasn't on every night breaking down, analyzing and comparing the top teams. But each week the coaches and players of the teams the Huskers and Sooners played inevitably would be asked by reporters to compare the two teams. When Tagge got his Sunday newspaper, the first thing he'd do was look for those comments, reading with great interest.

Sports Illustrated came to Lincoln to watch the Huskers take on ninth-ranked Colorado in a cold and wet nationally televised game, figuring the Buffs would be a good measuring stick for comparing the two teams. After the Huskers had breezed to a 31-7 win, the magazine figured the Sooners had gotten the best of the comparison, at least statistically. Buffs players, however, tended to favor the Huskers because of their physical play, offensive balance and superior defense. Regardless of how things came out on Thanksgiving, the magazine concluded, "somebody is going to be the turkey."

On November 13, the Big Eight powers had their final tune-ups. Oklahoma routed Kansas 56-10 on ABC. Nebraska bashed K-State 44-17, NU's 29th straight game without a loss. In the locker room in Manhattan, the Huskers finally could focus on the team everyone else in the country had been talking about for weeks. Bring on the Sooners.

The stakes were clear. Devaney made no bones about it. He told reporters the Huskers' next game would determine the 1971 national champion. "This is our season," said Jim Anderson, the NU defensive captain. "This is the one we want. Everyone knows that." Thus began the 12-day buildup to the Thanksgiving Day clash between the nation's top-ranked teams.

On the Tuesday after the K-State game, the Huskers returned to the practice field to begin their preparations for Oklahoma. And they did so in secrecy. Devaney decided to lock the gates to Memorial Stadium. He always had kept his practices open to anyone. Once when asked why he was willing to do that, he replied, "Half the time we don't know what we're doing, so how can anyone else?"

Devaney was interviewed by ABC's Bill Flemming before the Colorado game in Lincoln.

There was no joking around this time. It was time for Kiffin and his staff to begin implementing their weeks-in-the-making plan to crack the Sooner wishbone — a plan that would alter the very structure of the Nebraska defense. The secrecy and the magnitude of the planning were among the first signs to Husker players that this week indeed would be different.

Kiffin thought he needed to throw something different at Oklahoma, and the template for his plan came from watching film of Missouri. The suddenly lowly Tigers went only 1-10 on the season, but they had been the only team to slow the Sooners in a 20-3 Oklahoma victory. The Tigers did so by taking away the outside pitch.

Kiffin likewise came to believe the key to beating Oklahoma was stopping Pruitt on the outside. Kiffin saw him by far as the most dangerous Sooner. Almost every element of Kiffin's plan started with that premise.

To keep Pruitt and his halfback counterpart Wylie contained, Nebraska defensive ends Harper and John Adkins were to line up wider than normal and flow outside with the Sooner pitch men, marking their every step. That would force Mildren to keep the ball and funnel more of the Sooner offense into the middle of the field.

Linebacker Bob Terrio was assigned to shadow Mildren, trying to stay outside his shoulder and further force things into the middle. Tackles Jacobson and Bill Janssen and middle guard Rich Glover needed to tie up the OU linemen, keeping them from getting their mitts on Terrio. If Mildren gave it to fullback Leon Crosswhite — the quarterback's initial option — those interior linemen needed to get off their blocks and make the tackle. And even if Crosswhite didn't get the ball, the interior linemen needed to get him on the ground. That would keep him from getting to the Husker linebackers, freeing them up to make tackles.

> "Our offense requires somebody with complete composure to operate it. In my opinion, Jack Mildren is the greatest quarterback in the country."
>
> — Oklahoma coach Chuck Fairbanks

In another critical element of the plan, the Huskers would drop out of their traditional zone pass defense and play the OU split end and tight end man to man. That would allow the monster and safety to both play closer to the line like linebackers, giving the Huskers nine men dedicated to stopping the run game.

The Sooners passed only 82 times all season, completing 39. But when they did throw, they got amazing results, averaging 27 yards per reception, with 10 touchdowns. Still, Kiffin thought the Huskers would be able to handle the two Sooner receivers one-on-one. He didn't really think Mildren was a strong enough passer to beat the Huskers. Kiffin saw him as more of a grenade-thrower than a pinpoint passer.

As the coaches drilled the Blackshirts on the plan a week before the game, the flaky Joe Blahak would recall that he fell asleep in one of the meetings. He was awakened when Powers fired an eraser at him.

Blahak needed to pay attention, because his role would be pivotal. Kiffin and Powers decided that he and his old high school teammate Bill Kosch would trade places, Blahak moving to Kosch's safety spot and Kosch playing corner. The purpose was twofold: Blahak was a great athlete and one of the surest tacklers in the open field. The coaches thought he would be needed to haul down Mildren, Pruitt and Wylie. And Kosch actually was the faster of the two Husker defenders. The coaches thought that made him a good candidate to chase the Sooners' split end one-on-one around the field.

The plan obviously called for some pretty drastic departures from the way the Huskers typically did things. But the coaches thought the Sooners warranted it. Kiffin, ever confident, was sure the plan would work, and Devaney signed off.

When game week arrived, the media attention that had been building for weeks exploded. Some 100 media members already were on hand in Norman by Monday. The number of reporters gathered in Lincoln for Devaney's daily chats with the press also swelled, the anticipation building.

Larry Jacobson

Everyone wanted to know what would happen when a nation-leading, 563-yards-a-game offense went up against the nation's top defense, yielding only 172 yards a game. It was only the third time in college football history that the No. 1 offense and No. 1 defense in terms of yards would be meeting. The contrast in rushing yards was even more stark, the Sooners at the time averaging 481 yards on the ground against a defense that surrendered but 70 yards a game. Something had to give.

Sipping a Coke with his girlfriend at a campus restaurant, Mildren had no doubts. "I really think we're going to win," he said. "Our whole team thinks so." Mildren didn't see any way anyone could stop the wishbone. He just thought the Sooners had the horses.

Bill Janssen

The Huskers expressed equal confidence. Jacobson, the 6-foot-6 defensive tackle who wore math-nerd black-rimmed glasses but played like the class bully, had just recently been named the winner of the Outland Trophy, given to college football's top interior lineman. "Great," the South Dakota native said after Kiffin informed him of the award. "What is it?" While Big Jake didn't know the Outland, he had a pretty good idea how the 10-0 Huskers would perform. "There's no doubt in our mind that we'll beat them," he said. "There just isn't."

Sports Illustrated's cover that week showed Pruitt and Terrio going head to head. "Irresistible Oklahoma Meets Immovable Nebraska" read the headline. Inside, the magazine declared the matchup the latest "Game of the Decade," although it allowed it also could become the "Game of the Century." In fact, several college football observers, including the president of the United States, had noted that this one appeared to be the next Game of the Century, a title that had been affixed to many college gridiron battles over the years. Few, however, had lived up to such hype.

Rich Glover

The Las Vegas sports books had the Huskers as 1-point favorites. The AP's top football writer favored the Sooners. Jimmy "The Greek" Snyder, a Las Vegas sports betting expert, put his money on the Huskers. Computers weren't very sophisticated and were about the size of major appliances, but even they were put to use to guess the outcome. A Tulsa TV station put all available stats into a computer that picked the Sooners to win by 6. Union Pacific Railroad in Omaha put its computer to the test, coming up with a 6-point NU victory.

There was not a lot of trash talk during the week. The two schools were true rivals, having met each year since 1928, and they'd nearly evenly split the series. Each team respected how the other played the game.

Indeed, two speedy players who would play major roles in the game — Rodgers and Pruitt — soon would become fast friends. After first meeting at an All-American event just days after the Thanksgiving clash, they would for the rest of their college careers regularly talk on the phone, comparing their weekly performances and bragging.

On Wednesday, the day before the game, Husker fans staged a 45-minute pep rally at the Lincoln Airport, with cheers, signs and songs. Then the Huskers boarded an Eastern Airlines charter flight bound for Norman.

Along with the Huskers' equipment, the plane carried some unusual cargo: the food the Huskers would be eating in their pregame dinner that night. Adding to the game's intrigue, Devaney had picked up rumors that someone had wagered a tremendous amount of money on the underdog Sooners. The large sum created a buzz that someone could try to taint the Huskers' pregame meal. Whether it was just Devaney paranoia or legitimate concern, the coach took no chances. He called his friend Bob Logsdon at the Legion Club and had him cook and pack up steak dinners, with all the trimmings, for the entire traveling party. The Huskers even brought their own salt and pepper. It was yet another sign that this was hardly just another game.

Settling into Norman, Devaney and his coaches tried to stay calm, hoping that demeanor would carry over to the team. They felt pretty comfortable with their plans. "There's a lot of people who say you can't stop the wishbone," Devaney told reporters as his team went through its final walk-through on Owen Field the evening before the game. "If you're a coach, you can't go along with that. You have to stop it."

But if Devaney had known at that moment just how things would play out on Thanksgiving Day 1971, he might not have talked so confidently. As everyone soon would find out, the Huskers' plans to stop the Sooners contained a serious flaw.

Greg Pruitt and Johnny Rodgers developed a friendly, competitive relationship.

By game time, even the normally busy intersection of 72nd and Dodge Streets in Omaha was devoid of traffic.

Don't Look Back

AS MUCH AS THE TWO TEAMS HAD TRIED to downplay the hype, the magnitude of the day was right before their eyes as they stood in the tunnel on a cool and cloudy November 25 in Norman. Owen Field was packed, the crowd having filled in long before warm-ups had even concluded. And when the ABC network cameras went live and the Huskers and Sooners got their cue to storm onto the field, an estimated audience of 55 million tuned in — the largest ever to watch a college football game.

Who could resist this one? The sod-busting Huskers vs. the prairie-fire Sooners. No. 1 vs. No. 2. The two Big Reds. An all-star cast that included 17 of the 22 All-Big Eight performers. A showdown for the Big Eight championship. A de facto national championship game.

ABC, which had promoted the game all week during prime time, simply referred to it in a graphic as "The Game for No. 1." This was must-see TV, the greatest thing to come to Thanksgiving since canned cranberry sauce. The nation would pause during holiday festivities to watch. The blockbuster battle that had played out for weeks on coaches' chalkboards, in the press and around the water cooler finally was going to be decided on the field.

Bill Flemming, ABC's sideline announcer, introduced members of both teams' starting offensive lineups. One by one, many of the prime players in this drama stared into an ABC camera and into living rooms across America: Jerry Tagge. Jeff Kinney. Johnny Rodgers. Jack Mildren. Greg Pruitt.

Standing on the sideline, Kinney never had been more nervous before a game. He hardly was the only Husker who felt that way. Everyone's emotions were running high.

Kinney pawed at the artificial surface, different from the natural grass the then-sophomore tore up during his breakout game in Norman two years earlier. There was something else different, too. Today, in his final Big Eight game, Kinney for the first time had donned a tearaway jersey.

Kinney, Tagge and Rodgers all were wearing the special jerseys that would leave defenders holding nothing but torn cloth if they attempted to grab them. The special jerseys stood out, lacking the red shoulder stripes that adorned the jerseys worn by the other Huskers. Devaney had borrowed the idea for the tearaways from Oklahoma, which regularly used them. On this day, Devaney wasn't going to concede the Sooners any possible advantage.

In the stands, Kinney's father and 14-year-old brother were among the record crowd of 63,385 decking out the stadium in two shades of red — Nebraska scarlet and Oklahoma crimson. Back in Lincoln, Jeff Kinney's wife, Becky, now with two in diapers, watched nervously with several other players' wives in the married student housing near the Lincoln Airport.

> "We in Nebraska are all so proud of you, we are busting at the seams. Now go out there and give them the devil."
>
> — Nebraska Governor J. James Exon, in pregame talk to the Huskers

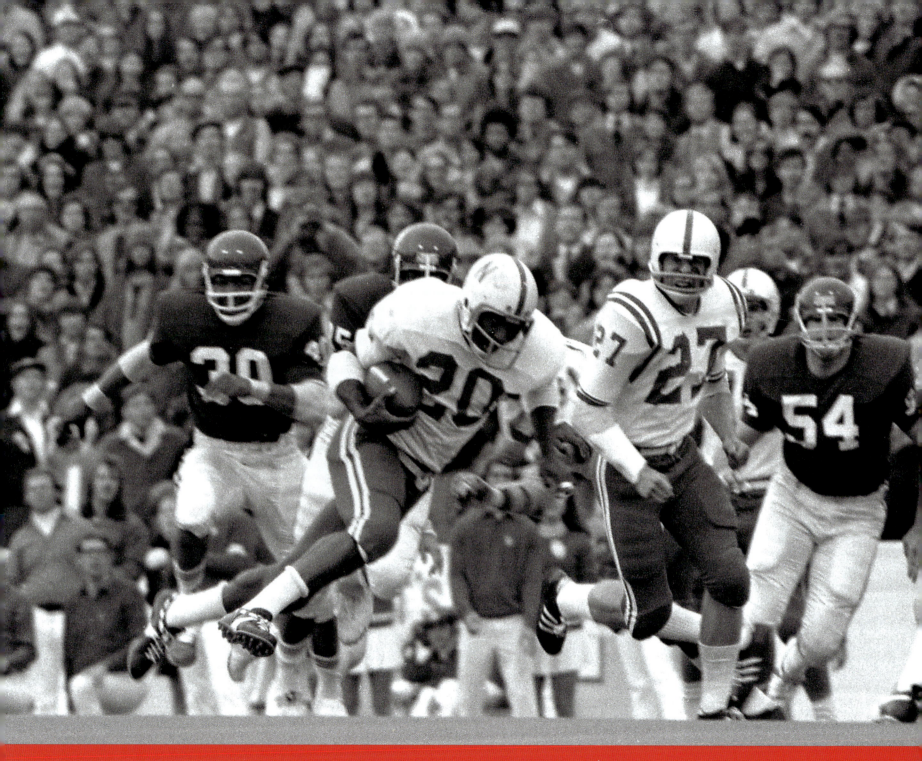
Johnny Rodgers escaped the grasp of the Sooners early in the first quarter and flew toward the end zone.

The Kinneys were typical of all Nebraska fans, a mix of excitement and fear. A cartoon in The World-Herald that day summed up just how excruciating this was. It showed a man watching a TV holding a #1 pennant in one hand and covering his eyes with the other. "What do you mean you can't look?" his wife says. "That was just the coin toss."

Up in the Owen Field press box, a record 500 media members packed the place to overflowing, ready to document what promised to be an epic college football game. Also in the press box were the representatives from the Orange and Sugar Bowls, who like the Sooners and Huskers had much on the line that day.

Rather than fight over the No. 1 team, the two competing bowls instead had brokered a deal. No matter what happened on Thanksgiving, the Sugar Bowl would get the Sooners while the Huskers would return to Miami. The outcome of this game would determine which bowl would get to host a national championship game on New Year's Day with the nation's No. 1 team. Now it was time to see which bowl had guessed right.

Joe Katz, the Sugar Bowl representative, had faced some criticism in New Orleans for arranging a deal for the then-No. 2 team. He defended it, publicly saying he had signed up the better team. "Oklahoma will beat Nebraska by 20 points," he said. Devaney read those words with more than a little irritation and took note.

> "We picked the national champion that still had the look of a champion. We couldn't turn our backs on continued success."
>
> — Bill Ward, president of the Orange Bowl committee, explaining his pick of Nebraska

Tom Osborne and John Melton were up in the press box, too, connected by headphones to the Nebraska sideline. There had been much less talk about Osborne and his multiple offense going into the game. But the NU attack also was a key when it came to stopping the Sooner wishbone. The Huskers' offensive plan was to mix the pass and run, particularly work the middle of the field with Kinney, sustain drives and burn up the clock. Devaney figured the best way to stop the Sooner wishbone was to keep it off the field.

Tagge's unit didn't have much success with that the first time they took the field. The Sooners twice swarmed over Kinney when he tried to pick up a short-yardage first down. The Huskers punted, setting up the first anticipated clash between the nation's top offense and defense.

Round one went to the Blackshirts, Kiffin's plan working like a charm. Twice Mildren took off on the option. And twice the Husker defensive ends took away his pitch man while the pursuit cut the Sooner quarterback down. Then it was time for the Huskers to fire up the Jet. One of the advantages of having a great defense: It creates more opportunities in your punt return game. And that was especially true if you were Bob Devaney and could send Johnny Rodgers back to field the kick.

Rodgers took his place as the lone Husker return man. He scared the Sooners to death. For that reason, they had worked hard all week on punt coverage. Sooner punter Joe Wylie had practiced getting the ball up high, giving the Sooners a chance to get downfield. Per his instructions, Wylie came up with a high boot, one that Rodgers settled under around the 28. It was the kind of kick you normally would expect a punt returner to fair catch.

Rodgers slips past Greg Pruitt (30) after fielding the punt, while teammate Jim Anderson (18) knocks OU's Robert Jensen out of the way.

But Johnny Rodgers rarely signaled for a fair catch. Devaney gave him the green light to return punts, even if he was standing in the shadow of his own goal line. Rodgers' attitude was, just keep them off me long enough for me to catch it. Then he would go.

The speedy Pruitt led the Sooner pursuit down the field, and like everyone else on the punt team, the running back also had his instructions. Stay in your lane and "break down" — hang together with the rest of the pursuit — so they all could be in position to bottle up Rodgers. Better to go at him as a team than have everyone trying to snare him on his own.

Unfortunately for the Sooners, Pruitt couldn't resist the chance to get in the first shot on Rodgers, a move that could have given him bragging rights in their soon-to-be friendship. Pruitt blasted Rodgers the instant he caught the ball. It was a mistake the two buddies would share laughs about for the rest of their lives.

Pruitt's hit would have knocked most any return man off his feet. But not a human gyroscope like Rodgers. He spun off the hit, put his left hand to the ground and was able to steady himself. It was a move one teammate later would describe as "physically impossible."

Pruitt's early hit had the added benefit of knocking Rodgers out of the way of the rest of the Sooner pursuit, including 236-pound offensive lineman Ken Jones, who appeared ready to demolish him. Jones lumbered harmlessly by.

The Husker return was set up to go to the right, but after Pruitt's hit Rodgers was completely improvising, reacting to whatever was in front of him. He first dodged backward in retreat. Then he juked very hard to the left. This was all instinct. If Rodgers had taken even a moment to think about all of his gymnastics, he already would be down on the turf. But with those two split-second dance moves, Rodgers suddenly had escaped the clutches of the nine Sooners who had surrounded him. Rodgers was free.

He started moving upfield, veering to the right and sidestepping a referee. He cut back left behind a midfield block by John Adkins. Then he made an even harder lateral cut toward the left sideline to avoid Sooner Tim Welch, whom he left standing flat-footed. Welch was the last Sooner between Rodgers and the end zone. The estimated 5,000 Husker fans on hand roared as he broke into the clear and started racing down the left sideline.

Rodgers always had another rule on punt returns: Don't look back. You know they're coming. Just keep running. And indeed,

Nebraska's John Adkins (57) takes OU's Joe Wylie out of the play with what might have been a clip. Rodgers' helmet and shoulder are visible just beyond Adkins.

with all the cutting slowing him down, there were five Sooners in pursuit. A couple had a head of steam and appeared to be gaining on Rodgers, who was running out of breath. It was about at that point that Rodgers, out of the corner of his eye, saw Joe Blahak.

Blahak, the cornerback-temporarily-turned-safety, had been doing as much running on this play as Rodgers himself. He didn't get a block on anyone after Rodgers caught the punt, mainly because Rodgers was moving around so much he faked out his own protection. That was the downside of blocking for Rodgers on a return, not knowing which way he was going. The good part was you might get chances to block two or three guys before Rodgers was finished.

Blahak was well used to what a Rodgers return was like. Once Rodgers broke away, the speedy junior raced after him, nearly colliding with Rodgers when the return man made his cut toward the sideline. Blahak got about 10 yards out in front. Then he peeled back toward the sideline, looking to get an angle on Rodgers' pursuers.

Blahak put his laser sights on swift Sooner receiver Jon Harrison, the man closest to Rodgers, and went at him full-bore. Blahak knocked him off Rodgers' back at the 30. The Husker star coasted the rest of the way into the end zone to complete his electrifying 72-yard play. It sparked pandemonium on the Nebraska sideline and in holiday households from border to border in the state.

With the game on TV, the audience was limited for the live radio call of Husker play-by-play man Lyell Bremser. Nonetheless, Nebraska fans would get plenty of opportunities to hear it later. Replays of his call still thrilled them even decades later. "He's all the way home!!" Bremser exclaimed. "Holy moly! Man, woman and child! ... Johnny the Jet Rodgers just tore them loose from their shoes!"

Blahak takes Jon Harrison out of the play as Rodgers races to the end zone.

Rodgers immediately was grabbed by a male Husker cheer squad member and then by big Larry Jacobson, and they all danced around the end zone. Even the normally reserved Tagge raced out on the field to give Rodgers a hug. Rodgers got another big hug from Devaney when he reached the sideline. And then he went over to the bench and threw up. A lot of Sooner fans at that point felt the same way.

Some Sooner fans later would claim Blahak's block was a clip, something even Harrison would discount. But Adkins' midfield block definitely was questionable. OU coach Chuck Fairbanks thought it was an illegal block in the back. Even Devaney later would admit it was a call that could have gone either way. But for the Huskers, it was a good no-call.

Rodgers' return would become the signature play of his incredible Husker career. But for many of his teammates, another play he'd make later in this game would stand out almost as much — one that would prove just as crucial in the outcome.

The Huskers led 7-0 less than four minutes into the game. It was an impressive statement play for a team playing on the road. But the Sooners later would say the return really didn't faze them much. It still was so early. They had ample chance to get the ball into the hands of their own playmakers.

But the Huskers on the Sooners' next possession continued to keep the ball out of the hands of OU's biggest playmaker, Pruitt. Whenever Mildren went left on the option, all-star defensive end Willie Harper fought the urge to go after him. Do not get sucked in, coaches repeatedly told him. Instead, Harper was taught to actually backpedal away from the quarterback, keeping a bead on Pruitt and taking away the pitch option. "They just wouldn't allow me to get the pitch and get outside," Pruitt lamented afterward.

> "I'm glad I'm on this side of the field. They've got some great guys over there, but I wouldn't take anything for anyone on our team."
>
> — Jack Mildren

For the game, the Sooner game-breaker would get his hands on the ball only 10 times, gaining 53 yards. In that way, Kiffin's strategy worked, essentially ripping the big outside running play right out of the Sooner playbook. "I sure can't run 70," Mildren said after the game.

The Huskers also were effectively taking away Mildren's first wishbone option, the middle dive to big fullback Leon Crosswhite. And for that the credit largely fell to Rich Glover, the Huskers' nose man. Largely unsung at the start of the season, he had emerged as an All-Big Eight performer. This was the game that would turn him into a bona fide All-American.

Glover had come to Lincoln two years earlier when Kiffin found him at Henry Snyder High School in Jersey City on his first recruiting trip to New Jersey. Jersey City was a rough place. One of Glover's games ended with an on-field melee that had to be broken up by mounted police. Another time the coach asked the players to bring garbage can lids on the bus so they could protect themselves from rocks thrown by opposing fans.

Kiffin loved what he saw in Glover's film, even though the Huskers and the University of Iowa in the end would be the only big schools to offer him a scholarship. Glover went on to become a standout on a talented 1969 freshman defense that included Blahak and Harper. But he largely disappeared as a sophomore, lost on the depth chart at tackle behind Jacobson.

Then in the spring of 1971, looking to find a replacement for Ed Periard, coaches moved Glover over to nose guard. Sports Illustrated going into the 1971 season called nose a position of concern for the Huskers. But the 6-foot-1, 234-pounder blossomed into one of the nation's most fearsome defenders. Big, strong, quick and aggressive, he was an absolute rock in the middle, controlling the line of scrimmage in every game he played. He didn't go around centers. He'd mostly go right through them, sometimes throwing in a head slap for good measure.

Glover would finish the 1971 season second only to linebacker Bob Terrio in tackles, an unusual stat for a defensive lineman whose main job was tying up as many offensive linemen as possible. By the end of his career, Devaney would say he'd never had a player who was so consistently good. "I can honestly say Glover never played a bad football game for us," he said. "He was always between outstanding and super."

Glover never would be more super than he'd be during this game in Norman. Glover lined up head to head against Sooner center Tom Brahaney, himself an All-American. But despite the stoutness of Glover's opponent, Husker coaches didn't believe there was any way Brahaney would be able to match up one on one. Glover simply was too strong and too quick.

During warm-ups, ABC had Brahaney and Glover pose head to head at midfield. Brahaney stared right into Glover's face, then smiled. Glover could see the Sooner had no idea what he was in for.

Setting up so close to Brahaney their helmets practically were welded together, Glover started coming off the snap like a ball of fire. The Sooner center simply couldn't block him.

On OU's first play, Glover teamed with Jacobson to bury Crosswhite. Glover continued to smother everything up the middle but also ranged to make plays end to end along the line.

Bob Terrio (45) brings down Oklahoma quarterback Jack Mildren, one of his 17 tackles.

Before this day was over, Glover would rack up 22 tackles — a stunning figure on the biggest of stages. The ABC cameras couldn't stay off him, constantly replaying his athletic stops. "Glover has been giving Brahaney a hard time," observed ABC color man Bud Wilkinson, the former Sooner coach.

But in football, anytime you scheme to take something away, you potentially open something else up. As the Huskers took away the fullback dive and pitches to the halfbacks, Mildren found other ways to make the Huskers pay.

On the Sooners' second possession, Mildren carried on the option for several big gainers, taking punishment but bouncing right back up. And then in the biggest surprise to Devaney and Kiffin, Mildren hurt them with his arm. The quarterback the Husker coaches had seen as a grenade-thrower instead started firing precision-guided missiles.

The Sooner coaches had noticed very early in the game that Nebraska was covering their receivers one-on-one, with the safety Bill Kosch now on Jon Harrison. Mildren and Harrison had been throwing and catching balls together for years, having been teammates together in high school in Abilene, Texas. So on the key play of the drive, a third and eight, they decided to test Kosch.

Harrison put a move on Kosch and ran a simple corner route. And despite having a Husker right in his face, Mildren heaved the ball 40 yards and dropped it right into the hands of Harrison, who had a step on Kosch. The completion was good for 31 yards. The drive eventually stalled, the Sooners forced to kick a field goal that cut the Husker lead to 7-3. But the Sooners had found a hole in Nebraska's defensive game plan, one the Sooners would continue to exploit at critical times.

Kosch had been named an All-Big Eight safety that year. But by moving the Columbus, Nebraska, native to corner and then asking him to cover a receiver one-on-one, the coaches were asking him to do something he'd never done in college.

As a safety in the Huskers' zone defense, Kosch was used to playing about six yards off the receiver and shading him to one side, denying him one side of the field. That way he was responsible for covering only a small section of the turf.

Rich Glover (79) tosses aside a blocker as Mildren (11) fakes a handoff to Leon Crosswhite (17) and eyes the outside with back Roy Bell (35).

Now coaches were asking him to play 10 yards off Harrison and straight over him, and then to follow him wherever he roamed all over the field. While the other Blackshirts played 10-on-10, Kosch was alone with Harrison. As Kiffin would put it in an interview years later, "In fairness to Bill, what we did wasn't at all fair to him."

Kosch had practiced the new scheme in the days leading up to the game, but he never had been comfortable with it. He felt like a rookie out there. And he couldn't believe how well Mildren had thrown that pass. In film, it seemed like he'd miss by 5 yards on a 5-yard pass. Now he put it 40 yards right on the numbers. Kosch went back to the sidelines with an uneasy feeling in his stomach. He felt a little better when the Blackshirts sent the Sooners packing three-and-out on their next possession.

Bill Kosch

The next time the Sooners got the ball, Glover delivered his first huge play of the day. Frustrated by their inability to get Pruitt loose outside, they tried running him up the middle. Glover tore the ball loose as Pruitt ran by, and Jim Anderson pounced on it at the Nebraska 46 just before the first quarter expired.

To this point, the NU offense had gone nowhere. During the first quarter, they had not picked up a single first down and not once entered Sooner territory. But the turnover seemed to put a spark in the unit. Tagge, Kinney and fullback Bill Olds all ripped off nice runs. Then the quarterback under a heavy rush found a leaping Rodgers down to the Sooner 20. Tagge, his torn jersey hanging on him like a poncho, later got it to the 5 on a nice keeper. Kinney took over from there, following a bruising block from Kansas City native Olds and leaping over the pile from a yard out. The Huskers led this game of games 14-3.

Seemingly undaunted, Mildren again countered Nebraska — and he did so by running counters. Barry Switzer and other coaches in the press box clearly could see the way Glover was dominating. Heck, everyone in America could. So they decided to start using his quickness against him. On second down, Mildren and the rest of the backfield went right and the quarterback handed to fullback Crosswhite going left. He ran right by Glover and burst through a gaping hole for a 24-yard gain. The counter gave Glover and the other Huskers in the middle something to think about as they came off the snap, slowing their pursuit. In this game of chess, the Sooners had the pieces and schemes to match the Huskers.

Mildren then repeatedly called his own number, mixing in options and quarterback counters where he went in a different direction than the rest of the OU backs. He'd carry six times for 43 yards as the Sooners drove 80 yards, every single one on the ground. From the 3, Mildren, with Harper back-pedaling away from him, waltzed in without anyone laying a finger on him. With 5:10 left in the half, the Husker lead was cut to 14-10.

After the way the Sooners had been running the ball on the Huskers, Kiffin huddled up the defense on the sidelines. And in an unusual move, a fiery Devaney came over and got in the Blackshirts' faces. "I see Glover tackling the dive, the quarterback and the pitch," Devaney said. "What the hell are the rest of you guys doing?"

The Blackshirts soon were back out on the field. For the fourth time in six first-half possessions, the Sooner defense had sent Tagge and his offense back to the bench without a single first down. This time, they again stopped Kinney on a short-yardage third down. The Sooners were stuffing the Husker running game like a Thanksgiving turkey.

Oklahoma took over at its own 22 with just 55 seconds left in the half. Switzer sent down word to the field for Mildren to just run out the clock, not wanting to risk a turnover just before halftime. The coach took off his headphones and headed for the elevator that would take him to the locker room. Mildren, however, had other ideas.

After a couple of runs netted a first down, the clock was stopped. Harrison had been telling Mildren he could beat Kosch one-on-one again. Mildren thought this was a good time to take his old high school buddy up on it. They decided Harrison would run a route toward the goalposts.

Mildren faked a handoff to Crosswhite and then quickly dropped back three steps. His pass was more like the kind the Huskers had expected going in, a wounded duck that hung up in the wind. Kosch overran the ball, turning around to see it falling into Harrison's hands. Kosch's helmet went flying off as he and Blahak brought Harrison down. The play gained 44 yards to the Husker 24.

The Sooners huddled and Mildren again asked Harrison what route he wanted to run. This time they decided to go for the end-zone flags on the opposite side of the field.

Harrison at first headed for the post, Kosch dipped in, and then Harrison cut and headed for the flag. Mildren again threw it like a pro,

Fullback Bill Olds gained 22 yards in four carries in the Game of the Century.

dropping the ball right over Harrison's shoulder just as he crossed the goal line. A dejected Kosch, head down, headed for the Husker sideline. And Owen Field exploded into a frenzy. After going 74 yards in just four plays, the Sooners suddenly led 17-14 with 28 seconds left.

The final seconds of the first half ticked off the clock. "I wouldn't have believed this," ABC's Wilkinson said to play-by-play man Chris Schenkel. The Huskers couldn't believe it, either. As they left the field in Norman, for the first time all year, the No. 1-ranked Nebraska Cornhuskers trailed in a football game.

One for the Ages

AS THE HUSKERS GATHERED IN THE LOCKER ROOM in Norman, Warren Powers could see on the Blackshirts' faces that they were shaken. The Sooners had gained 312 yards in the first half, more than any team had picked up in a whole game against the Blackshirts. Amazingly, 122 of those yards had come through the air. And all three Sooner scores had come after long drives, covering 85, 80 and 78 yards. No one did that to Nebraska.

The Blackshirts weren't the only ones who were shell-shocked. The NU offense had managed an anemic 91 yards, with just 69 yards on the ground. Jeff Kinney had been held to 17 yards on nine carries. Jerry Tagge's passing game never took flight.

Going in, the Oklahoma defense had not gotten much attention, and the numbers suggested that they were sieve-like in comparison to the Huskers. But while young, the Sooners also were stocked with tremendous athletes. Players like sophomore Lucious Selmon, a naturally strong kid who grew up dirt poor on a farm in Oklahoma plowing fields with mules and digging post holes. Now he and his gang-tackling Sooner teammates were shutting down the Huskers' 39-points-per-game juggernaut. If it weren't for that Johnny Rodgers punt return, Nebraska would be in dire straits.

When Bob Devaney walked into the locker room, he saw that assistant coach Bill Thornton had Willie Harper against a locker, a finger in his face. Rich Glover thought Devaney would be equally fiery. But the head coach just told all the players to go get some water or juice. They were going to win this game.

"Get your heads up," Devaney said. "We've got a ballgame to play. We're the best team, and we're going to go out in the second half and prove it."

Then the units broke up to discuss adjustments. The changes on defense were surprisingly minor, mostly line shifts aimed at slowing down Jack Mildren's counter plays. The coaches still thought it was important to stick with the overall plan, taking away Greg Pruitt's outside run threat.

Bill Kosch went to Monte Kiffin and Powers and asked if he could tweak his assignment. Let me play my usual technique and shade Jon Harrison to one side, he told them. Or let me go up to the line and chuck him a couple of times. No, the coaches wanted Kosch to continue to play off Harrison and prevent him from getting behind him. They encouraged him to stick with it. They had faith in him. But after the three deep passes the Sooners had hit, Kosch's confidence was flagging.

> "We were trying to create some bad plays for Nebraska (but) Jerry Tagge did a great job. ... They are strong, and they assaulted us more in the second half."
>
> — Oklahoma coach Chuck Fairbanks

Quarterback Jerry Tagge huddles with coaches Mike Corgan, Carl Selmer and Bob Devaney in the fourth quarter, trailing 31-28.

Offensively, Tom Osborne decided to toss out most of the game plan. The Huskers' plan to mix things up in the first half clearly hadn't worked. They had thought they needed to pass to loosen up the Sooner run defense. Instead, the scheme kept the offense from getting into any kind of rhythm, as Tagge completed only 3 of 8 passes for 24 yards.

Osborne decided the Huskers needed to get physical with the Sooners in the second half, to run it right at them. To do that, they also adjusted the way the Huskers would be running their I-back isolation plays into the Sooner line — a change that seemed small but would prove crucial. With the Sooners jamming up the middle, Osborne moved the point of attack on the line from the guard hole out one spot to the tackle hole. Now Jeff Kinney would key off the blocks of the tackles in deciding which way to cut his runs. During the second half, Tagge would give the Sooners a heavy dose of those Power 48 and Power 42 plays.

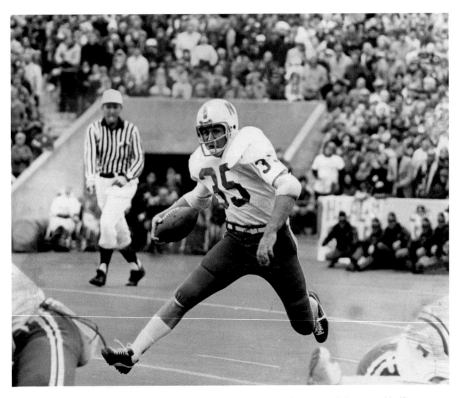

Jeff Kinney, held to 17 yards in the first half, ran for 22 yards on his first carry of the second half.

The Huskers knew their whole season now boiled down to 30 minutes of football. They were determined not to give up all they'd worked for, not without an incredible fight. And almost no one was more determined than Jeff Kinney. As he sat in the locker room, he psyched himself up for the physical battle he knew was ahead. *I'm not going to be stopped,* he told himself. *I don't care what happens to me. I'm not going to be stopped.*

Kinney showed just that kind of drive the first time the Huskers got the ball in the second half. Cutting off the tackle's block, he powered for 22 yards to the Sooner 42. In just a single play, Kinney already had exceeded his rushing output from the first half. He got eight more on his second carry.

A motion penalty — the only flag on either team in the game — pushed the Huskers into a passing situation, and then Tagge was sacked. The Huskers were thwarted. But they now believed they could get their running game going.

Thanks to John Adkins, the Huskers got the ball back just four plays later. The player teammates called "Spider" would go on to write one of the more compelling personal success stories on this team. The son of a Lynchburg, Virginia, garbageman later became an emergency room physician, a great example of the opportunities college sports represented for blacks in a new era of civil rights. The two-year starter put a vicious hit on Mildren, who coughed up the ball. Monster Dave Mason, one of three NU starters from Green Bay West, picked up the Blackshirts' third turnover of the game. Tagge and the offense were set up at midfield.

Kinney picked up where he'd left off, spinning for six and then going around the left for five. On a third-down play, Tagge faked the pitch to shake the defensive end, turned upfield and broke a tackle at the 22. By the time the rumbling quarterback was dragged down, he'd gained 32 yards to the Sooner 3. It was one of the longest runs of Tagge's career. Kinney put a helmet right to the chin of Sooner linebacker Steve Aycock and twisted in from there for a touchdown. With the six-play, 53-yard drive, Nebraska was back on top, 21-17.

The Blackshirts again ensured the momentum stayed with Nebraska. Mildren attempted a third-down pass but was buried by Harper for a 12-yard loss. The Blackshirts, too, were finding their mojo.

Kinney was just getting warmed up. He went off left tackle, broke to daylight and gained 15. That little hole adjustment at halftime was working. And the focus on the running game was allowing the Husker offensive line to fire off the ball every play. They were in attack mode.

Tagge then twice found Rodgers on passes, hitting him in stride for 20 off play action and then connecting again for 10 to down inside the 1. Kinney submarined into the end zone from there, his third short touchdown of the game, to cap the 61-yard drive. The Huskers again were up by two scores, 28-17.

With a dominating third quarter, it seemed to the Huskers that they had restored the proper order of things. Husker fans suddenly were feeling pretty good about this one, clapping in the stands as the pep band played a lively version of "Dear Old Nebraska U." But part of what would make this game a classic was that the wobbled Sooners refused to fold. Through some trickery, they found a way late in the third quarter to get back in the game.

Glover demolished two Sooner running plays in a row, on one beating the double-team the Sooners had been forced to use because Brahaney couldn't block him alone. Then on third down, Harrison took a handoff from Mildren on a reverse and suddenly reared back to throw. The Huskers were surprised but actually had prepared for it.

If Kosch saw the receiver he was covering go into the backfield on a reverse, his job was to call out "reverse" and then take off in a 45-degree angle the opposite direction looking for the tight end, the likely target if Harrison was to pass it. But Kosch called out "reverse" twice before turning, and he later figured just that split second cost him. He got to tight end Albert Chandler just a tick too late. Chandler broke loose and got all the way to the NU 16, a 51-yard gain.

> "You never know what helped in a game like this. Everything did."
>
> — Jeff Kinney, responding to a question about Nebraska's tearaway jerseys

ONE FOR THE AGES

Mildren carried four straight times from there. On the last one, Mildren zipped in on the option while Harper backpedaled himself out of the play. The star Husker end threw his head back in obvious frustration after Mildren crossed the goal line. Going into the final 15 minutes, Oklahoma now trailed just 28-24.

Undaunted, Nebraska stuck with what was working on offense and again powered the ball down the field. A 16-yard reverse by Rodgers and an explosive 17-yard burst by Kinney had the Huskers again knocking on the door at the Sooner 24.

One of the reasons Nebraska was riding this two-year unbeaten streak was that the Huskers simply did not beat themselves. And a big reason for that was Tagge, a quarterback Devaney could count on to avoid mistakes. However, on the next play, Tagge would make a big one, and it dearly hurt the Huskers.

Tagge had taken to doing a little hidden-ball trick sometimes when faking handoffs. He'd reach the ball behind his back with one hand to hide it from the defense, reach back and grab it with the other, and then take off running. He had performed the slick move in the national championship game against LSU and in the first half of this game. Now Tagge decided to employ his dipsy-doodle ball trick while faking to Rodgers on the scissors.

Unfortunately for Tagge, Sooner linebacker Danny Mullen caught him while the ball still was behind his back. It spurted to the turf, lying like a grenade about to go off. Much to the dismay of Husker fans across the country, it did. Lucious Selmon fell on the ball.

The unflappable Tagge put on a rare show of emotion after the Huskers' first turnover of the day, punching the air with his fist. "It was stupid," he'd later say.

The Blackshirts then chose an inopportune time to lose their containment on Pruitt. Harper had grown tired of watching Mildren gouge the Huskers while he just backpedaled away from him. He had hardly hit anybody all day. So the lightning-quick end decided to try to make a play on the quarterback. Mildren just as quickly slipped a pitch around Harper to Pruitt. The Sooner busted loose around the edge for 18 yards down to the Nebraska 33 — by far his longest run of the day.

Mildren kept the drive alive by converting a crucial fourth and 2 from the Nebraska 25, getting four yards on a counter. A minute later, the Sooners found themselves facing another fourth down, from the Husker 16. And for the fourth time, Mildren burned the Huskers with a surprise play-action pass.

Harrison headed for the post, then cut right toward the flag. He was wide open, this time getting several steps on Kosch. Once again, Mildren's pass was right on the money, and Harrison snagged it in stride in the corner of the end zone.

Harrison tossed the ball high into the air and was mobbed by his teammates, while the capacity crowd in Norman went into hysterics. Kosch wanted to climb into a hole. Oklahoma's gutty comeback from an 11-point deficit was complete. With 7:10 to play, the Sooners' 69-yard drive put them back on top, 31-28.

> "I was giving him a lot of room because I wasn't sure of myself. I just couldn't find the ball."
>
> **— Bill Kosch on his coverage of Jon Harrison**

Jack Mildren (11) pitches to Greg Pruitt (30) after Nebraska's Willie Harper (81) mistakenly went after the OU quarterback.

The light was fading and a gray, misty rain fell as Tagge, Rodgers and Kinney trotted out to the field, 74 yards separating them from the Oklahoma goal line. The Sooner band was playing "Boomer Sooner." The Oklahoma fans were imploring the Sooners with chants of "Defense! Defense!" For the Husker offense, this was do or die. With the way the Sooners were moving the ball, fail here and Nebraska might never see the ball again.

Such grand stages are where legends are made. Over the next six minutes, Tagge, Kinney and Rodgers indeed would step up in a big way, cementing their places in Husker lore.

A calm confidence permeated the Nebraska huddle. They knew they would score. Until the Tagge fumble, the Sooners had hardly stopped them the whole second half. They also all had been in this same spot against LSU just 11 months earlier, trailing late in a must-win game. That big-game experience was the biggest advantage Nebraska had over Oklahoma. It was time for the offense to finish again. Husker guard Dick Rupert, one of Osborne's West Coast juco recruits, looked to the sideline at his teammates. He put his finger in the air, made a circular motion, and pointed to the Sooner end zone.

Jerry Tagge had a rough day passing but rushed for 49 valuable yards.

Tagge had by now shed his rag of a tearaway for his normal No. 14 road jersey. At the moment, after that costly fumble, he faced the potential of being the goat. But the cool quarterback was unruffled by recent events. As he'd say later of his thoughts at that moment: "We never think about losing. We only think about scoring."

In the huddle, neither Tagge nor anyone else said anything particularly heroic. Nobody needed to. Everyone knew what they had to do. And everyone — including the Sooners — knew what the Huskers were going to do. They were going to give the ball to Jeff Kinney.

After that miserable first half, Kinney already had picked up more than 100 yards in the second. He didn't plan to stop now, even if the Sooners knew what was coming. They're not going to stop me, he told himself again.

The Husker drive started with Rodgers picking up four yards on a reverse. Then Kinney shook off Sooner defenders to gain five yards over right tackle, setting up third and 1.

It was a down and distance where the Sooners might have suspected another thrust into the heart of their defense. But Tagge instead called for a pitch to Kinney outside, catching the Sooners in an overshift into the middle of the field. Kinney broke into the open and shed no fewer than four Sooner tacklers before being brought down along the Nebraska sideline. With the 17-yard gain, the Huskers already had cracked Sooner territory.

But as the officials set the chains, the Huskers suddenly were without their workhorse. Kinney still was down on the ground along the sideline. Both his legs had painfully seized up with untimely cramps. While trainers furiously worked on the sideline rubbing down Kinney's legs, his backup, junior college transfer Gary Dixon, went in.

Dixon got two yards on first down. Then Tagge missed with a pass on second. Fortunately for the Huskers, Kinney was back on his feet. "I'm ready to go back," he told Mike Corgan. With the Huskers facing a crucial third and eight, Kinney ferried the next play call into the huddle. It was 71 Wingback Pass, that same pass play to Kinney that had keyed the winning drive against LSU. But this time, thanks to the Sooners, it would get completely fouled up.

Oklahoma rushed only three and dropped everyone else back into coverage. Yet Raymond "Sugar Bear" Hamilton still managed to shake free and come in on Tagge. He made a dive for the quarterback's feet, but Tagge escaped. The play was still alive, though the timing was shot.

Tagge rolled to his right under pressure, looking for someone open amid the eight Sooner defenders in the secondary. He saw a gap between the linebackers and heaved the ball there.

Devaney called Kinney's performance the best he'd seen. "He ran over people, through them, broke tackles and everything else," the coach said.

By now, Tagge and Rodgers had played together long enough that it was like they were telepathic. Tagge knew that Rodgers had a knack for finding those holes, and Tagge put it there. "He knew what I was thinking," Tagge later would say. "I knew what he was thinking."

Sure enough, Rodgers found the same spot, breaking for it just as Tagge released the ball. Kinney, running his delayed crossing pattern, also saw what was developing in front of him and slowed down to avoid carrying his defender into the play. With a dive, Rodgers clutched Tagge's sinking liner to his chest just before it hit the turf.

Rodgers' crucial 11-yard catch gave the Huskers new life at the Sooner 35. The pass was one of only four Tagge would throw the entire second half. The quarterback later would recall it as the most critical play he'd ever make during his Nebraska career.

With the Huskers now just 35 yards from the Sooner end zone, they knew these next few minutes were going to be like primitive warfare. But they were ready for it.

This was the time of the game where their strength and conditioning advantage would show through. Center Doug Dumler, guards Rupert and Keith Wortman, and tackles Daryl White and Al Austin — the latter filling in for the injured Carl Johnson — sensed that their steady pounding in the trenches was wearing the Sooners down.

At one point during the final drive, Dumler would recall looking into the stands and somehow spotting his brother. Out of 63,000 people, to see his brother at a moment like this. They looked at each other, and Dumler flashed him a No. 1 sign. He and his teammates soon proved that they were.

On the very first play after the Rodgers catch, Kinney slashed through the Sooners for 13 yards.

One of the lasting images of this game would be the valiant Kinney charging through the Oklahoma line, his jersey shredded and his shoulder pads flapping with every stride. The senior appeared to just get stronger with every carry.

Tagge then changed things up and gave to Rodgers on the scissors, the wingback using some slippery moves to shake two Sooners and gain 7. After that, Tagge just started calling Kinney's number, again and again and again.

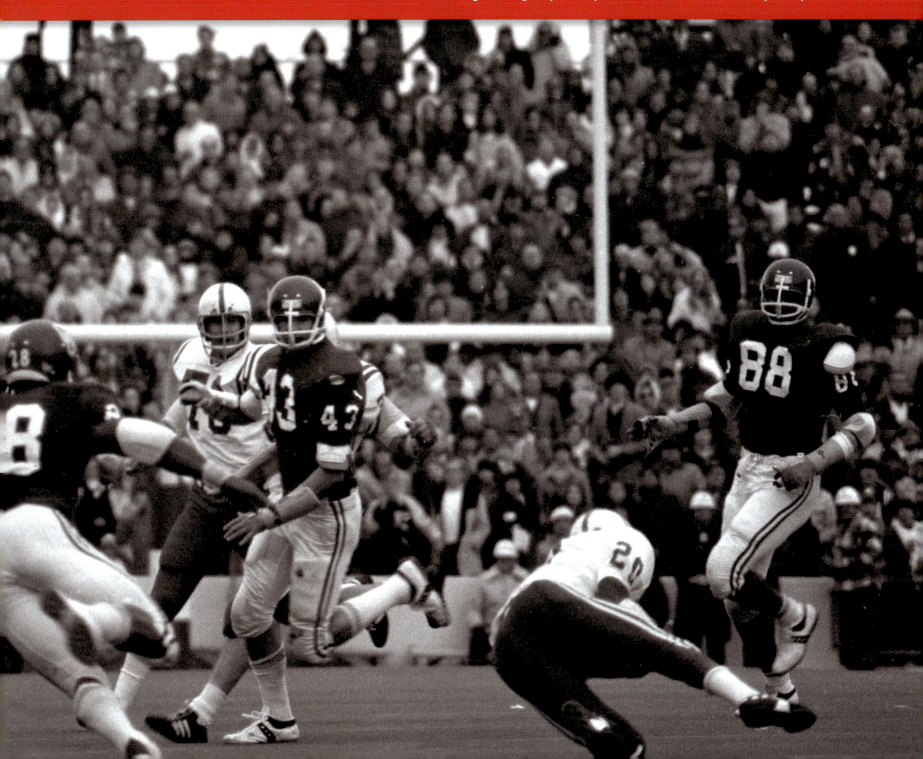

Rodgers' diving reception keeps the Husker drive alive late in the fourth quarter.

Tagge would go into the huddle, call Power 42 or 48, come to the line and look at where the safety was lined up. If he needed to, Tagge audibled to the side away from the safety. Then he'd take the snap and hand Kinney the ball. It literally became that simple. There was no reason to stop. Kinney on the first one pounded for 7, brought down inside the 10. And then he got 2 more to the 6.

The savvy Tagge was in control. He was ever mindful of the clock. He reminded teammates to keep their heads on straight. "No mistakes! No mistakes!" he'd admonish. And now facing third and one, he decided Kinney needed a breather. The senior quarterback called a timeout and went to visit with Devaney on the sideline.

Devaney, wearing a red cap and letterman's jacket, said the Huskers weren't even going to consider a field goal try. There wasn't going to be any tie on this field. Tagge assured him the Huskers would put the ball in the end zone.

"I know we can score, Coach, but I've been worried about eating up the time," Tagge calmly told Devaney. He didn't want to leave Mildren and the Sooner wishbone even a minute to work with.

"What's your best play?" Devaney asked.

"I think it's off-tackle with Jeff," was Tagge's unsurprising reply.

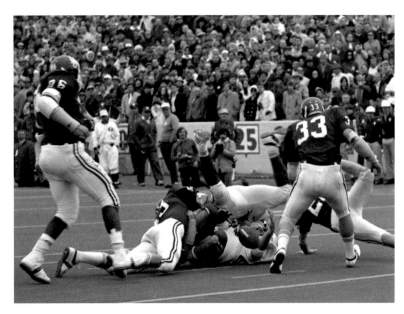

The ball popped out at the 2-yard line, but officials said the play was dead.

"OK, let's run it," Devaney said, "without any mistakes."

The Huskers returned to the line, and Kinney took the ball behind big left tackle White for 4, down to the 2. A desperate Sooner pried the ball out of Kinney's hands after the play was over, the OU defenders pleading for a fumble call. But the officials were emphatic that the ball had been blown dead, and replays indeed showed his knee was down before the ball came out. Still, during an era before video reviews, referees had been known to blow such calls. "If they had ruled it was a fumble," Tagge told an interviewer years later, "you'd be talking to Oklahoma right now."

From the two, Tagge handed off to Kinney one final time — his fifth carry in the last six snaps. His No. 35 jersey was in tatters. The numeral 5 on the back was totally gone, and there wasn't much left of the 3, either. But by now, everyone in the country recognized who this lionhearted Husker was, jersey numerals or not. Behind crushing blocks from White and backup fullback Maury Damkroger, Kinney pushed the ball over the goal line. Damkroger bear-hugged Kinney from behind as the Husker sideline broke into triumphant screams.

Kinney's 2-yard run capped what would go down as the most epic march in the history of Nebraska football. It was true grit. Five and a half minutes. Twelve plays. Seventy-four yards. Fifty of them on the tireless legs of Jeff Kinney.

Kinney blasts across the goal line for the game winner.

When kicker Rich Sanger tacked on the critical extra point, the Huskers were up by 35-31. The game wasn't over yet. The Sooners still had 1:38 left on the clock and one more chance to send heartbreak blowing north up the Plains. The Blackshirts, having already taken their biggest beating on the scoreboard in nearly three years, needed one more stop.

Kiffin huddled with the Blackshirts during the TV commercials. And when he sent his unit back out onto the field, they gave the Sooners a new look. Knowing the Sooners almost surely had to pass, Kiffin switched the Huskers into their base zone pass defense. That also meant Kosch and Blahak were back at their regular positions.

Mildren had put up big numbers on Nebraska, running for 134 yards and more amazingly throwing for 137. But now he was backed up at his own 19 with little time left and facing a must-pass situation. The wishbone wasn't made for times like this. He tested the Huskers' new alignment right away, on first down cutting loose with a long throw to Harrison. And the receiver once again got a step on his defender, outrunning Blahak down the field. Jim Anderson watched in horror from the other side of the field as the ball arced through the air. But under pressure from tackles Larry Jacobson and Bill Janssen, Mildren missed this one. It landed well beyond Harrison's reach. Anderson never was so happy to see a ball hit the turf.

> "We were just a bunch of seniors, juniors and sophomores out there who knew we had to win. It was our whole season, our whole careers."
>
> **— Jeff Kinney**

"I got beat," Blahak said with a laugh when he got back to the huddle, as if it had been a meaningless play out on the schoolyard. There was a reason teammates called him Airhead. Nothing could shake him.

Mildren kept the ball for four yards on second down. Then on third, Jacobson smothered the quarterback for a huge loss of 8 yards back to the 15. Much like their offensive counterparts, the NU defensive line now was overpowering the spent Sooner front. Boyd Epley was surely smiling.

On fourth down, Mildren dropped back again. And while the Huskers rushed only three, Jacobson came free straight up the middle. Mildren sidestepped him and in a frenzy tried to get the ball to his outlet on the play, Pruitt. But Rich Glover, making his final spectacular play of the day, came with a rush right after Jacobson and batted Mildren's throw to the turf. This Glover play was a true showstopper.

Jacobson lumbered off the field with arms raised toward a delirious Nebraska sideline and jumped into the arms of Kiffin, almost crushing him. Kiffin actually hadn't seen the final play by Jacobson and Glover, having been anxiously looking downfield to see if Blahak was on Harrison. Even after winning a Super Bowl later in his career, Kiffin would say he never was part of a bigger defensive stop.

Tagge worked the last minute off the clock, not trying to score despite taking over on the Sooner 15. Then the Huskers hoisted Devaney onto their shoulders, ecstatic but relieved to get off that field with their No. 1 ranking intact.

This one had been rough on the fans, too. Two patients were admitted to an Omaha cardiac unit with chest pains brought on by the day's heart-stopping action. But for the Huskers and their fans, the dream season lived on. A spectacle Husker players would find almost as unforgettable as the game itself was the crowd of 20,000 Husker fans and "We're No. 1" chants that would greet them at the Lincoln Airport hours later.

Jeff Kinney lingered on the field after the game and met up with his father and brother. He was exhausted. During his gutsy second half, he'd carried the ball 22 times for 154 yards. His final numbers: 31 carries for 171 yards and four touchdowns. Sometime during the second half, he had even surpassed Bobby Reynolds to become the Huskers' all-time career rusher. Quite a day.

His eye black smudged on his cheeks, Kinney pulled from his shoulder pads the tattered remains of his tearaway jersey and gave them to his dad. Those scraps one day would be proudly displayed in a case back home at McCook High School, a testament to his heroics that day. "This was the most important game of my life," he told reporters afterward. "Of anybody's life."

Devaney made his way to the postgame interview room. The Sugar Bowl's Katz was standing outside, and he extended a hand of congratulations to the Husker coach. Without even breaking stride, Devaney told Katz the dark place he could stick those 20 points he'd favored the Sooners by.

Devaney right off the bat called it the biggest win of his career. He praised the effort of both teams.

The Huskers lift Devaney onto their shoulders at game's end.

He said he never doubted that the offense would score at the end. Both during his press conference and afterward, Devaney couldn't stop talking about what a great game Kinney played. "He ran over people, through them, broke tackles and everything else," he said.

When it came to defense, Devaney said the plan to take away Pruitt had worked. But he took the blame for the flawed plan to play the Sooner receivers man-to-man. While it was Kiffin's design, Devaney had the final say. The buck stopped with him. "If I had to do it over again," he said, "I sure as hell wouldn't."

At some point in the game's aftermath, during a private moment, Devaney sought out Kosch and put his arm around the senior.

"Billy, I apologize for putting you out of position," the coach said. Kosch told him it was OK. "We won the game," he said. But even decades later, Kosch still would feel bad about what happened. Tagge and his teammates would continue to encourage Kosch to get over it. It wasn't his fault that the coaches put him in a tough spot. And everyone made mistakes that day. "I fumbled in the game, and all I had to do was hand the ball off," Tagge said.

Kosch eventually would come to accept what happened. He's now part of the lore of one of the greatest games ever played. "Someone had to keep Oklahoma in the game," Kosch said with a laugh during a 2014 interview. "Otherwise, it wouldn't have been the Game of the Century."

Rodgers' punt return was much spoken of immediately after the game, particularly by the Sooners. They knew it had been the difference. The offenses largely had played to a draw, with the Sooners out-gaining Nebraska 467 yards to 362 and each unit scoring four touchdowns. The Sooners, though, had no match for Rodgers and his dazzling return. "We feel we're national champions right now, right now!" a sweat-drenched, beaming Rodgers said in the locker room. "And ain't nobody stopping us."

Rodgers and the happy Huskers doused Devaney, all their other coaches, the university chancellor and even Nebraska's governor in the showers. Amid the hijinks and howling, no one realized that the phone was ringing. Someone finally picked it up and urgently went to find Devaney. It was the nation's College Football Fan in Chief.

President Nixon had watched the game while spending the holiday at home in California and wanted to give his regards to the winning coach. Nixon told Devaney that this was one "Game of the Century" that had lived up to the billing. "Yes, Mr. President," Devaney told him. "They sold a lot of popcorn. Nobody left."

The president of the United States wasn't the only one who felt that way. It was sinking in for both the participants and the millions who watched that this game had been a true classic. With four lead changes, 60 minutes of unending offensive fury, gallantry under fire and last-minute drama, it not only lived up to the Game of the Century hype, it surpassed it.

After dressing, Jim Anderson hurried out back onto the field to take one last look. The Owen Field stands were empty. He was all alone. But he took five minutes to soak it all in, savoring his part in the once-in-a-lifetime football game. The senior knew he never would see another like it.

The sentiment of the day probably was best summed up by football writer Dave Kindred as he sat in the Owen Field press box that night batting out his game dispatch for the Louisville Courier-Journal.

"They can quit playing now," he typed. "They have played the perfect game."

Devaney and Chuck Fairbanks shake hands at the end of the Game of the Century.

Going on a Bear Hunt

AS BOB DEVANEY'S 10TH SEASON on the Nebraska sideline wound down, he possessed the highest winning percentage among any active coach. He had won a national championship. He'd claimed seven Big Eight championships in 10 years. He'd won a pair of Orange Bowls. But there was at least one thing still lacking on his college coaching résumé: He never had beaten the Bear.

Unlike in pro football, it's the coaches, not the players, who lord over college football. The players cycle through their programs in four years, whether they achieve a degree or stardom. But the coaches endure, at least the good ones do, looming large on fall afternoons. And within the fraternity of college coaches in 1971, there was no bigger name than Bear Bryant.

Bryant was a true giant of the gridiron. He wore his trademark houndstooth hat and spoke with a gruff, menacing drawl. Bryant was so tough, it was said he was the only coach in America who had a large mammal named after him. He was a wily bear, too, ready to spring a trap when you least expected it. There was substance to the Bryant mystique. No coach in the game in 1971 had more career wins than Bryant's 210, on his way to becoming college football's all-time victory leader. His Alabama teams had particularly terrorized college football in the early 1960s, winning national championships in 1961, 1964 and 1965.

Bryant's most recent title had come at Devaney's expense, a 39-28 pounding in the 1966 Orange Bowl. The Bear had outfoxed Devaney in that one with two onside kicks and a tackle-eligible play. Only two late Husker scores made it halfway respectable. Then after talking Devaney into a rematch in the next year's Sugar Bowl, Bryant piled on the humiliation, smacking him 34-7.

But Devaney now had a chance to begin to even the score. He and his Huskers were set to square off in the Orange Bowl with Bryant's Crimson Tide. What's more, it was going to be yet another No. 1 vs. No. 2 match. A second Game of the Century, as some would try to call it, with the national championship again on the line.

"Bryant is a great coach and good friend of mine," Devaney had said after the matchup was set. "But he's treated me poorly on the field. I'd like to get to him once."

Devaney's words only hinted at just how hotly he burned for this game. Those two previous losses to the Bear had been a big blow to Devaney's ego. Getting a Bear pelt would mean almost as much as claiming a second straight national championship.

Devaney frequently invoked his two losses to the Bear for laughs while out on the banquet circuit. But his words often were spoken only half in jest, such as when he said he had gone into hiding for a month after the Sugar Bowl loss. Members of the Nebraska press well knew how much those losses stung. A World-Herald columnist put together a whimsical list of Devaney's 10 biggest coaching embarrassments, with six of them revolving around losses to Bryant. Among them: the first onside kick Alabama recovered in the Orange Bowl; the second onside kick Alabama recovered in the Orange Bowl; the trap Devaney fell into trying to replicate Alabama's small, quick linemen. "Alabama has been the burr under Devaney's saddle," Gregg McBride wrote.

Johnny Rodgers' lead was so big he could look back before reaching the end zone on his punt return touchdown against Alabama.

Devaney's coaches, and even his players, were well aware of how important it was for him to beat Bryant. Recalled Tom Osborne: "We all really wanted that one for Bob." For the Huskers in Miami, helping their coach exact some revenge on the Bear became a driving force. The bowl game in Florida would be the Huskers' second stop on a tour of sun-splashed vacation paradises after the climactic victory over Oklahoma. Six days after the win in Norman, the Huskers flew to Honolulu for a December 4 game against the University of Hawaii's Rainbow Warriors.

The trip was a true four-day holiday for the Huskers. Everyone knew the Rainbows' only prayer was for Johnny Rodgers, Jerry Tagge and Jeff Kinney to be eaten by sharks. The Huskers risked such a fate, the players spending lots of time on Waikiki Beach. The players got kisses from native beauties in leis as soon as they got off the plane. They basked in the sun. The Honolulu paper photographed a bare-chested Tagge holding a pineapple like he was about to pass it downfield. Rodgers shared some of his own dance moves with hula girls. Devaney set no curfews until the night before the game. The atmosphere could not have been more different from the week leading up to the OU game. The Huskers needed that kind of break.

For Hawaii, the arrival of the Cornhuskers was compared in a local newspaper to the Japanese attack on Pearl Harbor, almost 30 years earlier to the day. One local columnist suggested that the undermanned Warriors show up in Lincoln on game day and say, "We thought the game was here." Other suggestions for surviving the Big Red included using a 22-man defense or, alternatively, an 11-man defense, with one armed with a rifle. As expected, the game turned into a luau on the beach for the Huskers, who coasted to a 45-3 win.

Rodgers holds a native Hawaiian weapon at NU's hotel near the beach.

Two weeks later, the now 12-0 Huskers again were packing their sunscreen for Miami and their matchup with the 11-0 Crimson Tide. Alabama was coming off a 31-7 walloping of arch-rival Auburn, a win that vaulted the Tide to No. 2. The Tide had beaten five other bowl teams during the year, including a win over USC on the road to start the season. This would be only the third time in college football history that the nation's two top teams were meeting in a bowl.

In Alabama, the Huskers again would be facing a wishbone team. Much like Oklahoma, Alabama had switched to a wishbone after Bryant endured two straight six-win seasons. But the Alabama wishbone did not strike the same kind of fear in Devaney and Monte Kiffin that Oklahoma's did. Alabama was averaging a more pedestrian 324 yards a game. The Tide wishbone was built to pound it inside rather than race around the end. Bama just didn't have the speed to go outside, no Greg Pruitt-like threat to take it all the way. In fact, for the first time in his meetings with Bear, Devaney figured he had the team with superior speed.

One reason the Tide lacked the kind of speed and athleticism that Nebraska and Oklahoma possessed: Alabama still had almost no black players. Alabama for the first time in 1971 had a pair of black recruits on its roster, a first-team defender and a No. 2 running back. Osborne said the Alabama coaches seemed to believe that black high school players in the South did not possess the skill and discipline to play the game. Now that the school was open to recruiting black players, one of the Tide assistants asked Osborne where Nebraska found its great black players. Osborne told him he bet there was a wealth of talented black players within 50 miles of Tuscaloosa. The coach looked at him as if he'd just sprouted a third eye.

Alabama did have some tough inside runners, including All-America halfback Johnny Musso. And they had 273-pound guard John Hannah to throw blocks. By this time, in an age of increasingly big and fast players, even Bryant had given up on the idea that you could win with little gremlin offensive linemen. His offensive line was now as big as Nebraska's. But Kiffin was betting that with Rich Glover, Willie Harper and Larry Jacobson up front — all of them by now landing on various post-season All-America teams — Alabama wasn't going to hurt Nebraska up the middle.

Nebraska's offensive line prepares for the Orange Bowl. From left, Carl Johnson, Keith Wortman, Doug Dumler, Dick Rupert and Daryl White.

The Huskers also thought they matched up pretty well against an Alabama defense that was receiving a lot of accolades after holding Pat Sullivan, Auburn's Heisman Trophy-winning quarterback, to 121 yards. But the Husker offense was far better balanced than Auburn's. With the All-America combo of Tagge, Rodgers and Kinney, Devaney figured he was well-armed for this Bear hunt.

The Huskers were welcomed at their arrival in Miami by bowl reps in orange blazers, beauty queens and an obnoxious Alabama fan who worked at the airport. "You boys gonna be showed how it's done," the fan proclaimed.

The game became a hot ticket, all 77,000 seats quickly selling out. That many requests reportedly had come from Nebraska alone. The media horde exceeded even that of the Oklahoma game. And despite Nebraska's impressive win in Norman and 31-game unbeaten streak, many of the national pundits were predicting that the Bear would continue his mastery of Devaney. Some figured the Bear had another surprise for the Husker coach hidden in his houndstooth. "Bama will dazzle them to death," wrote a scribe for Football News. "You may think I am off my rocker, but I don't think it will be really close."

The sharpest words — a direct jab at Devaney — came from a Minneapolis writer. Bama's big linemen are about 15 percent quicker than Nebraska's, he wrote, while Bryant's mind works about 15 percent quicker than Devaney's. Such comments, widely reported in the Nebraska media, could only have boosted Devaney's temperature from simmer to boil.

With the media crush, both Devaney and Bryant were meeting with reporters twice a day. Though reporters made much of Bear vs. Bob — the battle between the coach with the most wins and the one with the highest winning percentage — both downplayed any kind of personal rivalry or grudge. About the biggest highlight was when the two coaches traded hats for the photographers, Devaney putting on the Bear's houndstooth.

> **"If we can't be mentally ready for this game, we'll never be ready."**
>
> — **Devaney during preparations for Alabama**

Nebraska's players seemed to be much more relaxed than the coaches. This was a team that had grown accustomed to playing with a target on its chest. And after the OU game, there was no such thing as pressure. Devaney made sure they stayed loose, again surprising them with tickets to a concert at a club, this time to Ike and Tina Turner.

The Huskers' looseness was reflected in a World-Herald career retrospective interview with Tagge and several other seniors set to play their last game for Nebraska. Offensive lineman Keith Wortman recounted his injuries, several of which, he said, came when the Huskers' hefty quarterback stepped on him. "When I was a kid, I always thought the players on the No. 1 team in the nation would be really something," Tagge said in response. "But here I am, playing on such a team, and we're nothing but a bunch of clowns."

The Huskers, favored by a touchdown by oddsmakers, didn't seem much interested in talking about Alabama. When Glover was asked what he thought of the Crimson Tide, he responded, "I'm just sitting by the pool listening to soul music on my radio." Also sitting poolside one day, Jacobson offered up a prediction of his own. "Come Saturday night, there won't be anything else to discuss," he said. "We'll still be No. 1, and Oklahoma will be back to No. 2."

Jacobson's prediction started looking good New Year's Day as the Huskers were holed up in the Ivanhoe on a rainy afternoon. They watched on TV as the Sooners pounded Auburn, 40-22.

The rain continued to fall in Miami all day, at times in torrents. The Alabama media figured the Bear would have the elements under control by game time, and sure enough, the rain stopped a half hour before kickoff. But soon, another kind of deluge began. As one scribe later would point out, this game indeed featured the nation's top two teams — one the Nebraska offensive squad, the other the Husker defense. With a showing of poise, power, balance and strength, Bob Devaney's Huskers would leave no doubt which college football team was No. 1 in 1971.

Jerry Tagge tries his luck at receiving at the Ivanhoe Hotel's pool in Miami.

Taking over at their own 47 after Alabama botched a punt snap on its first possession, Tagge quickly marched the Huskers toward the end zone. Kinney bulled over from the 2, a play that for him was now becoming so routine he could have patented it.

Then it was time for the incomparable Rodgers. Less than two minutes after Kinney's score, he dropped back to field a punt. He once again was surrounded by enemy red jerseys when he picked up the bouncing ball at his own 23. And then he showed that he may have picked up a few new moves from those hula girls a few weeks before. A dart right allowed him to escape Musso's diving tackle attempt. He made another hard cut, and he once again was running in the clear. Several great blocks gave him a clear lane down the sideline, Rodgers streaking right past a disgusted Bear. This time, Rodgers broke his rule and did look back. He had that luxury. There was no way anybody on this Alabama team could chase him down.

The 77-yarder was Rodgers' fourth punt return for a touchdown in Nebraska's last seven games — surely some kind of record — and Devaney later would say it completely demoralized Bryant's team. If the punt return didn't, the next play surely did. On the ensuing kickoff, the Alabama return man was decked by reserve middle guard Monte Johnson and coughed up the ball.

Nebraska, already leading 14-0, recovered just 27 yards from the Alabama goal line. Seven plays later, Tagge offered an imitation of his touchdown sneak in the previous year's Orange Bowl, lunging over from inside the 1.

Bad as that turn of events was for Bryant, things only got worse. The Blackshirts again shut down Musso and the Tide wishbone.

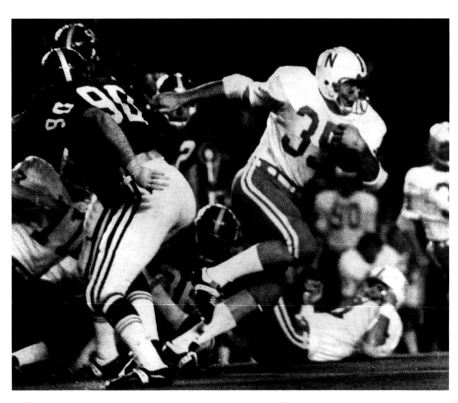

Jeff Kinney ran for 99 yards and a touchdown in his final game at Nebraska.

During the first half, Alabama would manage but 96 total yards. Despite often facing double teams, the ferocious Glover was dominating the middle of the field, where Alabama had made its hay all season. Kiffin later would say that Glover could have been playing in sweatpants that night, and the Crimson Tide still would not have been able to get past him.

With Tagge's flawless playmaking behind a man-handling offensive line, the Huskers again cruised right down the field. Tagge already could see: There isn't a play in our playbook that won't work tonight. Kinney, though limited by the flu, made two quick 8-yard runs to put NU near midfield. Then Tagge hit Rodgers with a 30-yard pass, but Rodgers was smacked as he tucked the ball away, and it bounded toward the goal line. Alabama recovered at the 2. Just two plays later, Glover made sure that was but a hiccup. He blasted the Alabama fullback, jarring the ball loose. Bob Terrio, the same Californian whose interception clinched the 1970 title, fell on the ball at the 4. He jumped to his feet and held the pilfered pigskin aloft, a moment that would land him on the cover of Sports Illustrated the next week.

Gary Dixon, in for Kinney, carried it in two plays later. The score capped a 28-0 Nebraska scoring barrage in the span of just over eight minutes. Almost nine minutes remained in the first half. But even the Bear knew this one was over. The Tide simply was overmatched against a pitiless Nebraska team that was bigger, faster and stronger.

By halftime, Rodgers and some of his offensive mates were talking about how they were going to celebrate later that night. To Devaney's credit, he resisted the urge to pour it on his old nemesis Bryant. The only Nebraska touchdown in the second half would come when Jim Anderson — the Tagge high school buddy who was starting his record 36th game for the Huskers — intercepted a pass and returned it to the Alabama 1. That provided one last moment of Husker glory for the forgotten Van Brownson. He sneaked over for the final points in Nebraska's 38-6 rout.

It was the worst defeat of Bear Bryant's Alabama career. And also Bob Devaney's finest moment. Four decades later, Osborne would choke up when speaking of what that night meant to Devaney. "That was a big moment for Bob," Osborne said, "so I will always remember that."

As he had against Oklahoma, Rich Glover overwhelmed a heralded opposing offensive line.

Devaney took that now-familiar ride atop players' shoulders back to the locker room, showered with "We're No. 1" chants. Husker fans were absolutely giddy. With back-to-back championships and a 24-0-1 two-year record, their Cornhuskers now were the undisputed kings of college football. As the school song proclaimed, there really was no place like Nebraska.

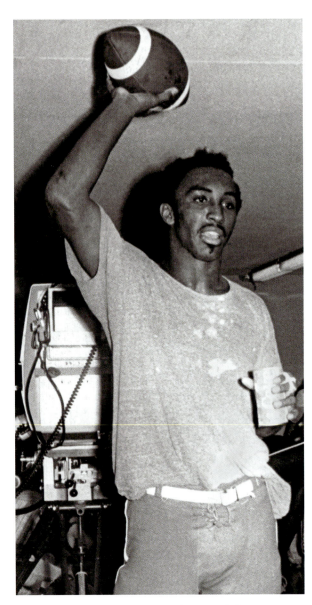

Rodgers announces the presentation of the game ball.

The locker room afterward was not quite the riotous place it had been after the win over LSU the year before. There was a lot of hugging but not a lot of screaming. This businesslike team had expected this result all year long. For players like Kinney and Tagge, there also was the bittersweet feeling that this was their last game as Huskers. "It's kind of sad knowing you won't be playing anymore for Nebraska," Tagge said. "But it's the greatest way in the world to leave."

Just as he did the year before, Johnny Rodgers stripped off his shoulder pads down to his sweaty T-shirt and climbed atop a bench. Perhaps someone might have expected him to again declare the Huskers "No. 1 in the world." Instead, he produced a moment that would speak to the closeness of this team — a crucial element in its run to two straight titles.

Rex Lowe

In the corner of the locker room, former Husker Rex Lowe sat in his wheelchair. The Milwaukee native had lettered at receiver for those turnaround 1969 Huskers. But at the end of that season, he'd been diagnosed with Hodgkin's lymphoma, cancer of the lymphatic system.

His teammates watched during the next year as Lowe's body withered away. The once-sturdy 200-pounder lost 40 pounds. But Lowe insisted on staying with the team during the 1970 season, coming to practice every day. Teammates were amazed by his positive attitude and resilience. "Rex was an inspiration to all of us," Kinney would recall.

And amazingly, Devaney even allowed Lowe to take the field on game days. He got in for a couple of plays in one early home game. And then during the home finale against K-State, he was introduced with the other seniors and again got to play a few snaps. Tagge even tried to hit him with a pass. Tears came to Devaney's eyes when he later was privately asked why he allowed the ailing Lowe to play. "He wanted so badly to be part of the team," Devaney had said. Indeed, those days with the 1970 Huskers, including being part of Nebraska's first national championship, would be some of the happiest moments of Lowe's life.

Soon after the 1970 season, Lowe graduated and returned home to Wisconsin, hoping to teach. He instead ended up back in the hospital, emerging in a wheelchair. Some Husker fans pooled money to help pay his airfare so he could watch his former teammates go for the repeat title in Miami. Lowe was now a wisp of his former self, his weight closer to 100 pounds. He was in such frail health that Devaney had arranged to have an ambulance bring him to the game. He sat watching on the Nebraska sideline before being rolled into the locker room afterward.

Lowe and the younger Rodgers weren't particularly close. But as members of the receivers position group, they were part of the same "club" on the team. And even now, to Rodgers and the other Huskers, Lowe still was part of that club and this team.

The 23-year-old Lowe watched from his wheelchair as Rodgers climbed atop that bench, holding a football high above his head. He shouted to shush his teammates and get their attention. "I know we always put it to a vote to see who gets the game ball," Rodgers said. "But I say it should go by acclamation to one of the greatest guys there is, Rex Lowe."

It was like a scene out of a saccharine sports movie. But this was real life. The room erupted in a thunderous cheer. Rodgers jumped down from the bench after his spur-of-the-moment gesture and swiveled his way over to the astonished Lowe. "Hey, Rex, this is yours ... from all the guys."

Lowe first tried to object. And then he started to cry. He buried his sobs in Rodgers' shoulder as the two embraced. "Thank you, thank you," Lowe said as tears rolled down his cheeks. Rodgers cried, too.

The image of Rodgers as just a pampered troublemaker disappeared in the embrace between the Huskers' spiritual leader and the inspiring Lowe. One reporter who witnessed it later would call it Rodgers' finest moment as a Husker.

More than any shower dousing or trophy presentation, that's the most vivid memory the 1971 Huskers would take from the post-game locker room scene. The poignant moment became even more meaningful six weeks later, when Rex Lowe died.

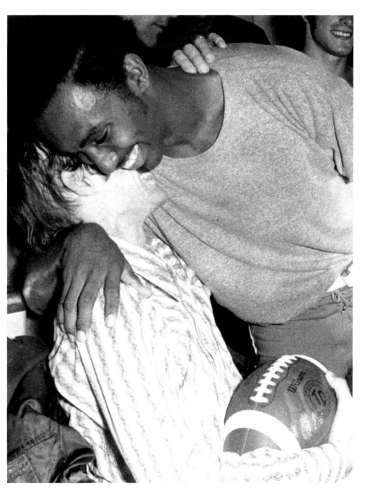

Rex Lowe embraces Rodgers, the ball firmly in his grasp.

In a more formal locker room ceremony, the Huskers accepted the MacArthur Bowl trophy, the award given by the National Football Foundation to the nation's No. 1 team. With No. 1 and No. 2 matched up in a bowl, the foundation had made the unprecedented decision to award the trophy right after the game.

Going into the Orange Bowl, the Huskers already had the United Press International national championship wrapped up, thanks to those early-voting coaches. But Nebraska's win over Alabama assured that the Huskers would not be sharing the 1971 championship with anyone. The release of the final Associated Press poll days later would be just a formality. In fact, the talk after the game quickly turned from who was No. 1 to another question: Were the 1971 Cornhuskers the greatest college football team ever?

Tagge, with Bruce Weber (61), ended his career as Nebraska's all-time total offense leader.

The Huskers were the first team to go 13-0 in a college football season. Other than Oklahoma, no team had played them closer than 24 points. And in the end, the Huskers had beaten the teams that would finish No. 2 (Oklahoma), No. 3 (Colorado) and No. 4 (Alabama) in the final AP poll. The last time any team had done that was … never. NBC's game announcers already had broached the best-ever subject while filling air time in the second half of the blowout. Others quickly were sharing similar thoughts.

"The only question left unanswered by Nebraska's efficient, often awesome display is whether the Cornhuskers are the most complete college football team ever," the New York Times said in its game dispatch. "Who can deny them serious consideration?"

Devaney himself weighed in after the game. "I thought going into this Orange Bowl game that our Nebraska football team was probably one of the greatest ever to play college football," he told reporters. "After tonight, I'm convinced of it."

Given their shared history, though, probably most meaningful to Devaney afterward was the assessment of the Bear. The humbled Alabama coach told reporters that Devaney's team "just flat-out whupped our butts in every way known to man." As to whether there had ever been a greater team, Bryant wasn't going to argue against Nebraska.

"I surely think they are one of the greatest, if not the greatest, team I have ever seen."

Nebraska Sen. Carl Curtis congratulates Kinney in the locker room after the game.

A Bittersweet Ending

IT SEEMED BOB DEVANEY HAD EVERYTHING perfectly scripted. He would announce that he would be stepping down after the 1972 season, making his 11th season on the Nebraska sideline his last. And then with another star-studded lineup that included the likes of Johnny Rodgers, Rich Glover, Willie Harper, John Dutton and Joe Blahak, his farewell tour of the Big Eight would end with a third national championship. He'd accomplish something no other coach had done in modern college football history — finish atop the polls three straight years. And then he would ride in his booster-supplied Cadillac happily into coaching retirement.

Nebraska's cheerleaders watch the Huskers' winning streak come to an end in Los Angeles.

But in the end, there would be no Hollywood ending for Devaney. That became clear in the Huskers' 1972 opener — a game that was played in the shadow of Tinseltown in the Los Angeles Coliseum. The Huskers' opponent that day, the UCLA Bruins, were quarterbacked by Mark Harmon, who would go on to become a twice Emmy-nominated TV star. Harmon would show that even back then he knew how to rework a script.

The Huskers went into that game huge favorites against a team that had won only two games the previous year. But with a stunning last-minute UCLA field goal, the mighty but mistake-prone Huskers fell, 20-17. Nebraska's 32-game unbeaten streak went poof. Moreover, the miserable night marked the start of a disappointing 9-2-1 Husker season. For Devaney and Nebraska's fans, whose expectations entering the season had been through the roof, 1972 would prove a major letdown. Not that it was something Devaney couldn't deal with. He'd shrug it off. Such was the game of football and life.

The course for Devaney's historic final season actually was set November 15, 1969, on the bus ride home from that stressful win over Kansas State. It was the young Tom Osborne whom Devaney called over to sit beside him. "Tom, I'm not sure how much longer I'm going to go at this," Osborne recalled him saying. "Maybe another year or so. And when I hang it up, I'd like you to take over."

UCLA quarterback Mark Harmon (7) tests the outside of Nebraska's defense.

Devaney indeed was ready to go. The job wasn't as easy or fun as it used to be, especially now that he had the additional duties of athletic director. The demands of recruiting were never-ending. And now there was off-season conditioning, too. Quite honestly, he'd later say, he was just getting tired of the grind. He was ready to settle full-time into his athletic director's chair.

Devaney was convinced that Osborne was the right man to coach the Huskers, a decision that had grown on him over time. He knew Carl Selmer, one of his offensive line coaches, badly wanted the job, and he felt he would have been a good coach. But Devaney didn't think Selmer was the kind of offensive innovator Osborne had proved to be. There was no doubt in Devaney's mind that, among all his assistants, Osborne had the best chance to be a successful head coach at Nebraska.

The indefinite nature of Devaney's declaration to Osborne, though, would make things somewhat uneasy over the next two years. When Devaney won that first national title the very next year, suddenly coaching didn't seem so bad. Devaney then decided 1971 would be his last year, only to have his Huskers repeat as champs. He again reconsidered, still not ready to hang up his whistle. With Rodgers and all those other great players coming back, he'd sure like to go for three.

Devaney appreciated how patient Osborne, now 34 years old, was being. Devaney wanted to make it clear to him there would be no more foot-dragging after the next season. Devaney also was becoming concerned around that time about the increasing interest Osborne was generating from schools looking for new coaches. We can't afford to lose him, Devaney thought. Devaney decided to make it official. The 1972 season would be his last.

He made the announcement in his office on Monday, January 17. One more year. Tom Osborne now will have the title of assistant head coach. And in 1973, he'll take over. "Next fall will be it, win, lose or draw," the 56-year-old Devaney said. "We certainly are planning on it being win."

David Humm

The news landed like a bomb in Nebraska. Devaney was at the height of his power and popularity. When Devaney headed back to Hawaii to coach in the Hula Bowl all-star game after the win over Alabama, one small-town paper suggested that he'd be able to walk to the island. During this election year, bumper stickers reading "Re-elect Devaney" also would become common sights in Nebraska. Everywhere he went to speak across the state, crowds gave him long standing ovations. (He'd typically thank them for it, saying, "It gives us all a chance to adjust our shorts.")

But because of their high regard, Nebraskans had faith that Devaney knew what he was doing. And any concern for the program's long-term health quickly was overwhelmed by excitement over the coming bid for a three-peat. "There's not a guy on the team who doesn't think it could happen," Devaney said that spring.

Indeed, there wasn't much reason to think they couldn't. Jerry Tagge, Jeff Kinney and Larry Jacobson were big losses off the championship teams. The roster remained loaded, though, including returning All-Americans in Harper, Rodgers and Glover. And though the Huskers needed to find a new starting quarterback, Devaney believed he had one in David Humm, a tall lefty from Las Vegas whom Husker coaches had been raving about for two years. Some said Humm, the nation's top 1970 quarterback recruit, threw the ball better than Tagge. He seemed more than capable of getting Rodgers the ball.

As Boyd Epley led the Huskers through their conditioning drills during the winter and spring of 1972, the players with each repetition would scream out their goal: "Three! Three! Three! Three!"

In retrospect, however, Devaney and his players later would say that some seeds of defeat were also being sewn heading into his last season.

Some later would consider Devaney's decision to serve as a lame-duck coach for a year to be a mistake. Selmer, Mike Corgan, John Melton and Cletus Fischer all had been disappointed when Devaney told them of his decision to name Osborne. And it led to tension. As Johnny Rodgers later would put it: "There were other coaches upset that they didn't get the job."

Humm threw for a school-record 2,259 yards and a Big Eight-record 18 touchdowns in his first year as a starter.

Osborne would agree there was some "uneasiness" on the staff during 1972. It was a difficult thing for coaches who had been with Devaney from the beginning to see him instead tap someone who had been in the business for far less time. Osborne said he didn't think the other coaches understood that he never had been angling to succeed Devaney. "I didn't seek the job," he said. "Bob put a lot of confidence in me, for whatever reason. I could see where it would be unsettling to some folks." Whether the feelings were justified or not, the staff unity that Devaney long had enjoyed was broken.

And with Osborne named the head coach in waiting, some players and coaches said they weren't sure whom to consider the boss. Selmer later would say he felt Devaney should have named his successor and immediately stepped aside or waited until after the year to announce his plans. "I think we lost a little something," he said. "Who do you pay attention to?" Harper later expressed similar sentiments. "It caused some confusion," he said. "I loved Osborne, but they were two different coaches."

Players believed in hindsight that there were other distractions going into 1972. Devaney and his entire coaching staff that summer coached a team of college all-stars in a game against the NFL's Dallas Cowboys. The staff spent a whole month in Chicago getting the team ready, and then practically came right back to Nebraska for two-a-days. That time in Chicago, players later said, could have been spent preparing for Nebraska's 1972 slate — including the UCLA opener.

After two years of demolishing every team in their path, the Huskers also lost some of their edge. "We weren't as hungry as we were when we started," Rodgers later would recall. Devaney later would say that some of the Huskers' success by that time also had gone to their heads. That's human nature. But it bred dangerous overconfidence. "We started to believe all the nice things that were written about us," Devaney later wrote. The coach admitted he may have been as guilty as anyone. He had seen the film of that 2-7-1 UCLA team from 1971. He was not impressed.

The Huskers were favored by 18 points when they took the field against a school far better known for John Wooden's championship basketball teams. While the Bruins' football coach was no Wizard of Westwood, he was a good one: Pepper Rodgers. Yes, the same sandwich-chucking, hard-luck Kansas coach the Huskers beat in 1969 to launch their current 32-game unbeaten string. The football gods knew irony when they saw it.

Combine a first-year quarterback and an oblong ball, and you are bound to get some crazy bounces. Humm threw two interceptions that night, and the Huskers lost three fumbles. It would become a season-long problem for Nebraska, which after collecting a school-record 26 more turnovers than they lost in 1971 would go -4 in 1972.

Meanwhile, UCLA's Harmon played like the son of a Heisman winner, which he just happened to be (Tom Harmon, Michigan, 1940). His first pass of the game went for a touchdown, a ball that ticked off Blahak's arm right into the hands of the receiver. The wishbone quarterback later ran for another score, staking the Bruins to a 17-10 third-quarter lead.

In spite of that, the talented Humm connected with Jerry List for a touchdown that tied the game at 17 early in the fourth quarter.

He and the Huskers, however, would generate little offense after that. Harmon drove the spunky Bruins from their own 43 in the closing minutes to set up Efren Herrera's game-winning field goal. It went through with just 22 seconds left. Bruins fans stormed the field, while the entire state of Nebraska was stunned. The unbeaten streak was gone. And so was Nebraska's No. 1 ranking. "We knew the winning streak had to end sometime," Devaney said afterward.

For the first time in almost three years, the Huskers had to learn to be gracious losers as well as graceful winners. And to the Huskers' credit, they would wake up and rally after that setback, knocking off their next seven opponents with the same machine-like precision of their 1971 kin. In fact, take away three games in 1972, and the Huskers won their other nine by an average score of 50-4. The seven straight wins helped the Huskers jump up to second and third in the polls — and back into the national championship picture.

> "It's not something you sit down and talk about. There's nothing that can be done about it now."
>
> **— Devaney, asked about the end of NU's winning streak**

Nebraska's Rich Glover (79) and Monte Johnson (37) watch the closing minutes of a disappointing 23-23 tie with Iowa State.

But then the Huskers traveled to Iowa State seeking Devaney's 100th career NU win and inexplicably laid another egg. On a sloppy field, NU made so many mistakes that only a CPA could total them, including eight turnovers, a critical penalty to stop a drive and a missed extra point. Then the Blackshirts allowed the Cyclones to drive the length of the field in the final minute for a touchdown that forged a 23-23 tie. That's the way it ended.

Afterward, Devaney couldn't remember being more disgusted with a Nebraska team, saying the Huskers played "like a bunch of farmers on a picnic waiting on somebody to bring their lunch." He was so mad that the players noted what bus Devaney was boarding and headed for the other one. As a further kick, Devaney whacked his head on the cargo door of the bus while tossing his bag on, drawing blood. It was a long ride back to Lincoln. Nebraska's reign atop the college football world clearly was over.

Devaney makes his last walk off the field at Memorial Stadium as Nebraska's head coach.

Two weeks later, the Huskers lost Devaney's final game in Lincoln, a Thanksgiving showdown with Oklahoma that could have allowed the Huskers to salvage at least a Big Eight championship.

With all the talent back on the field, it had been billed as another top-flight game. It was also seen as a head-to-head Heisman Trophy battle between two of the favorites, Rodgers and Greg Pruitt. But this one would not be confused for the classic the year before. OU lost four fumbles, two of them muffed punts that set NU up for both of its scores. The Huskers gained only 77 yards on the ground, manhandled by the Sooner front.

Late in the fourth quarter, the Huskers, just as they had a year earlier, trailed by 3 points. But there would be no last-minute heroics this year. Kinney was playing with the Kansas City Chiefs. NU's last two drives ended in interceptions, sealing the 17-14 defeat. It was Nebraska's first loss in Lincoln since the 1969 opener.

Rodgers grabbed Devaney's arm at the gun and said a few words, tears in the player's eyes. He and other Huskers were disconsolate over letting their coach down. Rather than being carried off in triumph one last time in Lincoln, Devaney walked out of The House That Bob Built alone in defeat.

The ballyhooed battle between the two Heisman candidates also was a dud that day. Pruitt, coming in hobbled by an ankle injury, carried only twice for 7 yards before leaving the game. Rodgers largely was shut down, stalked and chided all day by Pruitt's roommate, Ken Pope. Rodgers rushed four times for just 5 yards, caught three passes for 41, and his lone punt return netted 7 yards. Said Pope afterward: "I wonder if Greg will let me hold the Heisman Trophy sometimes." Just as for Devaney, it was a disappointing way for Rodgers to go out in his last home game.

In many ways, 1972 was a bizarre year for Rodgers. At one point he was engaged to a secretary for Playboy magazine, a former "Miss Sepia" he had met only weeks earlier while in Chicago to pose for the magazine's preseason All-America team. She quit her job and moved to Nebraska. But soon Rodgers and the young woman were fighting regularly, including one conflict, Devaney later said, where much of the furniture in Willie Harper's apartment was destroyed. She soon was back in Chicago. Rodgers later admitted the whole thing had been crazy.

Some also would argue that Rodgers by his senior year was no longer the same respected team-first player teammates earlier had praised. It seemed he truly believed he was Johnny R. Superstar. As Devaney would later put it, "By this time, John had become very impressed with his ability."

Defensive tackle Bill Janssen was even harsher when he popped off about Rodgers in a 1974 interview with a New York paper. "He was the greatest guy in the world when he was unknown, but as soon as he became famous he became impossible," Janssen said. "By the time he was a senior, he didn't have a friend on the team." Janssen two years earlier had been quoted saying how appreciative Rodgers was of the players who blocked for him on punt returns.

Janssen also described incidents of Rodgers during his senior year screaming at assistant coaches in practice. Devaney later would write of a dust-up he and Rodgers had in the locker room after the UCLA loss when Rodgers blamed the upset on the fact that the team had no black captain. Devaney gave him hell, telling him he was way off base. Osborne would recall another incident that year in which Rodgers grabbed the headphones from a coach during a game and complained to Osborne up in the press box that he wasn't getting the ball enough.

Oklahoma's Ken Pope hits Johnny Rodgers to break up a pass.

Rodgers also that year would get ruffled by bad publicity over his robbery conviction. After fielding few questions about it during the 1971 season, Rodgers was besieged before and during his senior year. The bogus marijuana arrest that spring and his driving under suspension conviction didn't help matters. The incidents made it easy for people to define him as a bad guy. Even many Husker fans were down on him, so much so that Rodgers was quoted as saying he had thought about quitting the team.

On the field during 1972, Rodgers also was a marked man. He didn't have the great supporting cast of years past. Teams did everything possible to keep from kicking the ball to Rodgers, with pooches, out-of-bounds shanks and even a third-down boot by Iowa State.

A BITTERSWEET ENDING 255

Rodgers pulls away from Kansas State's Fred Rothwell (59) on his way to a 52-yard punt return for a touchdown.

Despite all that, Rodgers again would put up huge numbers in 1972, scoring 16 touchdowns, including two more on dazzling punt returns. And his season capped one of the greatest careers in college football history.

The record book proved that. He set NCAA career marks for punt return touchdowns, kick return touchdowns and all-purpose yards. His 13.8-yard average each time he touched the ball on a run or kick return also was an NCAA record. And he scored a touchdown once every nine times he touched the ball. Only two players in the history of the college game had scored with more frequency, 1940s Army stars Doc Blanchard (8.2) and Glenn Davis (8.7). Devaney later would praise the way Rodgers performed in 1972 despite all the adversity he faced. "John Rodgers was a champion, in every sense of the word."

Going into 1972, Rodgers badly wanted to win the Heisman Trophy. In fact, years earlier Devaney had made Rodgers a deal: You drop your plans to play baseball at Nebraska, and when the time comes, we will promote you for the Heisman. When asked about his chances after the OU loss, Rodgers wasn't modest, referring to himself in the third person in proclaiming that no one was more deserving. "They may not give me the trophy," he said, "but Johnny Rodgers will always know that he won it."

At the time, a national debate was swirling around Rodgers' Heisman candidacy. Many argued his criminal past should disqualify him. Several voters who were members of the media proclaimed they would leave him off their ballots entirely. Devaney defended his star. "The Heisman is not a Sunday school or Fellowship of Christian Athletes trophy," he said. "It goes to the best football player on the field."

It was fortunate for Rodgers that with Pruitt injured at times, 1972 was a year without another clear standout Heisman candidate. And in many ways Rodgers would owe a great debt to brilliant Sports Illustrated writer Dan Jenkins, at the time one of the most influential voices in college football. In early November, Jenkins extolled Rodgers' on-field wizardry, saying the Husker had a knack for making a mere 6-yard run "into a journey into outer space."

"If the typesetters aren't careful," he colorfully wrote, "Nebraska's Johnny Rodgers may leap right out of this sentence, and then, like the hummingbird that he is, go flitting through ads, photographs, along the margins of the pages, in and out of other stories and maybe right out the back cover, if that is what it takes to beat somebody."

A BITTERSWEET ENDING 257

Most importantly, Jenkins chided Heisman voters who would make Rodgers out to be some kind of "mini-Capone." He concluded that the legal trouble Rodgers had run into in the three years since the robbery amounted to little more than running stop signs. Jenkins ended the piece: "Rodgers may not win the Heisman because no one knows how many of the 1,200 voters are anti-stop sign running. But there happens to be one — me — who intends to vote for the best player in the country, in or out of the courtroom, or in or out of a crowd of tacklers, and that player is Johnny Rodgers."

In a season where Rodgers caused a stir at one point by shuffling backward into the end zone on a TD against Missouri, he in the end didn't back into the Heisman. When the vote was announced December 5, he'd won in a landslide. He had nearly three times as many first-place votes as his buddy Pruitt. Rich Glover finished third — one of the best finishes ever by a defensive player. Glover's consolation prize would be winning both the Outland and the Lombardi Awards as the nation's best lineman — Nebraska's second straight Outland winner.

Rodgers actually was in New Jersey visiting Glover when he learned of the Heisman. Glover's brother drove him across the Hudson to the Downtown Athletic Club so he could be photographed that day with the award. It was an unbelievable moment for him to see the Heisman the first time, and it instantly changed his outlook. He was filled with gratitude for Devaney and all the others who had stood by him. "When I got underneath a punt or ready to catch a pass, it helped me to know there were about 80,000 fans there to help me," he told a reporter. "I know I haven't pleased everybody. But I now feel that I have more friends than enemies."

Rodgers thanked Devaney by asking him to stand in for his long-absent father at the Heisman ceremony a week later. Devaney was honored but had a prior commitment. Osborne went in his place, which Devaney considered more appropriate anyway, given the close mentoring relationship they'd had the past two years. "Sometimes when John didn't think he had a friend in the world," Devaney later would say, "Tom Osborne was there."

Rich Glover, Devaney and Rodgers show off their 1972 hardware.

During the black-tie gala in New York where Rodgers received his award, Rodgers teared up when thanking Osborne. The articulate Rodgers gave a good speech that night. He said the fact that he could win such an award after his past mistakes was an example for others who had been "crippled in life." He vowed to work to help others who were down. "On my way up, I'm going to try my damndest to reach down to younger people, black and white, and whoever grabs hold, I hope to pull with me."

At that point, though, there was only one person Rodgers was looking to pull up with him. In two weeks, during his final game in a Husker uniform, he wanted to help send out Bob Devaney with a victory. He wanted that even more than he'd wanted the Heisman.

Despite the disappointing season, the ninth-ranked Huskers were for the third straight year invited to Miami's Orange Bowl, this time to take on No. 12 Notre Dame. Even with no national championship on the line, going to a bowl still was a big deal. Winning a third straight Orange Bowl would be even bigger, something no school had ever done.

Devaney said he wouldn't be inspiring his team with any "win one for the Gipper" speeches, even if the opponent was Notre Dame, the school that gave the world the Gipper speech. Devaney joked that he'd already tried that against Oklahoma weeks earlier. Everyone saw the result.

Such speeches, of course, never were his style. And in reality, speech or not, Nebraska's players weren't even going to consider the possibility of losing their beloved coach's last game. "We could have beat anybody in the world that night, because we were not going to have Coach Devaney not go out a winner," Rodgers would recall. "It just wasn't going to happen."

When the game kicked off, the Husker offense took the field. And Johnny Rodgers left the huddle and lined up behind the quarterback in the I-back spot. Now everyone could see why the Huskers had again been practicing

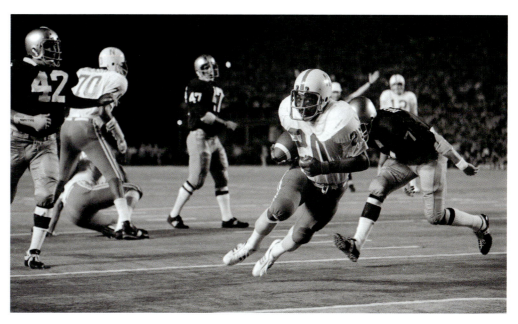

Rodgers darts past Notre Dame defenders on his way to one of his three rushing touchdowns.

in secrecy all week. On the game's first play, he tore through a hole for 13 yards. Minutes later, he took a pitch from Humm and pounded the ball 8 yards into the end zone. It was the start of a huge night for Rodgers and Devaney.

Rodgers had not played I-back since a few token snaps on the freshman team. Coaches didn't believe the 173-pounder could have taken the week-to-week pounding of the position in the Big Eight. But for one night, they thought it made sense, particularly after they'd seen the way the similarly slashing Anthony Davis of USC had sliced up the Irish a month earlier.

Putting Rodgers at I-back would make it easier to get the ball into his trusty hands. The move also showed that when it came to winning Devaney's last game, the Huskers were pulling out all the stops.

In the second period, Rodgers caught a lateral from Humm and surprised the Irish with a pass. His 45-yard heave hit a wide-open Frosty Anderson in stride. The 52-yard touchdown play put Nebraska up 20-0 at the half.

In the third quarter, Rodgers really cut loose. The I-back logged two more touchdowns on 3- and 5-yard runs. And then to cap his sensational Husker career, he took a short screen pass and did all the rest himself. He outran four Irish defenders and then beat the last one by cutting so hard the poor guy fell flat on his back. It was Rodgers' final college touchdown, coming on his final play as a Husker.

For the night, Rodgers had scored an Orange Bowl-record four touchdowns and passed for another — a performance that laid to rest any doubt as to whether he was a deserving Heisman winner. No previous winner had ever finished his career with such a flourish.

As a team, the Huskers again were playing like the national champions, with the Blackshirts also making the night a long one for the Irish. The final was 40-6, the worst loss Notre Dame had suffered since World War II. It was worse than the 22 points by which USC — the 1972 national champions — had beaten the Irish weeks earlier at home. If not for a couple of bad days, this Nebraska team had the talent to be right up there. In the end, Devaney's last team finished a respectable No. 4 in the final AP poll.

> "I just ran around thanking the boys and was so busy trying to reach them all I almost forgot our after-game prayer."
>
> — Devaney

As the final seconds clicked down on the 101st and last victory of Devaney's NU career, the smiling coach was pounded on the back by his players and then hoisted up for one last victory ride. In the locker room, he made a point of trying to thank every coach and player. He still wasn't ready when the press swooped in. He frequently interrupted his final post-game press conference to hug and thank players.

Reporters asked what it would be like to watch the Huskers from the stands from now on. "I can manage," he said. They pressed him, wanting him to offer some kind of dramatic career-ending statement. But Devaney said he didn't "go for drama." He did share this pearl: It felt a lot better to win than to lose.

If reporters were looking for Devaney to be sentimental, they should have been in Omaha a month earlier. The occasion was Devaney's weekly meeting with boosters where he showed film of the Huskers' latest game. Devaney usually would have a drink or two at such gatherings, and it would have been almost a necessity on this night: They were watching the Oklahoma film.

Whether it was the less-formal setting or the highballs, Devaney did turn a bit wistful that night before the 500 fans in Omaha's Elks Lodge. He confided that he had come into his final season with great aspirations for what it would have meant to him, his program and the whole state to win a third straight national title. "But I've been disappointed before, and I'll be disappointed again," he said.

Devaney also said he considered himself lucky. He was grateful he had been able to be part of something so great in his adopted home state. The Huskers couldn't have done it without the support of the people from Omaha to Lincoln to the state's far reaches. Then he expressed confidence in where the program was headed in the future, saying it was in good hands with Tom Osborne.

"After he's coached here a few years, you'll say, 'Who's that fellow Devaney?' " the coach said. "He'll be a lot better at figuring out what to do on Saturdays than I did.

"But the thing is, I had fun doing it."

Randy Borg (19), Jerry List (85), Mike Beran (62) and Joe Blahak (27) help Devaney celebrate his final victory.

Epilogue

BOB DEVANEY ALWAYS USED TO JOKE that the size of his funeral would be determined by the weather. Well, May 14, 1997, broke as a beautiful spring day in Lincoln. But that had nothing to do with making the final rites for the godfather of modern Nebraska football arguably the biggest funeral in Nebraska history.

There were some 700 people in attendance, and the proceedings were carried live statewide on TV. Surely thousands across Nebraska that day took time to remember the man who built a college football powerhouse and, in the process, lifted an entire state.

Osborne speaks at Bob Devaney's funeral in 1997.

Devaney's death at age 82 came nearly a quarter century after he coached his last game, but only four years after he'd finally stepped down as Nebraska's athletic director. Befitting a state funeral, the governor spoke, telling of the man whose accomplishments extended far beyond the football field. "He gave us a winning team, but he gave us something extra," Ben Nelson said. "He gave us pride in our state and in ourselves."

Not all the talk was so high-minded and serious. Of course, there were lots of stories and laughs, too. Tom Osborne joked of how Devaney used to punish players by having them run laps around the not-so-svelte John Melton. Jerry Tagge told how he knew when he was playing poorly. "All I had to do was look at the sidelines, and coach would have his arm around Van Brownson," he said.

The line likely invoked a chuckle from Tagge's old quarterback rival, who also was in the church that day. In fact, most of the coaches and key players from Devaney's 1970 and 1971 championship teams were there. Their names read like a list straight out of the Nebraska football hall of fame: Johnny Rodgers. Tagge. Jeff Kinney. Rich Glover. Monte Kiffin. Guy Ingles. Bob Newton. It was as if they had gathered at Schulte Field House for another team meeting.

In private moments, the old Huskers shared stories that day. Ingles liked to tell of how he served as Devaney's financial adviser in his later years. The first account status Ingles checked every morning was Devaney's. Even decades later, he still didn't want to let his coach down.

Steve Runty, who would mostly serve as a backup quarterback throughout his Husker career, had a favorite Devaney story, too. Of how in the late 1970s he found himself standing next to Devaney at a urinal in a downtown Lincoln hotel. Without any provocation, Devaney blurted, "I should have started you at UCLA in 1972." Runty knew Devaney didn't really mean it. But years after their Big Red days were over, Devaney still was trying to build up Runty. It was just Devaney's way.

Bob Devaney traveled to Nebraska's 1995 game at Michigan State, where he had begun his college coaching career.

Devaney in 1990 posed with commemorative trophies of his two national championships.

In fact, as those former Huskers sat in First Plymouth Church that day in 1997, each could reflect on how Bob Devaney and the Nebraska football experience had touched their lives in ways that served them long after they left Lincoln. That remained no less true in the many years after Devaney's 1997 passing.

TOM OSBORNE KNEW when he took over for Devaney in 1973 that it would be extremely difficult to follow a legend. There indeed were some rough patches early when his teams couldn't figure out how to stop that Oklahoma wishbone. Osborne appreciated how Devaney as athletic director always stood by him without interfering. In the end, Osborne would build a coaching legacy that would stand on its own as among the greatest the college game has seen. And he did it with a style that was profoundly shaped by those great Devaney years.

After the Orange Bowl had secured the 1971 national title, Osborne sat on the bus in a bit of a stupor, contemplating what the team had accomplished. This was supposed to be the sport's greatest achievement. Yet he couldn't help feeling hollow inside. He got back to the Ivanhoe and sat on the bed, driving wife Nancy crazy. "Everybody's celebrating," she said. "Let's go do something!" But he continued to sit and reflect. And he had an epiphany, one that would guide him through his own days leading the Huskers.

The real joy of athletics isn't the winning, he decided. Rather, it can be found in the process, the path the coaches and players follow as they strive toward a shared goal. The relationships they form. The life lessons they learn. The rings and trophies are nice, but they're just things. It's those experiences that will carry them through the rest of their lives.

That became Osborne's guiding philosophy during 25 years on the Husker sideline. Every year, he worked to instill in his players the values he believed would serve them in their lives' endeavors: Give great effort. Be disciplined. Do things the right way. Persevere. Stay humble. And keep your eyes on higher purposes.

Following his process each year, he developed close relationships with his players — a lesson he originally had learned from Devaney — and transformed countless boys into men. And in the process, he and his players won a lot of games.

Osborne would take the foundation that Devaney built and turn Nebraska into the most consistent winner in the history of college football. Not once during his quarter century on the sideline would the Huskers fail to win at least nine games or fail to go to a bowl. The streak of bowl seasons later would stretch to 36 years under Osborne's handpicked successor, Frank Solich.

And though it took awhile, Osborne eventually would bring Nebraska back to the very pinnacle of college football. Osborne won his own back-to-back national championships in 1994 and 1995. There are amazing parallels between those two championship years and Devaney's 1970 and 1971 Huskers. As with Devaney, the twin titles came after the head coach re-examined his program top to bottom in the wake of disappointing years. Like Devaney, Osborne's first national title was achieved by a two-headed quarterback, Tommie Frazier and Brook Berringer. Like Devaney, the second title came after one of the team's biggest stars, Lawrence Phillips, was arrested in a sensational criminal case.

Then in 1997, less than eight months after Bob Devaney died, Osborne led Nebraska to another national title, the school's fifth. He retired after that game. Osborne's record in his final five years: 60-3, with three national championships. No coach in college football history exited the sport on a higher note. Bob Devaney sure knew how to pick them.

LIKE MANY OF THE OTHER STARS of the championship Husker teams, Jeff Kinney dreamed of making it big in the NFL. He was off and running when Kansas City drafted him in the first round. But he soon learned why they say NFL stands for Not For Long.

He found the way coaches treated players to be degrading and dehumanizing. He went through a coaching change, and suddenly he was just another name on the roster. He got shipped to Buffalo and spent a couple of years blocking for O.J. Simpson. It wasn't much fun. One time a teammate gave him a hand slap after a good play. The coach turned around and kicked Kinney in the rear end. "We don't have that college crap here," the coach said.

"It definitely wasn't like Nebraska," Kinney said. He got out of the business. He spent his real professional career in the investment and banking business in Chicago, Kansas City and Denver.

Even outside Nebraska, he still would get asked about what it felt like during that last drive of the Game of the Century — still the only so-named game that lived up to its billing. He thought it was funny. They were just college kids living in the moment and playing a game, not thinking in terms of achieving great or timeless things.

But he remained proud of what he and his teammates accomplished. "We were just ordinary guys who had a special chemistry," he said. "You realize you were part of something special, and you're grateful for that."

> "We were just ordinary guys who had a special chemistry. You realize you were part of something special, and you're grateful for that."
>
> — Jeff Kinney

AFTER WINNING THAT SECOND ORANGE BOWL, Tagge was also drafted in the first round, and by his hometown Green Bay Packers. You would think that was a dream. But the Packers were an aging team past their prime, with receivers that weren't even as good as those Tagge had at Nebraska. He was soon out of the game, turning to a career in business.

He at first did investment and real estate work in the St. Louis area. Then he was offered a job in Omaha. "I thought, if I'm going into a sales field, maybe the people will remember who I am," he said. Did they ever. He indeed found the Tagge name still had luster in Nebraska. He eventually co-founded a successful investment firm.

Tagge and Rodgers enjoyed time with Devaney and wife Phyllis in 1992.

Late in Bob Devaney's life, Jerry Tagge reconnected with his old coach. It started in 1994 when they went on an autograph signing tour. Tagge couldn't begin to count how many times he signed pictures of himself reaching that ball over the goal line. But Tagge enjoyed seeing Devaney again work his magic with the public. He'd tell stories, charm the ladies and try to guess kids' ages. It was the same old Bob.

Tagge and his wife continued to regularly visit Devaney in Lincoln until his death. The coach had good days and bad. Sometimes it was, "Remember that Kansas game in 1969 when you threw the ball over McFarland's head?" Other times it was, "Who are you?" But Tagge treasured those last days they had together.

Unlike many of his former teammates, Tagge didn't wear championship rings. It's not that he wasn't proud of those days and fond of the guys he played with. But it did sometimes get a little old being a Nebraska football celebrity. All anyone ever wanted to ask him about was the Game of the Century. He would prefer to talk about his grandkids. In fact, he said he'd take having his grandkids fight about who gets to sit on his knee over a national championship ring any day of the week. "That's the real stuff," he said.

DESPITE BEING THE ODD MAN OUT in Nebraska's quarterback battle, Van Brownson still was drafted by the Baltimore Colts. He never made it out of camp. His football days were over. His drinking days were not. It finally reached the point where he could imagine drinking himself to death. In 1977, he sought help.

Adrian Fiala would recall working with Brownson in 1980 for a Lincoln radio station that broadcast Husker games. They flew to Penn State for a game and went out that night. When the waitress got to Brownson, he ordered a soft drink. "I'm pretty impressed here, my friend," Fiala told him. As of 2014, Brownson had been sober for 37 years.

Brownson eventually went back to Shenandoah to take over the family implement business. Then in 2001, he decided to return to the university, cleaning up the academic mess he'd left in Lincoln three decades before and getting his degree in business.

Even four decades after his playing days, Brownson looked like he could play quarterback, fit and still at his playing weight of 190 pounds. "Believe me, sometimes I could convince myself I could play," he said in a 2014 interview. "At least until somebody hit me."

He truly had no bitterness about how his Husker career turned out. "It seems like everything is hard to deal with when you're 18 to 22 years old," he said. "But it wasn't anything I held anyone else responsible for. It was something only I was responsible for." And Brownson remained proud of what they all accomplished as a team. He knew he contributed to those twin championships, even though most Husker fans just think of him as Tagge's backup.

"Because of the way it played out, the course of history has me as the backup quarterback," Brownson said. "But I never, even my senior year, thought of myself as the backup quarterback. And I don't think Jerry or anyone else on the team did, either."

It seems Bob Devaney appreciated Brownson's contributions to his best Nebraska teams. Long after he retired, on the wall of awards and mementos that hung in his rec room was a copy of that staged World-Herald photo of Brownson and Tagge. They still were both clutching that single pigskin.

Tagge and Brownson proved from the beginning of their careers that they were willing to share the load to help their team.

JERRY MURTAUGH DIDN'T ATTEND Bob Devaney's funeral. But he said it wasn't because of his sour relationship with Devaney — he was out of town. In fact, he says, he and Devaney long before had buried the hatchet on their conflicts as player and coach.

When Devaney retired as coach following the 1972 season, the school held a big retirement party. Devaney's wife phoned Murtaugh and asked him to attend the event, even though she acknowledged Devaney didn't want him there. "That makes two of us," Murtaugh told her. But out of respect for her, Murtaugh went.

Murtaugh was there shooting the bull with some ex-teammates when someone grabbed him by the ear. It was Phyllis Devaney, and she dragged him across the floor over to her husband. "Bob. Jerry. Talk!" she said, leaving them together. They stood there for a time awkwardly looking at each other. Then Devaney asked, "Do you want a beer?" They walked over to the bar. And over drinks, they shared the best conversation they'd ever had. It was a great time. Murtaugh would remember one thing in particular that Devaney said that night.

"Everyone talks about what a great coach I was. They're throwing this party and doing this and that for me," he recalled Devaney saying. "I'm not a great coach. But I was smart enough to hire the eight greatest assistants in the country."

Murtaugh spent 30 years as a railroad conductor before retiring. Over the years, he mellowed. He stopped drinking as much. He started hosting a Saturday morning radio show in Omaha where he interviewed Husker legends of years past. "He didn't talk much in college," Tagge said in 2014. "He won't shut up today."

And the mean Husker who hit like a ton of bricks showed he had a soft spot. He formed the Husker Greats Foundation, which raises money for former Huskers who have fallen on hard times. His teammates said they were more proud of that Jerry Murtaugh than the one who helped lead them to the 1970 national championship. "I made a lot of mistakes," he said years later. "But I had a great time. I won't take anything back."

JOHNNY RODGERS IN 1973 WAS DRAFTED by the NFL's San Diego Chargers, but he spurned their offer to instead sign with Montreal of the Canadian Football League. Why? They offered him a $100,000 contract. He finally got that $100,000 he dreamed of as a kid. Rodgers won rookie of the year and went on to win a CFL championship before going to the Chargers.

Johnny the Jet had some jet-set years as a pro. After the relative deprivation of college ("NCAA — No Cash At All," he'd say), he now had big bucks to go with his fame. There were fast cars. Fur coats. Drugs. Women. He still was the same daring guy who once had caught BBs with his hands, hated fair catches and robbed for sport. "I was wild," he'd say of those days. "Just wild."

Injuries soon ended his pro career. For a while, the entrepreneur was doing well in San Diego as founder and publisher of a cable TV guide. Then, ironically, in 1985 he had a conflict with a cable TV installer at his home and was arrested on suspicion of assault. While that conviction was thrown out on appeal, Rodgers still was found guilty of being a felon in possession of a handgun. He was considered a felon because of that Lincoln robbery, "10 minutes of insanity" that continued to haunt him. Rodgers' fall was steep. His legal and financial problems eventually led to bankruptcy.

In 1989, Rodgers returned to his native Omaha. He said he was coming back to start a youth foundation to help kids in north Omaha. But it also was a chance for Rodgers to make a new start in life.

In Omaha, the Rodgers name still was worth a lot. He found success as a sports marketer, his "Jetwear" company developing new licensed retail products bearing the Husker logo. He's been devoted to his five children, four of whom were born before he left Lincoln. He's received praise for his foundation's work in north Omaha.

During his work with kids, Rodgers would encourage them to stay in school. There was one problem, though. Rodgers never had finished his own college degree. So he returned to Lincoln and actually earned two bachelor's degrees, in marketing and broadcasting.

Rodgers also established the "Jet Award," each year recognizing the top kick returner in college football and feting him at a charity banquet. While some might think it a bit presumptuous to give an award named after yourself, in Rodgers' case it fit. He's still arguably the best kick returner college football has seen. No single kick return in football history has been written about, spoken of or broadcast more often than Johnny's amazing trip during the Game of the Century.

And in 2013, a state board voted the imperfect Rodgers a full pardon for his 1971 robbery conviction. Finally after more than 40 years, his criminal slate was wiped clean.

Rodgers still had regular contact with his old teammates. His latest goal in 2014 was to see all his 1971 teammates recognized by having the entire team inducted as a group into the school's athletic hall of fame. He still valued and treasured those years.

Rodgers gets a hug from his mother, Ardella Rodgers, after gaining a pardon in 2013.

"Those are the greatest days of my life," he said. "White guys, black guys — we were just guys. We played together, hurt together, laughed together and won together."

THE 1971 HUSKERS GATHERED in Lincoln in 2011 for a 40th anniversary celebration. As was typical when the men — by this time in their late 50s and early 60s — got together, they spent as much time talking about grandkids and Social Security as they did football. Rodgers was speaking at the podium when he was interrupted by a man bearing an envelope. He encouraged Rodgers to open it.

It was from the editors of Sporting News magazine. They thought the anniversary celebration was the appropriate time to let those old Huskers in on some news: The magazine soon would be naming the 1971 Nebraska Cornhuskers the greatest team in the 125-year history of college football. Naturally, a big cheer went up in the room. And again, they felt the pride. The Sporting News is not the only organization that has looked back at the 1971 Cornhuskers and decided they passed the test of time. ESPN five years earlier went through a similar exercise and also ranked those Huskers as the best. In 2002, the Sagarin ratings computer looked at every team's performance and strength of schedule since 1956 and determined that 1971 Nebraska ranked second-best, behind only Tom Osborne's 1995 Nebraska team.

There's no question, the legacy of Devaney's final Nebraska teams has endured in Nebraska and beyond. Generations of Nebraska fans who never lived during the Devaney days would come to know that the school won back-to-back titles in 1970 and 1971. Those titles stand as pillars of Nebraska football history as much as Osborne's later 1990s titles.

Of course, no empire stands forever. While Nebraska football in the 21st century remained a cultural phenomenon and a tremendous source of state pride, it had lost its place among the true elite of the sport. In 2013 — the year the school erected a long-overdue statue of Devaney outside Memorial Stadium — Nebraska had gone 14 years without winning even a conference championship. Several times it had seemed to Nebraskans that their beloved Huskers were on the cusp of returning to past glory, only to see them stumble at a key moment. It became a source of consternation among fans longing for the greatness of the past.

If Devaney still were alive, what would he have thought of that state of affairs? It's hard to think he would have gotten too worked up about it. His thinking might be in line with some words he said just days after that 1971 national championship had put him at the very top of his sport.

During a speaking engagement in Lincoln, he was surprised with a plaque thanking him for his contributions. He first joked that he'd hang it in his living room in place of the picture of his father-in-law. Then he said he'd hang it in his rec room with his other career mementos. Something else he could gaze upon to fondly recall those unforgettable years. "If we lose one sometime," he said, "I'll pour myself another drink and say, 'We were pretty good at one time.' "

Other than being familiar with the names Rodgers, Kinney and Tagge and perhaps seeing the Game of the Century on the ESPN Classic network, most Nebraska fans who came along after the Devaney years would know little of the real story behind his championship teams. They'd have no idea that those great years arose from the ashes of the coach's 47-0 flameout in Norman in 1968.

The story of how Devaney went from his career low point to just three years later fielding the greatest team of all time ranks as one of the remarkable turnaround stories in sports. Under Devaney's leadership, there came a convergence of extraordinary people and exceptional events. "It starts with a leader. The catalyst was Bob," Tagge said years later. "But if Tom Osborne wasn't on the staff, none of this would have happened. Put Johnny Rodgers on the other team, and we might lose two games a year." Tagge could have mentioned his own vital contributions as well.

When you get down to it, the story of how Devaney engineered that stunning turnaround is also the story of how Nebraska football became Nebraska football. Many of the elements that stood for decades as hallmarks of the Husker program were born during those final Devaney years: the offensive innovation of Tom Osborne; the cutting-edge weight training program; Outland Trophy-winning linemen; the driven walk-on kids who provided a special edge; the epic head-to-head Thanksgiving battles with Oklahoma; that iconic red N on the sides of the helmet; the perennial contention for national titles.

They became as much a part of Nebraska football as stadiums packed with red-clad fans and Go Big Red chants. Those great Devaney years marked the birth of the Big Red dynasty.

"There's nobody that deserves a statue more than Bob Devaney," Osborne said when the bronze artwork was unveiled in 2013.

Acknowledgments

After The World-Herald published the 2012 book "Unbeatable" — the story of Tom Osborne's national championship teams at Nebraska — I told my editors that at some point we should consider writing the "prequel." That is, the story of Bob Devaney's championship teams. I have to thank our book editor, Dan Sullivan, and the paper's executive editor, Mike Reilly, for giving me the chance to do that.

As a Nebraskan who came along after the Devaney years, I knew little about the history behind NU's 1970 and 1971 teams. How pleasantly surprised I was to find a wealth of fascinating characters and amazing story lines: Devaney's 1968 career nadir; the two young geniuses he turned to; the powerlifting pole vaulter who revolutionized football; the timely arrival of the "super sophs"; the team rebel who willed the team to No. 1; the flawed but incomparable kid from Omaha's ghetto; the stars aligning on a warm night in Miami; and the epic clash in Norman that still resonates with fans today. All combined to give birth to the Big Red dynasty.

Like "Unbeatable," this book is a historical narrative that taps the memories of many of the principal participants. Among those who generously gave their time in more than 70 hours of interviews were Jerry Tagge, Johnny Rodgers, Tom Osborne, Jeff Kinney, Jerry Murtaugh, Van Brownson, Guy Ingles, Monte Kiffin, Mike Green, Adrian Fiala, Jim McFarland, Ken Geddes, Bob Newton, Dave Morock, Steve Runty, Bill Kosch, Wally Winter, Warren Powers, Don Bryant, George Sullivan and Boyd Epley. Mike Devaney also provided some new insight into his father's life. It was a pure joy to get to know those men and have the chance to share their stories.

Understanding that memories can fade, their words were backstopped when possible with The World-Herald's archives and the great writings of reporting legends like Wally Provost, Tom Ash and Gregg McBride. Special thanks to World-Herald librarian Jeanne Hauser for helping me dust off those archived accounts. I also utilized many other resources, including several books written of those years: Devaney's own memoir, "Devaney"; "Go Big Red" and "Bob Devaney" by James Denney, Hollis Limprecht and Howard Silber of The World-Herald; Michael Corcoran's "The Game of the Century"; Robert Knoll's "Prairie University"; Bryant's "Tales from the Nebraska Sidelines"; Osborne's "More Than Winning"; Dave Newhouse's "After the Glory: Heismen"; George Mills' "A View From the Bench"; and Rodgers' "An Era of Greatness." Other useful information was found in the colorful pages of Sports Illustrated, in dispatches from the Associated Press, Miami News, Sporting News and New York Times, and on the Huskers.com and HuskerMax websites.

Devaney posed in 1972 with a bronze bust commissioned by the Omaha Chamber of Commerce to honor him for Nebraska's two national championship teams.

Devaney emerges from a shower after the Game of the Century.

Special acknowledgments are due to retired World-Herald photographer Rich Janda, whose old negatives produced never-before-seen images from some of Nebraska's greatest games, to Jolene McHugh, for digitally cleaning up old prints in the World-Herald archives, and to Paul Jacobsen and his unmatched library of Husker videos.

Special thanks, too, to my wife, Susan, and daughters, Thelma and Lucy, for indulging me in this pursuit, particularly in the final frantic weeks. I would also be remiss if I did not thank the fans of Nebraska football, whose passion drives the entire enterprise and makes books like this even possible.

I've heard from many who enjoyed getting new insight into the Osborne years through "Unbeatable." I hope fans find this account equally illuminating. Of course, what NU fans would really like is for their beloved Huskers to once again ascend the throne in college football. For their sake, I hope to be able to come back one day and write a book that completes a Husker football trilogy. Who knows?

ABOUT THE AUTHOR

Henry J. Cordes has spent more than 30 years as a reporter for The World-Herald, covering crime, the Statehouse, politics, regional and national public policy and, on occasion, Nebraska football. He also is the author of "Unbeatable," a book about Tom Osborne's championship teams at Nebraska. Four times he has received the University of Nebraska-Lincoln's Sorensen Award for distinguished Nebraska journalism. A graduate of Omaha Central High School and the University of Nebraska at Omaha, he lives in Omaha with his wife and twin daughters.

Credits & Photographers Index

BY HENRY J. CORDES

EDITOR
Dan Sullivan

DESIGNER
Christine Zueck-Watkins

PHOTO IMAGING
Jolene McHugh

CONTRIBUTING EDITORS
Rich Mills, Pam Thomas, Bob Glissmann, Jim Anderson, Kathy Sullivan

RESEARCHERS
Jeanne Hauser, Sheritha Jones

INTELLECTUAL PROPERTY MANAGER
Michelle Gullett

PRINT AND PRODUCTION COORDINATORS
Pat "Murphy" Benoit, Wayne Harty

DIRECTOR OF MARKETING
Rich Warren

DIRECTOR OF PHOTOGRAPHY
Jeff Bundy

PHOTOGRAPHERS
Allan, Tom: Front cover, 14, 27, 49, 103, 137
Associated Press: i, 15, 47, 50, 107, 129, 140, 159, 161, 215, 239, 241, 249, 258, 259, 261
Batson, Bill: 31
Beiermann, Jeff: 262
Breci, Sebi: 105, 131
Bundy, Jeff: 266
Burnett, James R.: 117
Haas, Clark: 6
Hall, Pat: 41
Janda, Richard: Back cover, ii, 63, 95, 170, 174, 188, 209, 212, 225, 226, 227, 228, 230, 231, 233, 235, 246
Johnson, Phil: 96, 99, 118, 150, 176, 189, 207, 263
Machian, Chris: 271
McGaffin, Ronnie: 6
Melangagio, Yano: 28
Paskach, Robert: 73, 125, 126, 127, 128, 238, 264, 267
Plambeck, Tom: 29, 62, 180, 197
Savage, John: 32, 72
Smith, Rudy: Back cover, 76, 119, 198

REPRINT INFORMATION
Omaha World-Herald photos are available from the OWHstore.
Call 402-444-1014 to place an order or go to OWHstore.com.

Relentless Jeff Kinney takes another step toward the end zone on the final drive of the Game of the Century.

Index

Adkins, John 142, 150, 159, 163, 172, 204, 212, 213, 223
Alvarez, Barry 124
Anderson, Frosty 196, 260
Anderson, Jim 61, 150, 151, 167, 200, 203, 211, 218, 232, 234, 243
Armstrong, Neil 46
Ash, Tom 272
Atlas, Charles 44
Austin, Al 228
Ayala, Ron 126, 128
Aycock, Steve 223

Babcock, Gib 42, 116
Barnes, Walt 15
Bauer, Henry 5
Bell, Roy 217
Benning, Don 111
Beran, Mike i, 190, 261
Berringer, Brook 265
Bible, Dana X. 5
Blahak, Joe i, 54, 148, 150, 152, 188, 189, 204, 212-214, 219, 232, 248, 252, 261
Blanchard, Doc 257
Booker, Michael 53
Booth, Bummy 4
Boozer, Bob 108
Bordogna, John 68
Borg, Randy 261
Bowles, Glenn 72, 73
Brahaney, Tom 215, 223
Branch, Jim 192
Bratten, Jim 78
Bremser, Lyell 117, 213
Briscoe, Marlin 108-110
Brockington, John 158
Brown, Bob 11, 16, 97
Brown, Ralph 53
Brownson, Van 29, 56-65, 68, 69, 76, 78-84, 88-90, 92, 94, 99, 101, 106, 115, 116, 120, 125, 126, 132-141, 144, 148, 157-159, 167, 168, 192-196, 243, 262, 266, 267, 272
Broyles, Frank 38
Bryant, Anita 160
Bryant, Don 20, 70, 74, 158, 176, 272
Bryant, Joan 20
Bryant, Paul "Bear" 2, 15, 50, 51, 93, 118, 129, 236, 238-240, 242, 243, 246
Buchanan, Pat 174

Cardwell, Lloyd 5
Carlson, Dennis 37
Carstens, Jim 126, 142, 189, 190

Casanova, Tommy 162
Chandler, Albert 223
Christie, Dick 111, 112
Claridge, Dennis 11
Coffee, Al 167
Cole, Bobby 149
Corgan, Mike 3, 12, 18, 27, 36, 84, 91, 92, 99, 101, 172, 177, 221, 227, 251
Cosby, Bill 130
Crosswhite, Leon 204, 214, 215, 217-219
Crowder, Eddie 150
Cunningham, Sam 129
Curtis, Carl 247

Damkroger, Maury 230
Daugherty, Duffy 8, 9, 11, 15, 32, 46
Davis, Anthony 259
Davis, Clarence 118, 129, 130
Davis, Dick 27, 110
Davis, Glenn 257
Dawson, Fred 4, 5, 10
DeRogatis, Al 165
Devaney, Bob i, 1, 2, 3, 6-38, 40, 42, 44, 46, 48, 50-56, 58-66, 68-74, 76, 78-81, 83, 84, 86, 88, 90-94, 96-99, 101, 102, 104-106, 113, 115, 117, 119-122, 124-126, 130-132, 134-138, 141, 142, 145, 146, 148, 150-160, 162, 163, 165, 167-170, 172-177, 179, 180-184, 186, 188-192, 194-196, 198-200, 203, 205, 206, 208, 210, 211, 213, 215, 216, 218, 220, 221, 224, 227, 230, 232, 233-236, 238-240, 242-244, 246, 248, 250-255, 257-268, 270-273, 278
Devaney, Mike 8, 172
Devaney, Phyllis Wiley 8, 21, 266, 268
Dickey, Lynn 83, 142-144, 150, 152
Didur, Dale 52, 53
Dietzel, Paul 169
Dixon, Gary 193, 227, 243
Donaldson, Carl 6
Douglas, Paul 178, 182, 183
Douglass, Bobby 59
Duda, Fred 17
Dumler, Doug 144, 147, 148, 150, 167, 170, 193, 228, 239
Dutton, John 54, 55, 189, 248
Dvorsak, Tony 63, 65
Dye, Tippy 9, 10

Elliott, Bob 9
Epley, Boyd 43-46, 150, 190, 192, 232, 251, 272
Exon, J. James 208

Fairbanks, Chuck 86, 88, 93, 198-201, 204, 213, 220, 235
Ferragamo, Vince 53
Fiala, Adrian 16, 74, 82, 84, 88, 98, 99, 101, 266, 272
Fischer, Cletus 12, 40, 42, 43, 45, 113, 148, 251
Flemming, Bill 203, 208
Flippin, George 96
Foldberg, Hank 9
Fonda, Henry 76
Fonda, Peter 76
Foster, Amos 4
Fouts, Dan 186, 187
Frazier, Tommie 265
Frost, Larry 64, 68, 88
Frost, Scott 64, 65
Fryar, Irving 54

Garrett, Mike 118
Geddes, Ken 39, 43, 70, 78, 83, 88, 89, 96, 98, 272
Geraghty, Mark 72
Gibson, Bob 108
Gibson, Vince 83, 90, 145, 198
Glass, James 178, 182, 183
Glover, Rich 53, 54, 188, 189, 201, 202, 204, 205, 214-218, 220, 223, 232, 239, 240, 242, 243, 248, 250, 253, 258, 262
Grange, Red 5
Gray, Mel 69
Green, Mike 55, 69, 80, 88, 91, 93-97, 99, 101, 110, 272
Greer, Steve 101
Gregory, Ben 33, 34
Griggs, Glen 178, 182
Gutzman, Dennis 61

Hamilton, Andy 167, 172
Hamilton, Raymond 227
Hannah, John 239
Hardin, Clifford 9, 10
Harmon, Mark 248, 249, 252
Harmon, Tom 252
Harper, Willie 54, 143, 150, 152, 159, 163, 165-167, 170, 172, 187, 202, 204, 214, 218, 220, 223-225, 239, 248, 250, 251, 255
Harrison, Jon 213, 216, 218-220, 223, 224, 232

Hatcher, Jim 73
Hayes, Woody 2, 157, 174
Henderson, Joe 55
Herrera, Efren 252
Herron, Mack 24
Hicks, Emery 72, 73
Hooper, Bert 19
Hughes, Jeff 97
Humm, David 250-252, 259, 260

Ingles, Guy 17, 68, 73, 78, 79, 81, 92, 126, 137, 138, 146, 162, 167-169, 172, 177, 196, 262, 272

Jacobsen, Paul 273
Jacobson, Larry ii, 129, 150, 159, 163, 165, 187, 202, 204, 205, 213, 215, 232, 239, 240, 250
Jamail, Doug 128, 190
Janssen, Bill 166, 204, 205, 232, 255
Jarmon, Sherwin 88, 89
Jenkins, Dan 257, 258
Jennings, Bill 6, 9, 11, 24, 31, 36, 174
Jensen, Robert 211
Jeter, Tony 18
Johnson, Carl 53, 228, 239
Johnson, Lyndon 94
Johnson, Monte 54, 55, 189, 242, 253
Johnson, Rudy 13
Jones, Bert 170, 172
Jones, Biff 5, 6
Jones, Bob 157, 190
Jones, Jimmy 118
Jones, Ken 212

Katz, Joe 210, 233
Kelly, George 3, 12, 35
Kiffin, Monte 30, 36-38, 40, 53, 54, 73, 78, 84, 93, 98, 119, 137, 148, 150, 165, 172, 198, 202, 204, 205, 210, 214, 216, 218, 220, 232, 233, 238, 239, 242, 262, 272
Kindred, Dave 234
King, Bobby Joe 170
King, Dr. Martin Luther Jr. 94
Kinney, Becky 91, 208
Kinney, Jeff 60, 65, 68-70, 73, 75, 89-92, 94, 95, 101, 116, 120, 121, 126, 139, 145, 167, 169, 172, 186, 188, 189, 193, 195, 197, 208, 210, 218, 220, 222-224, 226-228, 230-233,

238, 239, 242-244, 247, 250, 254, 262, 265, 270, 272, 275
Kinney, Jeffrey Scott 91
Kirby, John 13
Klutka, Skip 60
Kosch, Bill 126, 150, 204, 216, 218-220, 223, 224, 232, 234, 272
Kratz, Dean 26

Larson, Al 39, 70, 78, 88
Lee, Buddy 163, 165-167
Liggett, Bob 24, 78, 88, 99
Linder, Max 60
List, Jerry i, 148, 162, 168, 169, 252, 261
Logsdon, Bob 20, 206
Lombardi, Vince 61
Lorenz, Tom 151
Lowe, Rex 244, 245
Lucky, Marlon 53

Majors, Johnny 202
Martinez, Taylor 53
Mason, Dave 61, 62, 223
McBride, Gregg 10, 236, 272
McCall, Randy 178, 182, 183
McClendon, Charlie 160, 168, 169
McElroy, Hugh 189
McFarland, Jim 16, 17, 40, 66, 72-74, 80, 85, 88, 266, 272
McGhee, Donnie 43, 144, 148, 170
McGuire, Mike 60
McKay, John 2, 15, 21, 34, 53, 118, 128, 129
McKinley, Frank 55
Melton, John 12, 18, 19, 24, 26, 38, 124, 172, 178, 184, 198, 210, 251, 262
Meylan, Wayne 16, 87
Mildren, Jack 88, 200, 201, 204, 205, 208, 210, 214-220, 223-225, 230, 232
Miles, Barron 54
Miller, Arthur 10
Mira, George 14
Moore, Bobby 186
Moore, Joe 136
Morock, Dave 42, 80, 98, 106, 115, 121, 124, 130, 150, 151, 172, 272
Mullen, Danny 224
Murtaugh, Jerry 39, 40, 44, 78, 82, 87, 89, 115, 118-126, 129, 130, 139, 141, 142, 149-152, 165, 172, 174, 175, 188, 268, 272

Musso, Johnny 239, 242

Namath, Joe 142
Nelson, Ben 262
Newton, Bob 43, 48, 49, 51-54, 84, 128, 144, 147, 148, 150, 151, 172, 262, 272
Nixon, Richard 10, 104, 174, 175, 188, 234
Novak, Tom 124

Olds, Bill 189, 195, 197, 218, 219
Orduna, Joe 23, 27, 64, 65, 90, 102, 110, 116, 117, 126-128, 130, 137, 145, 163, 164, 167-170
Osberg, Chuck 60, 62
Osborne, Nancy 264
Osborne, Tom 19, 24, 26, 28-32, 34, 35, 38, 40, 42, 45, 46, 51-55, 62, 66, 68, 72, 76, 78, 80, 84, 90, 91, 93, 96, 97, 102, 107, 115, 117, 122, 126, 137, 144, 146, 158, 162, 169, 172, 178, 179, 181, 184, 192-194, 196, 210, 222, 238, 239, 243, 248, 250, 251, 255, 258, 260, 262, 264, 265, 270-272
Owens, Steve 2, 28, 36, 86, 88, 89, 92, 202

Parseghian, Ara 2, 154, 173
Patrick, Frank 33, 34, 59, 61, 68
Patterson, Glenn 103
Pavoris, Ed 15
Penney, Tom 33
Periard, Ed 149, 150, 154, 158, 159, 163, 165, 188, 214
Peter, Christian 54
Peter, Jason 54
Peterson, Kelly 15
Phillips, Lawrence 53, 265
Pitts, John 150, 182
Plunkett, Jim 158
Pope, Ed 173
Pope, Ken 254, 255
Powers, Warren 26, 38, 42, 78, 165, 198, 204, 220, 272
Provost, Wally 81, 180, 272
Pruitt, Greg 200-202, 204-206, 208, 211, 212, 214, 218, 220, 224, 225, 232, 233, 238, 254, 257, 258

276 INDEX

Reynolds, Bobby 90, 222, 233
Riggins, John 70, 123
Rockne, Knute 4
Rodgers, Ardella 269
Rodgers, Johnny ii, 17, 18, 54, 97, 104-117, 121, 122, 126, 128, 130, 135, 137, 138, 144-146, 148, 152, 163, 167-169, 172, 176-185, 189-194, 196, 206, 208-214, 218, 220, 223, 224, 226-229, 234, 237-239, 242-245, 248, 250-252, 254-260, 262, 266, 268-270, 272
Rodgers, Pepper 59, 74, 126, 138, 252
Rogers, Paul 70, 71, 100, 101, 129, 162, 169, 170
Ross, Jim 12, 18, 19, 38, 115
Rothwell, Fred 256
Royal, Darrell 156, 200, 201
Rozier, Mike 54
Runty, Steve 42, 132, 151, 196, 262, 272
Rupert, Dick 53, 144, 148, 163, 195, 226, 228, 239
Ruud, Barrett 125

Sage, John 169
Sanger, Rich 232
Sargent, Conde 115
Sayers, Gale 108-110, 202
Schenkel, Chris 219
Schneiss, Dan 73, 75, 81, 84, 85, 88, 126, 128, 144, 145, 147, 152, 153, 158, 163, 168, 174, 175, 190
Schultze, Donald 22
Schultze, Larry 22
Selmer, Carl 12, 18, 49, 148, 169, 221, 250, 251
Selmon, Lucious 220, 224
Sevigne, Frank 43, 44
Simpson, Jim 160
Simpson, O.J. 34, 118, 265
Sims, Billy 31
Slough, Greg 126, 130
Smith, Bubba 65
Smith, Tody 65, 128
Snyder, Jimmy "The Greek" 205
Solich, Frank 265
Sorensen, Ted 22
Stai, Brenden 53
Starkweather, Charles 174
Starr, Bart 61
Stephenson, Dana 74, 78, 84, 88, 94, 102
Stiehm, Jumbo 4
Stith, Carel 17
Sullivan, George 42-44, 76, 150, 192, 272

Sullivan, Pat 194, 239
Swanson, Clarence 10
Switzer, Barry 200, 218, 219

Tagge, Jerry 56-58, 60-66, 68-70, 72, 73, 76-84, 102, 106, 115-117, 120, 124-126, 128, 132-136, 141, 144, 148, 150, 157-160, 162, 163, 167-172, 176, 186, 188, 189, 190, 192-197, 202, 203, 208, 210, 213, 218, 220-224, 226-228, 230, 232, 234, 238-244, 246, 250, 262, 266-268, 270, 272
Taucher, Bob 11
Taylor, Steve 53
Terrio, Bob 52-54, 142, 148-150, 172, 192, 204, 205, 215, 243
Theisen, Dave 13
Theismann, Joe 157
Thornton, Bill "Thunder" 11, 13, 38, 40, 96, 165, 178, 220
Tolly, Harry 12
Topliff, Paul 93, 95
Turner, Ike 240
Turner, Tina 240

Vactor, Frank 90
Varner, D.B. "Woody" 104

Wallace, George 94
Walline, Dave 78, 136, 143, 150, 159, 167
Ward, Bill 210
Ware, Frederick 5
Washington, Charles 115
Wead, Rodney 180
Weber, Bruce 193, 246
Welch, Tim 212
White, Daryl 53, 54, 228, 230, 239
Wilkinson, Bud 36, 215, 219
Winter, Wally 94, 124, 148, 272
Wooden, John 252
Wortman, Keith 53, 228, 239, 240
Wylie, Joe 200, 201, 204, 210, 212
Wynn, Mike 39, 78, 123

Yary, Ron 52

Zee, Dr. Jay B. 194
Ziegler, Mick 25

Devaney, right, listens in as Monte Kiffin gives instructions to Jerry Murtaugh in 1970.

INDEX 277

"We helped make winning something that is expected, rather than just hoped for, at the University of Nebraska."

— Bob Devaney,
asked in 1989 how he wanted to be remembered